Heritage and Tourism in 'the global village'

Tourism is now a global phenomenon, set to become the world's largest industry and already crucial to many national and local economies. To a great extent it feeds off a wide range of heritage – obvious monuments, movable treasures, indigenous cultures, ideas and images.

How can heritage sites be protected from, while being enjoyed by, 'the ravening hordes'? What are tourist operators' responsibilities, intellectually as well as to the monuments and museums which provide their attractions? How are various heritages presented to not just increasing numbers of tourists but an increasingly wide range of culturally-differentiated people visiting heritage through armchair travel – and indeed while eating and shopping? And how does and should the interpreter approach this increasingly complex and sensitive field, giving meaning to structures, artefacts and ideas for global villagers with different backgrounds, motivations and expectations?

The book identifies a host of practicalities among a plenitude of examples from around the world, specifying good and bad practice in the inevitable, often uncomprehending culture clash. The discussion, including such sensitive issues as ethnicity, loot, eco-tourism and interpretive relativism, is firmly bedded in the concept of a dynamic global village, where all the inhabitants can and do visit each other and are everywhere faced with the challenge of communication – not just linguistic, not just how to converse, but *what* to convey to each other.

Priscilla Boniface worked for many years for the Royal Commission on the Historical Monuments of England, and is now a freelance consultant in communications and heritage. **Peter J. Fowler** is Professor of Archaeology at the University of Newcastle upon Tyne.

THE HERITAGE
CARE
PRESERVATION
MANAGEMENT

Editor in chief Andrew Wheatcroft

The Heritage: Care–Preservation–Management programme has been designed to serve the needs of the museum and heritage community worldwide. It publishes books and information services for professional museum and heritage workers, and for all the organizations that service the museum community.

The programme has been devised with the advice and assistance of the leading institutions in the museum and heritage community, at an international level, with ICOM and ICOMOS, with national and local museum organizations and with individual specialists drawn from every continent.

Forward Planning: *A handbook of business, corporate and development planning for museums and galleries*
Edited by Timothy Ambrose and Sue Runyard

Heritage Gardens: *Care, conservation and management*
Sheena Mackellar Goulty

The Industrial Heritage: *Managing resources and uses*
Judith Alfrey and Tim Putman

Museum Basics
Tim Ambrose and Crispin Paine

Museum Security and Protection: *A handbook for cultural heritage institutions*
International Committee on Museum Security/ICOM

Museums 2000: *Politics, people, professionals and profit*
Edited by Patrick J. Boylan

Museums and the Shaping of Knowledge
Eilean Hooper-Greenhill

Museums Without Barriers: *A new deal for disabled people*
Fondation de France and ICOM

The Past in Contemporary Society: Then/Now
Peter J. Fowler

The Representation of the Past: *Museums and heritage in the post-modern world*
Kevin Walsh

Heritage and Tourism in 'the global village'

Priscilla Boniface and
Peter J. Fowler

LONDON and NEW YORK

First published 1993
by Routledge
11 New Fetter Lane, London EC4P 4EE

Simultaneously published in the USA and Canada
by Routledge
29 West 35th Street, New York, NY 10001

Typeset in 10 on 12 point Sabon, Linotronic 300 by
Florencetype Ltd, Kewstoke, Avon
Printed in Great Britain by
Butler & Tanner Ltd, Frome and London

∞ printed on permanent paper in accordance with American NISO Standards.

British Library Cataloguing in Publication Data

A catalogue record for this book is available from the British Library

Library of Congress Cataloging in Publication Data

Boniface, Priscilla.
    Heritage and tourism in 'the global village' / Priscilla Boniface & Peter Fowler.
        p.   cm.
    Includes bibliographical references and indexes.
    1. Tourist trade – Social aspects.   2. Culture.   3. Ethnocentrism.
    I. Fowler, P. J.   II. Title.
    G155.A1B555   1993
    338.4'791 – dc20   92–14577

ISBN 0–415–07236–0
0–415–07237–9 (pbk)

To the global villagers

Contents

Illustrations

The photographs are the authors'. The illustrations have been chosen to exemplify themes rather than to show a geographical spread or specific sites. Illustrations appear between pages 42 and 43.

Illustrations

Preface

Tourism is fast becoming the biggest industry in the world, 'The Greatest Show on Earth'. The life blood of much of that industry is heritage.

Technology has made world citizens of us all. Yet, though indubitably and irrevocably in a 'one world' situation, 'the global village' depicted by Marshall McLuhan, we may still be deeply different, conditioned by cultures of extraordinary variety and disparateness. In this book, our intention is to explore the sensitivity of circumstances surrounding the interpretation and presentation of heritage to tourists across the world at the current time. In so doing we hope that we may assist in some small way in informing the generation of *sympatico* cultural interactions between those who visit and those who are visited.

Our concern with the topic has developed as we have watched, with an increasingly absorbed interest, not just the concurrent emergence of mass tourism and of widespread usage of heritage imagery – the commodified cladding of symbols of antiquity – but also the apparent burgeoning of a symbiotic relationship between the two. Much of its interest to us, and we believe its significance in global terms, is that it seems a relationship compounded of two divergent elements: a potential for increased intercultural understanding, and a capacity for intercultural conflict and transformation. It is the second of these that we explore in particular here in what we see as an ambivalent and powerful matrix of nuances, subtleties, expectations, misunderstandings and ignorance.

We recognize all too well our own ignorance about and inexperience in many of the subject territories into which we dare to wander in this book. Despite our travels, we do not know most of the world at first hand; despite our best intentions we cannot really escape from our own cultural viewpoint. Our temerity notwithstanding, we believe

Preface

that it might be useful to the wider debate on tourism and culture in the present age to articulate *our* particular perceptions of these matters; perceptions conditioned by our variety of activity in the profession of heritage – 'old-style'.

Compared to that of the past, the crucial element in the heritage experience for the cultural tourist nowadays is that on his or her journey of historical *curiosity* he or she is likely to be presented with a fixed narrative or interpretation, a history story; whereas in 'days of yore', as time past would be described by many nowadays, a comparable historical encounter would be, *solely*, with one or more ancient objects and sites – the real things in positivist terms. Extremely salient also to the new situation we describe is that fast and economical communications have enabled many people to travel the globe, *physically* at least crossing cultural frontiers quickly and easily.

In essence, what we wish to investigate here are the cultural crosscurrents in this new situation of mass tourism characterized by the presentation of a set historical opinion to peoples of different countries and cultures. Nevertheless, it is important to our discussion of the contemporary relationship between tourism and the communication of heritage that we should take account of its own cultural context, that is of what has gone on before. As we have already indicated, our own backgrounds lie in traditional fields of heritage. We therefore consider it appropriate that the main focus of the book should be the situation of heritage interpretations – in their widest sense – to a global audience.

We have sampled the heritage of many countries and visited many heritage sites in the UK and abroad. However, such is the efficacy of the communications media worldwide and so prevalent is their use as vehicles for heritage interpretation that, essentially, all that would have been necessary to our study tour would have been armchair travel. Indeed, that this is so is fundamental to the premise of this book. The imagery of heritage, *sui generis* escapist, has been manoeuvred into such a position in our lives that from its treacly grasp there is little chance of escape, not least when any one of us indulges, anywhere in the world, in that activity so characteristic to our time, tourism.

Priscilla Boniface and Peter J. Fowler

Acknowledgements

First and foremost, we gratefully acknowledge the media, through whom, in this global village, we were enabled to 'reach' a lot more places than would otherwise have been possible. Our wholehearted thanks, therefore, go to the many often unknown journalists, writers and researchers, for their prose and images in newspapers, on screen and in countless information leaflets and the like.

Our gratitude extends also to the many people who have helped us as tourists, arranging our travels, travelling with us and talking to us on site, in museums and generally in their own countries. Of the arrangers, hosts and participants from many parts of the world, of various events and occasions, for inspiration, hard data and useful ideas: P.J.F. would like to thank those at the World Archaeological Congresses in Southampton, England (1986), and Barquisimento, Venezuela (1990), and the Heritage Interpretation International Congress at Warwick, England (1988); and we both thank all those involved in the Third Global Heritage Interpretation International Congress at Hawaii (1991). We have had to make very few large demands on individuals in writing this book, but we would like especially to thank the following for critical help: Professor John, and Bryony, Coles; Billy Folk; Brigid Fowler; Hallett Hammatt; Andrew Lawson; Professor Charles Thomas; Patricia F. Young.

We thank Trevor Ermel of *Monochrome*, Newcastle upon Tyne, who has printed our photographs with care and attention.

P.J.F. would like to acknowledge financial assistance for some of his journeyings from the Research Fund, Department of Archaeology, and from the Staff Travel Fund, University of Newcastle upon Tyne.

Introduction: setting the global scene

In 1961, when the era of package travel was in its infancy, Lewis Mumford, an American polymath, depicted a 'new human personality – that of "One World Man" '.[1] He continued, describing the new world citizen thus: 'The old separation of man and nature, of townsman and countryman, of Greek and barbarian, of citizen and foreigner, can no longer be maintained; for communication, the entire planet is becoming a village; and as a result, the smallest neighbourhood or precinct must be planned as a working model of the larger world.'

In the modern world, politicians, economists, businessmen and the people on whom they depend, those primed in the skills of marketing and communication, have heeded this creed. The message has been: to get big, think global. As the head of the luxury goods conglomerate L.V.M.H. Moët Hennessy Louis Vuitton, Bernard Arnault, has said, 'Nowadays you have to launch a product worldwide, if you hope to recover the costs of creating and marketing it'.[2]

And in the area of tourism, countries have courted a world market; their chosen object of enticement, more often than not, heritage. How else to be a distinctive 'product', distinguished from others, on a world scene? So far so easy, but of a heritage, what features should be selected? What is attractive to a chosen market? And, just as important, what will be repulsive and to whom?

These are some of the questions posed by the projection of a heritage as a tourist lure for foreign consumption. But what, meanwhile, of the home crowd?

How, and by whom, these questions have been answered, and why, is the subject of this book. For, an attempt to present a homogenized, yet locally satisfying, heritage may go against grains, rooted deeply in time.

That travel has become very big business, and very quickly at that, is now a truism. According to the chief executive of Forte plc, Rocco Forte, 'Travel and tourism is now the world's largest industry'.[3] At the beginning of *The Good Tourist* the authors inquire, sharing the amazement of many, 'Who would have thought, even one generation ago, that tourism and travel would be the largest industry of the 1990s?'[4] And within this burgeoning industry, multiplying too, is the industry of heritage, richness and recognition through roots, economic amelioration by means of ethnicity: cultural commodification as a cure for all.

But dangers are rife. And warnings of these have been made. Already by the mid-1970s, in their book *The Golden Hordes: International Tourism and the Pleasure Periphery*, Louis Turner and John Ash were stating unequivocally, 'Tourism is, everywhere, the enemy of authenticity and cultural identity'.[5] They comment on the situation of Haiti: 'Haitian culture is in danger of being prostituted as tourism prospers; it is already falling victim to the "deep-frozen folklore" syndrome. The "primitive" paintings are already being mass-produced for tourist consumption, and voodoo ceremonies are staged purely for the benefit of tourists.'[6] Little difficulty exists in bringing similar examples to mind. It is a premise of this book that, essentially, such interactions have inbuilt potential *to debase both presenter and onlooker*. We regard the Caribbean as particularly interesting in tourism and heritage terms, and in Chapter 3 we shall consider it further.

From an anthropological point of view, the problems of commodification of culture are only too apparent. Cultural marination is profound. In alluding to different practices in different parts of the world, Edward T. Hall cites the example of 'American city planners and builders . . . in the process of designing cities in other countries with very little idea of people's spatial needs and *practically no inkling that these needs vary from culture to culture*' (our italics).[7] Later in the book, Hall comments: 'We learn from the study of culture that the patterning of perceptual worlds is a function not only of culture but of *relationship, activity* and *emotion*.'[8] His conclusion is *'people cannot act or interact in any meaningful way except through the medium of culture'*.[9] Anthropologist Dr Desmond Morris believes we find it difficult to identify even with *national* groupings. In *The Pocket Guide to Manwatching*,[10] he offers the view that cultural groups are innately small. If this *is* still so in the modern age, the possibilities for culture clash in touristic, and other, situations multiply correspondingly. Morris opines in his book:[11]

Today each nation flies its own flag, a symbolic embodiment of its territorial status. But patriotism is not enough. The ancient tribal hunter lurking inside each citizen finds himself unsatisfied by membership of such a vast conglomeration of individuals. . . . He does his best to feel he shares a common territorial defence with them all, but *the scale of the operation has become inhuman* [our italics].

How then is our experience of heritage tourism affected and effected by our various culture sets?

Why then is there all this activity of heritage tourism? On the part of the presenters it usually boils down to one or both of two reasons: money; status. On the part of the user it is customarily escapism and/or status that are the essential components of the experience of heritage and tourism. With such high stakes, such a big investment in the situation, it is scarcely surprising that it is desirable that any element of chance be removed from the scene. But in the very effort, all too understandable in the circumstances, to find a formula and fix it, to remove any element of doubt or variability, can be the roots of disaster; *for not all the people can be pleased all the time, and in the service of one group, offence may be given to another.* Who to 'be' or who not to 'be' is a difficult question. What a dilemma to be in, if your livelihood or self-esteem, as continent, nation, region, city, organization, individual, depends upon it.

As has been mentioned, a prominent feature of contemporary life is the 'global product', borne of a high-tech, fast-moving society, frequently allied with the motive to maximize profit.

Such global products can be services as well as things. In the Western world, generally agreed star of the 1991 Gulf War in media terms was CNN International. Its slogan is 'For a global perspective': CNN is a North American organization. A precursor, albeit disinterested, as purveyor of information to the world is the BBC World Service, upon which returning Western hostages showered praise. The Service is a voice of civilization no doubt, but is nonetheless emblematic, wreathed in tones of a certain Reithian 'Queen's English' British mode of civilization.

Images projected on to sites across the world are a potent force. In his book *Ideology and Modern Culture*,[12] John B. Thompson gives the view that '*in the era of mass communication, politics is inseparable from the art of managing visibility*'.

3

As well as on its TV screen, the First World can have the whole world on its dinner table. A massed feast of cultural images are placed before us. Ingredients of many cultures, divorced from context, are blended into a hotch-potch global dish. Comparable are the *uprooted* buildings grouped in 'history parks' such as the North of England Open Air Museum at Beamish in the UK, and museum collections the world over: aliens put together, and thus in the process telling a new cultural story; that of their presenters.

Whether we stay at home as armchair tourists, or venture from home as field tourists, our view of foreign places may be coloured by what we have been told in the media. Guidebooks have their particular character and emphases. The advertising description for *The Cambridge Guide to the Museums of Europe*[13] is interesting in several respects. Assuredly it is the 'unique guide' it is claimed to be, since each tourist guide has its own perspective. No doubt, too, *to people of the same mind as Cambridge University Press*, it is 'the perfect travelling companion' of the advertisement claim. Finally, it claims to provide 'a cultural tour of Europe in one convenient . . . volume': how easy to 'paint in' Europe with the same brush and in one sweep of the brush at that. No nasty idiosyncrasies to grapple with. Such a book can be seen as a, doubtless unconscious, attempt at cultural colonization.

We shall explore the subject of cultural colonization in a touristic context more fully in Chapters 2 and 3. Here, in this general introductory chapter, we would mention in passing that the family credited with founding the tourist 'package', the Cooks, were colonizers of a kind, more especially in Egypt. As Alex Hamilton has judged of the Cooks,[14] 'Their effect was to be the bellows of a phenomenal leisure blaze and as the inevitable corollary, to tame travel and domesticate the exotic'. As early as 1873, the 'Cookii', so-called by Arabs in Egypt, reportedly inspired the contempt of boatmen. By the later nineteenth century, aversion to tourists had arisen in various places.

As we have seen, a view may be projected or imposed consciously or unconsciously. Where it takes root, there is cultural empathy; where it does not take root, there is cultural difference, and potentially disharmonious clash. To cater successfully to tourists from other cultures, a producer must avoid offending his customers. His product must be 'market-led'. But how much will his product have to be fashioned in an alien image to suit his audience? And in satisfying one market, will another be repelled?

Thompson[15] reminds us that 'human experience is always historical'. He warns too that 'The residues of the past are not only a basis upon which we assimilate new experiences in the present and the future: these residues may also serve, in specific circumstances, to conceal, obscure or disguise the present'. An example would be areas of obsolete industries, where the only lucrative way forward seems to be to start up an industry romanticizing for outsiders the old industrial society. The tale, told for tourist consumption, may, *or may not*, be remembered differently by those who experienced the real thing. As Professor Stuart Hall, a Jamaican by birth, observed in his televisual guide to the islands of the Caribbean *Redemption Song*,[16] 'tourism distorts reality, obliging people to produce themselves for tourist consumption'. Just how 'never-never' a story may be can depend; sophisticated editing can result in a cleverly contrived production.

Fundamental variables are the elements peculiar to a tourism situation. As Douglas Pearce has noted, the *context* of a tourism experience is influential. He says 'the social and cultural characteristics of a host society will influence its attractiveness to tourists, the process of development and the nature and extent of the impacts which occur. A distinctive culture may appeal to certain groups. . . . Class and political structure may also determine the type of tourist development that occurs.'[17] Pearce reproduces the tourist-type table from V. Smith (ed.) *Hosts and Guests: the Anthropology of Tourism*;[18] in which, essentially, the level of sophistication of a tourist is matched by the level of his/her integration with a 'host' life-style. So, the perceived degree of gullibility/education of an audience may influence the presentation offered.

A revealing case study was that portrayed by Robert Chesshyre in the *Telegraph Magazine*:[19]

> Advertised in its early days as 'exotic', The Gambia is scarcely that now. A western diplomat said: '. . . If you think you're coming to Africa, you're going to be very disappointed. . . . The average tourist doesn't know what Africa is anyway. Most couldn't find The Gambia on the map.'
> Given some of the in-hotel entertainment, such imprecision is hardly surprising. On Night One we were offered a Doncaster group dressed as cowboys who mimed country and western songs, games such as throwing darts at balloons, and a Russian pop band on a cultural exchange.

> Ten minutes away in Banjul, with its pitch-black rutted streets,

shops were still open selling individual cigarettes and sticks of chewing gum; garment makers worked at treadle sewing machines, creating shirts from tie-dye cloth; a ripe stench crawled from the sewers.

Whether it is more dangerous to separate or attempt to integrate in the presence of cultural chasms is debatable. By 1975, Turner and Ash had concluded, 'ultimately tourism will only survive if it helps create societies which are less divided than they are at the moment'.[20]

Below is a haphazard collection of quotations exemplifying cultural dissonance in heritage contexts.

Alexander Frater on the trail of 'the Olde Civil War' in Virginia, USA:

> I talked to a man who said the wrong side had won. You get into conversations like this on the Virginian Civil War circuit, though it occurred to me afterwards that he may have been talking about another war entirely – the one against the British.[21]

Keith Elliot Greenburg in Pennsylvania Dutch country, USA:

> When a tourist from New York saw the Amish farmer, with his long beard, 18th century-style black hat and horse drawn plough, she removed the lens cap from the camera, 'Why don't you bring your horse over here, get off that plough and take a picture with me?' she said.
>   As the farmer's faith preaches being a 'stranger and a pilgrim' in the world, he ignored the request and the tourist reported him to a Pennsylvania state trooper. 'She thought he was in costume to entertain her,' says Catherine Emerson, a museum educator in Lancaster County. . . . 'The Amish live this way all the time, whether tourists are around or not, but she just didn't get it.'[22]

Advertisement (decorated with, amongst others, Pharaonic sphinxes) for Windsor Safari Park near (Royal) Windsor in Berkshire, UK:

> An African Adventure . . .
>   . . . in Berkshire?
>   The new Windsor Safari Park is all this and more.
> You'll find everything from a Moroccan Bazaar to the Serengeti Plain and discover a host of thrilling rides in the Port Livingstone Village.[23]

Sean O'Neill at a pub rodeo in Camberwell, London, UK:

> Big Ray . . . [whose] cowboy hat has a battery motor to power
> flashing red and green bulbs which illuminate Old Glory on its
> front.
>   His wife of 43 years, Diamond Lil ('I don't know where he got
> the name, I haven't got any diamonds') explains, 'It's not just for
> tonight, he dresses like that all the time.' Big Ray causes quite a
> stir on Camberwell High Street.
>   'The gang is small tonight. . . . But as Crystal, Bronco's sister
> explains: 'a lot of them are on the social. Once a fortnight you get
> more cowboys in because they've just got their giros.'[24]

This last example seems to indicate that if circumstances do not
permit travel for an experience of heritage tourism, then where
there's a will a way is found for the sensation to be experienced on
home territory.

The contra-thrusts of individuality versus homogeneity are a constant
in the contemporary world of heritage tourism. From among the more
culturally civilized, individualistic, societal groups, many will favour
distinctive locales.

Referring to Europe, Paddy Ashdown, Leader of the Liberal
Democrats in the UK, has indicated he wants to maintain variety, to a
point. Describing what sounds like a sort of cultural theme park, he
has said: 'What I want to see is a sort of European village. Each
national or regional family will live in our private and different homes,
enjoying our separate traditions.'[25]

Difference has a place, but for many people the crucial element in a
touristic experience is that it should not threaten, or allow them to feel
uncomfortably deprived of the comforts of home. On the whole, when
holidaymaking, as opposed to making what is avowedly a journey of
discovery, we want a state of what Jean Baudrillard and Umberto Eco
have called hyper-reality. We want extra-authenticity, that which is
better than reality. We want a souped-up, fantastic experience. We
want stimulation, through simulation of life ways as we would wish
them to be, or to have been in the past. As is clear, the travel industry
knows it is dealing in dreams. An advertisement in the UK (the
nationality of the audience is relevant) for India is a case in point.
Beneath the culturally ambiguous illustration of elephant polo (exotic
colonial dreams of the Raj) is the caption 'A world of difference only 9
hours away' (we know you want to believe that you want to see
something different). In the small print, further on, reassurance is at

hand that it is, however, not *too* different (the words in italics are ours): 'Darjeeling [*colonial left-over and you know the tea*] and Sikkim to the east. To the south, Caribbean-style, sun-soaked beaches stretch for mile upon mile, yet leafy hill stations [*here's that old Empire again*] are close at hand. And everywhere, [*final reassurance this, that simultaneously you can have your fantasy and your home comforts*] while fairy palaces, proud forts and bejewelled temples transport you to a lost world of romance [*when you were Imperial masters*], first class hotels are just around the corner.'[26] In other words, the best of both worlds, the present-day hyper-real (for who lives at home as in a premier hotel) and the past hyper-real (for it wasn't Delhi Durbar all the way). You might wonder, what of the reality of life, past and present, for Indian and Anglo-Indian of the sub-continent?

And how to better your competitors in the tourism market? For example, there's so much sun, sea and heritage around the Mediterranean. The 'washes whiter' bathos of the advertisement for the delights of Türkiye is revealing: 'Much More Exotic. . . . More Christian Heritage than the Holy Land. . . . More History, Myth and Legend. . . . More Coastline, More Sun, More Sea than anywhere else in the Mediterranean'.[27] In the small print are the usual reassurances: 'Türkiye has the latest hotels, the cleanest beaches and the history of our culture waiting to be explored. It has people whose traditions of hospitality are legendary.'

In post-Gulf-War slump, Greece brought the gods in on the act to resurrect its biggest foreign-exchange earner with a campaign asserting that 'The Gods could have made their beaches anywhere. They chose the coastline of Greece.'[28]

In the homeland of 'vive la différence', France, where there are 'Plans to build a "Renaissance-style" theme park',[29] alongside the Loire chateau of Chambord, certain difference is apparently unacceptable to 'conservationists' who 'have accused President Mitterrand's government of introducing an "Anglo-Saxon phenomenon which will trivialise the nation's heritage" '. The underlying culture clash here is, of course, scarcely new news, since the reality is, that the French nation's heritage is already riddled with Anglo-Saxon phenomena.

The British are among several European cultural groups who are becoming increasingly attracted to experiencing, through the medium of a second 'home' or retirement dwelling, a supposed way of life in the French countryside. A rural French idyll has recently been described in two books by Peter Mayle,[30] significantly perhaps, an ex-advertising man. Mayle's presentation of a particular portion of France has drawn many Britons to the area. The worry has been expressed, apparently not least by those erstwhile outsiders who have come to 'see' the place as in Mayle's books and are determined to continue to do so, that the place is now victim to a new culture, a tourism culture. Whatever were the various perceived 'realities' pre-Mayle, it seems likely that they will be a different set now.

Political change can quickly be reflected in a heritage context. Heroes can suddenly have 'feet of clay' as in the fast toppling by the Soviet people of a formerly sacrosanct statue of Felix Dzerzhinsky in Moscow following the failure of the hard-line coup.

Authentic cultural re-grouping may be difficult to effect overnight. New, or re-newed, cultural boundaries can, though maybe only super-ficially, be cemented through heritage. The project to restore the palace of Sanssouci at Potsdam and re-bury Frederick the Great at his former home there is an example. The palace was taken over by Stalin: 'Watchtowers went up over the majestic gardens'.[31] Now, in unusual cultural mix, Daimler Benz is reportedly a sponsor for the restoration of the Chinese teahouse at Sanssouci.

For political, or whatever, reasons, it can sometimes be expedient to ignore a culture clash. An example of a religious nature saw the Saudi Arabians during preparations for the Gulf War choosing not to see the red cross on British army ambulances because it symbolized for them another Western invasion, by the Crusaders, of their land eight centur-ies ago. As a sop, a red crescent was put alongside the red cross.

Status so often equates to political prestige. The north-versus-south-cum-north-versus-north heritage rushes for America by Viking and Columbus journey-cloners are cases in point. The new scrambles offer an arena for new and old status games to be played. The *Gaia*, replica of the *Gokstad*, travels beyond the known facts to such places as New York and Washington, and arrives sooner than the rival Santa Maria. A spokesperson for the Viking camp reportedly said:

> 'We got there first to begin with, so it would be silly if we arrived after the Spanish this time round. . . .
>   'And let's not forget that Columbus made a very different kind of impact on the New World. We didn't do so much damage when we came – we learned to live with the Indians instead of killing them.'[32]

Even in the home territory of the Santa Maria, there is some agreement with this view. A monument is to be placed in Puerto Real to ' "the victims of the European invasion of 1492" '. The mayor of the town is said to have described the explorer's achievements as ' "plundering, invasion or genocide, but never discovery" '.

Old northern national jockeying for ascendancy, meanwhile, has produced the compromise now about the heritage of the skipper Leif Eiriksson, whom those concerned have agreed to describe as 'a son of Iceland and a grandson of Norway'.

And consolidating their green lead, the northerners are restoring natural heritage, bringing trees to the islands of Shetland, Orkney and Faroe 'in compensation for the mass uprooting of foliage by the Vikings'.[33] Interesting ambivalence lies behind the perception there. In this case it is scientifically a moot point to what extent 'foliage' existed for the Vikings to 'uproot'; for the character of the present appearance of Orkney and Shetland was largely created by the depredations of successful, megalith-building farming communities some three to four thousand years earlier. So the 'green' good intentions of present-day northerners stem to a degree from the assumption of unnecessary historic guilt-feelings, though assuaging them may make modern 'Vikings' feel better. Yet, in another light, right or wrong there, the incident is part of a worldwide pattern. The now much vaunted Polynesian ancestors of present-day Hawaiians had drastically altered the character of the flora of those mid-Pacific islands within a few centuries of their arrival (see Chapter 5).

Travel vehicles are most useful heritage flagships, little capsules of culture voyaging into alien areas, allowing their passengers to remain uncontaminated by the territories to which they go. Classic among such are the grand trans-national trains, cruise ships and ocean-going liners. In her query 'When does this place get to New York?', Bea Lillie, the comedienne, made the point. In the UK there has been a recent revival, or creation, of travel and travel-related advertising in the old, inter-war-years, mode. These pastiches appear to play to an old, and some would say ineradicable, British instinct for superiority over peoples of other countries, and to a nostalgic élitist dream of a world of glamorously exclusive travel before defilement by mass tourism. An example is the P & O European Ferries flapper-style advertisement showing a couple propped languidly against a gleaming beast of a motor car, *looking down* upon a coastal scene, and captioned 'The FREEDOM of the continent. Discover the undiscovered continent, by car.'[34] Heritage is of course particularly useful when you don't particularly want to talk about present-day phenomena like lots of quick planes and the Channel Tunnel.

The Orient Express train began operation in 1881. The re-born, re-configurated, 'Orient Express' caters to a desire to dress up and play roles. It offers an environment of apparent safety such as to allow stage moves confidently to be pre-planned. It is enjoyable, escapist fun, for those on the inside looking out; but the tableau, though probably principally only a cause of outsiders' mirth, might just also inspire envy of the perceived wealth of those presenting the scene within.

As we have suggested already, colonial history can be distorted history, for either colonizer or colonized. A set-piece heritage presentation of whatever genre can provide an ideal opportunity, through its very fixedness, for promoting a point of view. A history book is an obvious, and fundamental, example. Moves in America to put Africans firmly into history are significant of pressure for history to be written from new, different, angles of multi-culturalism. Attacks on white colonization of history books have grabbed headlines. Among reaction has been that reported of a professor, Arthur Schlesinger Jnr, who apparently has said firmly, ' "I don't think that history should be used to improve self-esteem" '.[35]

We shall say more about colonialization in the context of heritage and tourism in Chapter 3.

It has been recognized that symbiotic groupings can be formed across national, even continental divides. The now clichéd example is of the citizens of certain 'society' sectors of Paris, London and New York who are said to share many of the same cultural tastes. The type of cultural connections that can happen are varied. Cross-boundary connections may be derived from a shared business/economic culture. Victims to a common threat can form links too. A clash can develop between inter-continental cultural groups with opposing viewpoints. An instance of these two types in a heritage context is that of anti-opencasters in the UK, among them those in the north-east of England, and Hopi and Navajo Indians from North America, establishing links when a site regarded as sacred by Indians was threatened by an attempt to mine it by a subsidiary company of a British conglomerate.[36]

It is apparent that heritage presentations may take many forms, and that they are susceptible to many sorts of distortion for many kinds of reason. Their audience too is diverse, maybe bringing to the situation of presentation a variety of aspirations of it as well as an innate assortment of cultural configurations. The situation is essentially difficult. In ensuing chapters we shall look at various areas in more detail: to see what heritage narrative is being selected for the purposes of tourism, and why.

We should indicate clearly that, in this book, we are looking at the collision, actual and potential, in the arena of tourism between what is to a greater or less extent a fabrication and that culture which is, or has been, to a large extent unself-conscious, which develops 'in the wild', without training or template, being, essentially, a 'pure' unsullied product. We hope this process will demonstrate the distinction between picked and presented heritage and tenaciously rooted heritage; though of course the paradox is that both are cultural products.

The remarks of Julie Burchill, writing of culture, albeit in the narrower sense of the word, in the circumstance of that self-consciously hothouse cultural venue, the Festival at Edinburgh, make the point:

> Ultimately, there is something sad and self-deceiving about a city that seeks its salvation in culture, or which believes culture can thrive in a roped-off area away from the real world. . . . True modern culture grows through the cracks in the cement, nurtured by daily conflict. It does not wish to exist in a playpen which is what the festival boils down to.[37]

Salutary words, with a message for all players with heritage imagery on the global tourism/leisure scene.

Home thoughts 2

Deep down, a lot of people travel to arrive where they came from. And if it's an improvement on the reality, hyper-real, an idealized version in terms of facilities, so much the better. They are the 'accidental tourists' of the eponymous film which so sharply satirizes an acute victim of the syndrome, who actually doesn't even want to leave his own country at all. Many business travellers are, or become through 'O/D-ing' on travel, accidental tourists.

A solution to the problem for holidaymakers who might want to travel to strange lands for status reasons – showing off to the folks back home, or to escape the down side of home life – is to occupy on their own terms, take over or colonize, that portion of the alien environment which they decide to visit. Some matters relating to colonization in the generally accepted sense of the word will be addressed in Chapter 3 when we discuss the relationship of indigenous and colonial in a tourism context. Here we would like to consider colonization in the sense that we have described above and in Chapter 1, that is of travelling and holidaying in a culture capsule or under a cultural umbrella.

Though the effort of catering to a tourism mass market could be said to have produced this type of protectionism, its inception can be seen to reside well back in history in any journey predetermined by cultural criteria. The erstwhile Grand Tour, a requirement of aspirants to the ranks of British civilized society, is an example. A motive for exclusivity is still a determinant in selecting a tourism experience, perhaps even more so now given the massed numbers of tourists from many, but by no means all, parts of the globe. Since a fundamental need for many is to be among their own kind, it is not just ABs who may want the selectivity, but any other holidaying cultural groups as well. Essentially, underlying that syndrome of travelling and/or holidaying in an environment which is considered sympathetic is the requirement for *security*, for segregation from potentially dangerous elements.

Perhaps paramount among heritage touristic experiences, one now with quite a considerable longevity, this in itself a signifier of its success in meeting a continued need, is the cruise-ship 'tour of visit' to historic sites. Thomas Cook's Nile boat tours of the later nineteenth century were progenitors of the type, which, in the UK at least, has become almost synonymous with the name of Swan Hellenic, whose boast of their Nile cruises is 'travelling . . . in modern comfort through the ancient past'.

The sheer hard work of the culture-vulturing 'holiday' activity as a feature on Swan's tours is almost legendary; and the Puritan ethic revealed, a cultural aspect of the culture of the tour itself, is doubtless with appeal for its particular market. The prevailing view on such tours is carefully cultured to dovetail throughout: from preparation of the tour organization's brochure, to achieving its chosen market of a particularly identified group; through the choice of guide lecturers. In a way, the sites visited scarcely matter, so long as they are picturesque and old, since the view of them will to a large extent be preordained, merely reinforced at every stopping place. No sense of their *present-day* cultural context is likely to be gleaned from such short, and so protected, visits. Alien elements, less resolutely in cultural control, may be the crew on board, but, since its members are in servile roles, it may matter not too much. Anyway, it is osmotically known by such tourists, whether from real or aspired experience, that servants are seen and not heard.

Swan Hellenic see fit to make the same point twice on the inside back cover of one of their tour brochures. Presumably, therefore, it is seen by them as important. In the first instance the words are: 'you can enjoy . . . the congenial companionship of your fellow travellers who will doubtless share your interest in and appreciation of the lands and cultures to be explored.' In the second instance, the text is as follows: 'With us, you can discover the world's treasures during a carefree journey with people whose outlook and objectives will almost certainly match your own.'

It is not all plain, mono-cultural, sailing, however. The small world of the global village *has* intruded into some of the less overtly selective of the cruise experiences. A Serenissima guided cruise of the Danube, a river in whose heritage 'Romans, Celts, Thraks, Illyrics and Ottomans have all played their part', for example, is aboard the MS *Rousse*. The ship is described by Serenissima as 'built in a Dutch shipyard . . . owned by Bulgarian Danube Shipping Company and . . .

on charter to our partners in Austria – Lüftner Reisen of Innsbruck'.

Upon the native life style on land, it is likely that such tourists' influence will be relatively slight, though a measure of envy or derision may be incurred. The impact will impinge, apart from isolated thrusts, scarcely deeper than the waterfront. Nonetheless, along the cruise routes will be channels, behaviourally conditioned to, and by, visits from outsiders. One wonders whether life styles in even a country of such outward unmalleability and phlegmatism, and wholesome, down-to-earth, common sense as Holland, are not a little influenced when subject to tourist influx, when one reads as follows (the words in italics are ours) of a bulbfield cruise in a Swan brochure: 'For a glimpse of Dutch villages as they would have been in the old days [*we have made sure they are preserved in aspic for your delectation?*], we travel to Edam and Volendam, filled with charming houses and residents in traditional costumes [*what, even when the boat has gone by?*]. The village of Zaanse Schans illustrates life in Holland *c*.1700, but is also home to a resident population [*just like Williamsburg?*].'

P & O see fit to mention, in relation to their Indonesian Expedition Cruises, that they provide 'Western and Asian cuisine' and that their staterooms 'serve as an elegant cocoon'; P & O assert, nonetheless, that their 'voyages of discovery tend to attract those with a curiosity about other worlds and other peoples, who want to . . . fly an Indonesian kite, bargain for magnificent weaving and experience new foods and old customs'. Is this, perhaps, more subverting of native life ways for touristic requirements? Though ostensibly at least providing, in the assertion of Swan Hellenic of their cruises '. . . the best of all worlds', such tours in reality appear to be experiences, essentially, on the terms of the visitors only. Showing most clearly the type of tourist to whom such up-market cruises and tours are designed to appeal is a retro-style advertisement for P & O – The Peninsular And Oriental Steam Navigation Company, as is long-windedly explained *à la*, nostalgia, *môde*. The advertisement plays to the present-day cultural notions, of exclusivity and, unstated, superiority, of its, perhaps newly, affluent audience with its world-cruise slogan 'Tour All Around The Known World'.

When a mass market is catered to with heritage, the product is different, though it is just as carefully tailored culturally to reach its chosen portion of the travelling public. The mass-market equivalent of the themed heritage cruise is the themed heritage coach tour.

Advertising, and the brochure especially, are the cultural bait for a holiday package. Guidebooks may, themselves, provide cultural frameworks to travel. Certain styles attract certain audiences. From the evaluations between the covers of these books, the effect may be of many people choosing a certain, similar, experience, going for the same view in every sense. A result, too, can be overload at sites, in terms of absolute numbers, or of a high preponderance of visitors distinguished by a particular culture. The influence of guidebooks on the demographics of tourism may be considerable. The impact of guidebooks upon heritage should not be underestimated.

Travelling with real, or fantasy-real, cultural baggage is one option for the 'accidental tourist'. Another is to find it on arrival, a 'home from home' experience. Benidorm in Spain has, ostensibly at least, culturally neutered itself and superimposed on to the bland backcloth accoutrements of a UK provincial High Street. Behind the scenes, inland, Spain reasserts its strong cultural character. Top-coats such as this, applied for the benefit of attracting visitors from another culture, are to be found in many parts of the world.

A portion of Italy is known in the UK as Chiantishire because of the large number of British who have moved into the area. Representatives of other nationalities have moved there too. It has been indicated by Italia Nostra that it does not care for 'the glib alteration of place names by foreigners for the purposes of tourism'.[1] And a spokesman for Italia Nostra, Professor Italo Moretti, is reported as saying: ' "There is also a real danger of us losing our identity if something is not done" '. A Tuscan comment was: ' "These are interlopers unprepared to leave behind their new culture and fall in line with local customs' '.

Visitors to Amsterdam from the UK *and* Holland can feel at home when they visit the British Madame Tussaud's waxwork presentation of Holland's seventeenth-century Golden Age and, in the modern section, of Queen Wilhelmina broadcasting from London to the Netherlands during the Second World War.

Tourist resorts know they are unlikely to please all sections of society simultaneously. A wide-eyed Italian, Beppe Severignini, author of *Inglesi* (1990), was amazed, and delighted, by the cultural characteristics of Blackpool, a UK seaside holiday town. He told Sebastian Kelly of *The European*:

> 'Blackpool is another world compared to Europe. . . . There the working class goes to nice places and tries to behave like the rich.
> . . .

'Going to Backpool is a bigger culture shock than going to many of the far-flung places which people spend lots of money getting to. I advise all the people of Europe to go there – although don't swim in the appalling dirty water. You don't go to Blackpool for that. You go for Brit-watching, and I think it should be advertised as a holiday activity in the tourist brochures.
. . .

'The British have frozen in time something which has gone elsewhere in Europe.'[2]

Forms of culture shock are many and varied. It can, for example, be disturbing to some visitors of western industrialized nations to find that a country's treatment of its historic monuments does not conform to the practice back home. Some travellers to Rome complain of the, to their eyes, too casual local attitude to the conservation and presentation of historic sites. Visitors from young countries, without a long history of their own, may be especially appalled by the native lack of recognition and appreciation of what the outsiders regard as exquisite ancient sites.

Predominantly synthetic and superficial cultural 'islands' abound in the tourism world: among these are holiday enclaves such as Club Med, many hotel chains and a whole range of theme parks. While some types are 'home from homes'; the essence of others is that they are 'alien', exotic, experiences.

By their very difference from their environs, *implanted* cultural 'islands' can be extraordinarily attractive to tourists. Examples are: distinctively foreign segments of a nation or area such as the French-speaking portions of Canada, Montreal in particular, 'Little Germany' in Bradford in the UK, Cajun Country in Louisiana, Santa Fé and surrounding areas in New Mexico, and the mass of Chinatowns worldwide. This group of 'islands' appeals in terms of tourism potential, since the 'islands' are not only different but, at least at base, real. The difference may need underlining, however, by synthetic embellishment with heritage veneer to produce an attraction that is sufficiently sensational and continuously quaint. Various Chinatowns in the UK – London, Manchester, Newcastle upon Tyne – have been augmented to make them more pronounced; for example, standard telephone boxes have been decorated with Chinese imagery. In Newcastle upon Tyne, the event to celebrate the 1991 Chinese New Year was orchestrated by the tourism development officer of Newcastle City Council 'as part of the *development* [our italics] of Chinese culture in the city'.[3] Equally, aspects that might seem too threatening may have to be toned down through sugar-coating. Remnant areas of formerly mainstream cultures, now regarded as extreme by contrast with their surroundings, such as souks and cas-bahs, may be both especially enticing and especially nerve-racking for tourists.

A smaller cultural home within another cultural landscape is exemp-lified by the American Museum in Britain (see also Chapter 8), de-scribed by Hugh Montgomery-Massingberd as 'a fresh corner of an English field that is forever America'.[4]

The sadness of the tortoise approach to travel, the cowering, sheltered, approach (taking your own 'roof') is that so often it appears as denial of that inter-communication which is sought to be embraced within just such a term as 'The Global Village'.

Indigenous and colonial

3

Tourism feeds on the colonial impulse. Part of the appeal, the *frisson*, of travelling to strange lands is the opportunity that it may afford to patronize the poor native unfortunates who may know no better way of life than that of their homeland. Tourism, in many ways, is a sort of neo-colonialism.

Visitors' patronage may be one thing. Quite another can be the condescension of residents of a colonized country to the indigenous peoples of the territory to which they have come to regard themselves as the rightful heirs. A fount of power in an area is similarly likely to be the dominant source of culture, often, apparently at least, to the exclusion of all other. Colonizers can come to regard as solely in their ownership the culture as well as the land mass.

In the USA, a long 'forgetfulness' about, or suppression of, the native culture and history, is coming to an end. This is being encouraged by a range of apparently discrete factors, such as archaeological survey and excavation of the renowned 'last stand' battle site at Wounded Knee, South Dakota; indigenous peoples' demands for the return of burial remains, now recognized in law (1989, 1990) and restitution or preservation of sites they traditionally regard as sacred; films and books such as Michael Blake's *Dances with Wolves*;[1] and Black pressure for history to be rewritten from a perspective unbiased against, if not positively pro, the Afro-American. But this process of questioning and historical revisionism is worldwide, a writing of history from points of view other than the colonizer and therefore, in effect, a rewriting of history.

Clearly such issues are involved with heritage; but tourism? In fact they are basic to tourism, less in terms of where tourists go than because of what is supplied for and taken away by tourists from all over the world as their particular 'experience'. In other words, it is not so much the physical or scenic qualities of the sites as the cultural overlay, the interpretation, which throughout the world is now increasingly called into question as a form of, often unconscious but sometimes deliberate, intellectual colonialism. However distasteful many may find such enquiry, the questions are now there and they will probably not go away. As the neo-colonialist tourist strikes ever further from home, so everywhere may the 'natives' become more restive about the interpretive packaging, the 'meaning', of what the tourist wants to see and what he or she is shown.

Where, for example, does the cultural tourist now go for such an apparently straightforward request as his or her 'American history experience'? Far from remaining matters of interesting academic discussion, 'Which America?', 'Whose history?' and 'What sort of experience?' have become by the 1990s real practical questions, of great import and considerable emotion to many seeking answers from different racial, ethnic, political and scientific viewpoints. It would be unfair to duck the questions by saying there is no American history; but it is certainly fair to observe that there is no longer any single, accepted version of American history (or of many other countries' histories for that matter, for example Britain's).[2] Native Americans and Afro-Americans, not to mention hundreds of other minorities, want their own histories, and they want American history rewritten in the light of those histories. Even that catalyst of the formation of the States, the Civil War, is 'up for grabs'.

The USA is perceived from the outside as providing a microcosm of the world in all this, which is readily confirmed inside. The Townsend Professor of History at Yale University, for example, writing of the National Parks, observed:

> Increasingly there will be a vocal American population . . . that
> may declare that the American Revolution was not their
> revolution, that the Civil War was not their war, that the
> women's rights struggle as commemorated at Seneca Falls was not
> their struggle . . . those [Parks] that subtly speak to a value
> system that is rapidly changing may not be the places of
> veneration that they are today.[3]

And the doubters who query what this has to do with heritage and tourism should just bear in mind that the National Parks of the USA, established to preserve part of the American heritage, are now themselves part *of* that heritage, all 323,760 square km (80 million acres) of it. Furthermore, that heritage is visited by some 300 million people *each year*. Such a size of operation smacks of heritage and tourism on the grand scale, not least since so many of the visitors, even if American, are from far away.

Unfortunately for those responsible for the original vision of the National Parks and its present administration, however, the whole of the land-take and much of its presentation represents a form of internal colonialism, and much the same is true of similar operations elsewhere. There is nearly always someone with claims of some sort on any piece of land and, as we are increasingly learning, interpreting that piece of land is increasingly a sensitive matter. Professor Winks continued in his article (the words in italics are ours):

> The Park Service is meeting this challenge in some measure
> through its hiring policies. . . . But it must look beyond . . . those
> who interpret to what it is that they interpret. Is it not time to
> speak the truth at Wounded Knee? Is it not time to admit to a far
> greater need for bilingual [*only two?*] interpretive markers . . .?
> More important, is it not time for serious projections where
> people will live, who those people will be, and what it is that they
> will wish to visit, commemorate, and protect . . .?

The first National Park in the USA, and the world, was established at Yellowstone in 1872; the second in the world was Royal National Park in New South Wales, Australia, in 1879. Some 514 National Parks cover 2.4 per cent of that continent's land surface. Issues similar to those in North America have arisen in Australia too, though understandably they do not feature largely in the official brochure.[4] It reminds us, however, of the 'battle' in the 1980s over the Franklin–Gordon Wild Rivers National Park, threatened by damming of the Franklin River which would have flooded 'the wild river and the ancient Aboriginal artefacts in caves along its course' (eventually the scheme was aborted and the area was designated a World Heritage Site). It seems appropriate to exemplify this park here, partly to illustrate that the USA National Park Service is not alone in its problems, partly because it was and is very popular, consists largely of cool temperate rain forest, and contains, not living indigenous peoples, but 'sites inhabited by Aboriginal people about 20,000 years ago'. So here, as in many parks throughout the world, stewardship and heritage interpretation involve 'dead' archaeology as well as concerns about living peoples and traditions.

Yet, as the brochure says, 'European settlement spreading across Australia for over 200 years has significantly altered over 70% of original plant and animal communities'. But surely not just the natural environment? – much of this land 'belonged' to native communities in a way which even today capitalist societies find difficult to understand. And the point is not met by acknowledging, as the brochure does, that 'Most national parks contain fragments of Aboriginal culture: paintings, burial grounds and ceremonial sites. Special provision is made to protect these sites'. Taken by itself that statement could represent a good old colonial attitude for, while protecting archaeological sites is one sort of proper response, much greater sensitivity than that alone is required in places where people live who still relate to what may appear mere 'cultural fragments' in Western eyes. And in fact some Australian parks are owned by Aboriginal peoples. Uluru (Ayers Rock) National Park, for example, 'is owned by the Aboriginal people whose ancestors lived there for thousands of years' (not that that is the way that such people would express it, their concept of time being non-chronological).

The Australian Parks, as the American, also consciously preserve colonial archaeology or, as the brochure puts it, 'Parks protect history', making an interesting distinction between 'fragments of Aboriginal culture' and 'remnants of early European settlement' – neither phrase suggests a conceptual integration of humankind, time and environment. Gurig National Park in the Northern Territory includes 'the historic remains of Victoria settlement established in 1838', equivalent to, for example, the US National Park Service's Skagway National Historical Park, Alaska. Similar too is the Mission Houses Museum, Oahu, in and around the 'oldest remaining houses in the Hawaiian islands today', built between 1821 and 1841 as the family homes and headquarters for the first Christian missionaries to Hawaii. Now 'an independent, non-profit educational institution', the Museum meets head-on in its mission statement several of the issues embedded in this chapter. It unequivocally states that its 'purpose is to collect, preserve and interpret to a broad public audience the social history of early, 19th century Hawaii, with special emphasis on the cultural encounter of Hawaiians, missionaries, merchants and traders'.

This is quite a bold and relatively rare facing up to the past in the present. It recognizes not just that tensions occurred historically when colonizer interfaced with indigenes, especially so when religion was involved as well as commercial exploitation; it also recognizes that the interpretation and presentation of the issues as well as the history create a considerable challenge. Even more is this so when, as in a location like Oahu, the 'customer band' of visitors to the place is likely to be very broad indeed in terms of race and cultural background, while the local communities watch critically at every stage (see Chapter 5).

This is certainly the case at Uluru. One of the interpreters there, Allan Fox, described the park programme to the 1991 Hawaii Heritage Interpretation International Congress (see Chapter 5):

> our group has been successively initiating a number of culture-
> oriented activities at Uluru which introduce visitors to 'The Edible
> Desert' and the Aboriginal cultural values of Uluru and the
> Peterman Range (previously closed to European ventures). These
> have been made possible because of our strict adherence to
> culturally sensitive guidelines or rules . . . preparing front-line
> guides is via education rather than training. Training allows for
> the provision of accurate, spot information, whereas education
> promotes understanding through creating a context for
> information.

That surely has to be the message for all management and interpret-ation of heritage parks and sites, and not only those with indigenous peoples in them. It certainly encapsulates one of the main points of this book. Uluru in the Australian outback is on more than one kind of frontier.

One of the most deeply rooted and inspirational beacons of recent (White) American history has been the idea of the 'West', the frontier forever rolling forward, reaching its apogee in the contemporary cultivation of the 'Californian dream'. Yet even this is now perceived to be flickering.[5] And as geography and environment conspire to halt the dream-like quality of the frontier waggon train on the shores of the Pacific, so is the very concept of the 'West' held up to public scrutiny. Cause, effect or symptom?

The demythologizing of the American dream *vis-à-vis* the West reached *its* apogee so far with the presentation in 1991, to establish-ment dismay, of the exhibition 'The West as America: Reinterpreting Images of Frontier' at the National Museum of American Art in Washington D.C., part of the hugely popular Smithsonian Museum complex. Present-day resonances were not missed. At the start of the exhibition this view was stated:

> Images from Christopher Columbus to Kit Carson show the
> discovery and settlement of the West as a heroic undertaking. A
> more recent approach argues that these images are *carefully
> staged fiction* [our italics], constructed from both superstition and
> fact. Their role was to justify the hardship and conflict of nation
> building. Western scenes extolled progress but rarely noted social
> and environmental change.

Journalist Martin Walker concluded of the exhibition, 'it has exposed the raw nerves beneath the fragile new patriotism, and the old guilts about the price the Indians paid for the imposition of the new white empire upon the West'.[6]

Eskimos rather than 'Indians' as traditionally understood are the local people involved over large tracts of the new American frontier which, in terms of colonization and exploitation, has now moved from the 'West' into the north-west. Alaska represents a vast challenge, and not just in tapping for oil, metal ores and other natural resources, the obvious targets. The fact that people already live there, perhaps because of rather than despite the scattered nature of the communities and their relative material poverty, presents an opportunity for the colonizer to do better by them now in the later twentieth century than predecessors in similar situations. Furthermore, not only is the area lived in but it also has seen other stages of intrusion; and, with the area being opened up to tourism as part of its modern phases of exploitation, the history of earlier exploitations is as much part of the Alaskan heritage as is the culture of the native peoples. The consequential challenge to and opportunities for heritage interpretation are enormous; and much was said on this at the Heritage Interpretation International Congress at Hawaii in November 1991 (see Chapter 5).

We can but note one example in action. The 'Klondike Gold Rush' is an emotive phrase, reverberating with echoes of frontiermanship in the grand manner; it is now the name of a National Historical Park at Skagway, Alaska, administered by the US National Park Service though the area of interest extends over the border with Canada into the Yukon Territory. Described as 'the last grand adventure of the 19th century' in the park leaflet,[7] the sudden and brief eruption of tens of thousands of White seekers of gold into this wilderness area provides a splendid example of the opening up of a new frontier in alien territory and a classic case now of the preservation and presentation of material culture, from parts of townships to 'rusty tin cans, . . . bedsprings [and] bullets', not least with a view to encouraging tourism into this outback. While clearly an example of colonization in one sense, on the other hand Skagway is irrelevant here because, if you follow the park brochure, no one was there beforehand. So, officially, there are no grounds for using it in a discussion of 'indigenous and colonial'; but we wonder whether in fact that does not make it particularly relevant.

But there is more to all this than 'Indians', 'Red' or otherwise. We have already mentioned 1992 as the 500th anniversary of what ought to be unequivocally and uncontroversially a major event of understanding across the world. Yet, while such would almost certainly have been the case had Columbus reached the West Indies thirty years earlier, such is very definitely not so – because he did not – in the 1990s. To celebrate simply such a manifestly 'good thing' as the discovery of America is no longer possible, conceptually as well as practically. Why? Why cannot the innocent tourist, historically interested or simply patriotic, plan his or her visits to take in appropriate junketings in the USA, or Spain for that matter? As a matter of fact, he or she could do exactly that, and doubtless many will; but to do so is no longer a neutral action, for to do so is to take sides. That is what is different now for the tourist wishing to partake of heritage in the global village; for the village is not just multi-ethnic but many layered and of many perspectives, with pastness itself not just ambiguous but conscious of its own ambiguities. Yet it is as important as the present and so often seen as portentous of the future.

In the *National Parks* magazine quoted above,[8] for example, is a quarter-page boxed advertisement encouraging collectors to buy 'The 1893 "Columbus" Silver Half Dollar': 'Celebrate the 500th Anniversary 1492–1992. . . . Minted . . . to honor the 400th anniversary of the *discovery* [our italics] of America, this vintage coin. . . .' Whatever it may have been possible to say in 1892, powerful voices dispute that word 'discovery' in 1992. Not all, by any means; the Pope, for example, was widely reported as praising Columbus for 'his brilliance, his perseverance and his faith that the people of the New World could open their hearts to the good news of the Gospel'. The fact is, nevertheless, that the 'discovery' and its quincentenary celebration cause genuine offence to some who, native to North America, do not regard themselves as having been 'discovered' any more than indigenous Celts think of themselves as having been discovered by the Romans or Anglo-Saxons think of themselves as having been discovered by the Normans. And many also do not regard as cause for celebration an anniversary of an event which, whatever else it led to, heralded processes which eventually saw the near extermination of the native peoples of North America and the enforced exodus of African native peoples to be slaves across the Atlantic.

In addition, the claim to discovery is disputed as history by others with their own claims to have got there first. They range from protagonists of various Old World civilizations (Egyptians, Phoenicians, Romans, Celts, etc.) to the rather better-attested claims of Vikings (see Chapter 1) and merchants of the City of Bristol in the UK (for example, one Jon Jay, a second generation Norwegian, 'who did a bit of trade with Iceland and Greenland', and correspondent of Columbus, notably about a voyage in 1477 across the North Atlantic during which the latter 'is thought to have learned about the American continent from Norse sailors').[9] The tourist therefore has a wide choice for this single piece of heritage, both of celebratory destination and interpretive experience. But depending on where you go – Seville, Genoa, the Caribbean, Bergen – your choice will determine the interpretation you are given. Perhaps it would be best to choose which version of history you prefer, and then go to the appropriate place. The truly global villager will, of course, spend 1992 on the Columbus trail on both sides of the Atlantic.

Celebrating Columbus's achievement, unequivocally 'the discovery of America' then, was simpler in 1892. For example, Genoa, his birthplace, staged an Italo-American exhibition expressing 'pride of the famous ancestor mingled with the happy prospect of a future of progress that would be accompanied by untold technological achievement . . . the native peoples of the Americas likewise had every reason to be happy: they were enjoying the benefits of civilization – previously unknown to them – and their conversion to Christianity'. On the reverse of a special medal struck to commemorate the exhibition, 'the American savages show their amazement at the vision of progress . . . carried on by America in four centuries'. 'Other pictures of the time illustrate the same bewildered expression on the faces of the natives acknowledging the superiority of Western civilization'.[10]

Bitterness, anger and different historical perspectives will characterize 1992 – in addition, that is, to 'normal' celebrations of the conventional version of the Columbus story and achievement. Under the headline 'Saint or Sinner?' *The European*[11] tried to summarize the dilemma fairly. Particulars included the suggestion from the European Parliament to Genoa, grant-aided to the tune of $3.5 million to celebrate the voyage, that it should 'invite native Americans to the city to discuss their views on European exploration'. Another was the difficulty for the Spanish Government, hosting the Expo '92 World Fair in Seville around the theme of 'discovery'. 'It is not our job to make judgements' an Expo spokesperson was reported as saying, as if the mere fact of the theme was not itself making a judgement. In the Dominican Republic, 'the blind octogenarian president' was building 'a gigantic 200-metre lighthouse . . . where he believed the Genoese explorer first landed in the New World'. That the historicity of any particular landing spot had not actually been established was small beer compared to the row over the enormous cost of *El Faro a Colon* to a country marked by dire poverty. It will become a tourist site anyway, so that might help. But behind such particulars – and of course the already large Columbus library is being swollen enormously by current controversy[12] – are general matters of relevance here: the globalization of an interpretive issue, the high political, ethnic and financial stakes, and the sub-text of a struggle not just for the tourist and heritage market but for the heritage 'truth' with which to influence tourism and the individual tourist.

Just as the tourist now accepts security constraints on his movements, so there are now also cultural ones. Reportedly referring to Columbus as ' "the deadest White male now offered for our detestation" ', Professor Gary Wills apparently said, ' "If any historical figure can appropriately be loaded up with all the heresies of our time – Euro-centrism, Phallocentrism, imperialism, élitism and all-bad-things-generallyism – Columbus is the man" '.[13] That behind the Columbus figure lie deep issues of heritage and politics, never mind just those of historical interpretation, is illustrated by another quotation exactly a year later from the highly respected American historian Daniel Boorstin. Decrying the revisionist vision of 1492 by then in vogue, he described it as a 'vulgar anti-Columbus vendetta'.[14] So the debate continued, a manifestation to the end of 1991 of intellectual 'pre-anniversaryism'[15] triggered through a historical event capable of gen-erating diametrically opposed 'meanings'. It was also one which, central to the way in which the world's dominant power sees itself, was marked and marketed in 1992 as a major tourist opportunity. The 500th anniversary of Columbus's 'discovery' of America exemplified *par excellence* heritage and tourism in the global village today – with the raw flesh showing.

In South Dakota, meanwhile, tourism is set to expand on the back of *Dances with Wolves*. The economic development officer for the area where filming took place has said: 'We want to take out an ad which will appear in every home video of *Dances with Wolves* identifying our region as the location and inviting people to come. It may cost a million but think of the millions in Europe and Japan that it will reach!'[16]

In the past, White European colonization of the United States has been replicated to the extent of dominating the heritage tourism scene. From the quasi-seventeenth-century Puritan fellowship of Plimouth Plantation to the houses carefully 'taken back' to a suitably colourful point in time, and around which tourists must be guided by ladies of gentility, such as Daughters of the American Revolution, heritage presentations on the east coast of America are essentially White, Anglo-Saxon and Protestant in character. In the south and west, the style remains White European, but tends to be mainly Spanish or French in content.

Latter-day Hispanic colonization of Miami in Florida, a state, incidentally, which was a 'last-stand' home for many American Indians, has been intense. The re-naming of the so-called 'Little Havana' district of Miami, where it is thought around 60 per cent of residents are 'of Cuban descent',[17] as the Latin Quarter produced a delayed reaction in 1991 to the perceived loss of identity. Among the comments was that of Mercedes Rodriguez who opined, 'They don't call Chinatown Asiatown. They don't call Little Italy Europetown. We deserve the name. It's ours'. An architect, named Willy A. Bermello, from a neighbouring, affluent, area commented, 'The whole purpose behind the name was to promote the area. . . . From a marketing standpoint, it was easy to pronounce, easy to relate to'.

Such pronunceability may or may not attract people to Miccosukee Indian Village, one of the saddest of 'last stands' in Florida. Though the Miccosukee are not actually indigenous to the Florida swamplands, having reached here as a result of colonialists' reshuffling of the geography of North American native cultures, the Miccosukee Village exemplifies a way along which indigenous peoples have been forced in their efforts to survive in a market economy. The Village's main attraction for tourist purposes is not its 'Indiana'; it is alligator wrestling.

North American Indians have not, in the past, had a fair press. The essence of Dee Brown's *Bury My Heart at Wounded Knee* (1970) and the book and film *Dances with Wolves* was reinterpretation not just of history as narrative but of history's assessment of native American peoples. The subtitle of *Bury My Heart* is 'An Indian History of the American West'. An aiming-to-be-sympathetic-to-the-Indian feature of the film *Dances with Wolves* was that Indians spoke in their own tongue, dubbed for the benefit of White Man audiences. The sophistication of the millennium-old Indian society, which later foundered, centred on Chaco Canyon, New Mexico, is only now becoming appreciated, both scientifically and in popular terms. Many of the cultural artefacts, and the techniques for building, in particular, visibly dispute the idea of the 'Indian' as a simple savage. Yet, in this state too, the Indian inheritance has become commodified and debased, illustrated for the tourist by such sights as the sad Indian 'trading post' alongside a main 'White' traffic route. The majority of Indians stay at home apparently idling time away with hulks of rusty American cars.[18]

For many of their counterparts with a Spanish heritage, the present-day experience is not so different. While steel-framed and concrete, 'mud-brick', buildings are erected in pastiche of the genuine articles in, for example, Santa Fé, a tourist honey-pot which trades on its Spanish and Indian associations, they abide, away from the tourist centres, in village communities infested with old vehicles, living still in genuine mud-brick buildings. Modernity and heritage, heritage and tourism, confront each other in discordant proximity if and when the world comes to look, perhaps not wanting to know too much about the physical and social realities behind the 'interesting' façades.

The extent to which tourism has influenced life for the Indian is indicated in the description by writer Veronica Horwell of a visit to Taos, near Santa Fé, which merits a Memorial Park to Kit Carson.[19] Horwell portrays the cold-weather scene which she encountered at Taos Pueblo. She describes an area there where 'For a thousand years the man-made low canyon of the pueblo buildings had been there on either side of it, the cells of baked earth perennially renewed, until they shaped a most modern outline'. Horwell purchased food from an Indian: 'Her poncho'ed mother explained they were living in the pueblo, though most didn't no more, 'cept at festival times when the craft business prospered; but you didn't get no artists paying you $30 posing fee this weather.'

The profound culture clash for contemporary Indians in North America is emblematic of that between many Third World and First World communities in the present day. The story of the 'Stone Age wife'[20] makes the point; a Venezuelan Hasupuweteri from 'a lost tribe of Yanomama Indians', transported, through marriage to an American, to New Jersey, 'she eats Kentucky fried chicken, drinks Coke and screams with delight when Madonna appears on TV'. Of the dramatic change of life way involved, her husband said tellingly, making a value judgement on behalf of his wife, 'It's hard for her, but people came from all over the world to live in America. Why should a Yanomama be denied this chance to adapt and grow?'

Caryll Phillips, who was born in the Caribbean, but who has lived mostly in England, opined:

> Europe's absence of self-awareness seems to me directly related to a lack of a cogent sense of history . . . history is . . . the prison from which Europeans often speak, and in which they would confine black people. It is a false history, an unquestioning and totally selfish one, in which Whites civilize and discover and the height of sophistication is to sit in a castle with a robe of velvet and crown dispensing order with justice.[21]

The peoples of the islands of the Caribbean have in the past undergone repatriation and colonization. Tourism is a key industry for them now but, in many instances, this new situation is essentially an old one of colonization and/or exploitation. Often, an island will present an exotic version of the European culture of its old colonizers to the present-day tourists from that same country. In Haiti, the heritage is formed of a spicy combination of the cultures of its aboriginals, people who were implanted on the island (Africans), and those who first implanted them and then colonized them (French). In Chapter 1, we quote Turner and Ash[22] on the subject of the Haitian culture.

Across the globe, colonizers may be tourists to the land from which they, or their ancestors, originated. Their expectations of their visits may be both different and greater than those of travelling companions who are solely on holiday. Turner and Ash appear to suggest that expatriates are disposed to delve more seriously into the local culture.[23]

Attitudes to Africa and India are cases in point. Africans and Indians who have lived away from their country of origin will be almost certain to have changed in the interim, as will their homelands. Similarly, those who once colonized India and countries of Africa, which are now independent, will find radically altered circumstances to those of their memory. Philip Norman, in an article adapted from his book surveying the 1980s in Britain entitled *The Age of Parody* (1990), opined:

> Nostalgic craving for books and films about British rule in India effortlessly added itself to the marketing mix. Classes whose forbears were no more than cannon-fodder to the Raj now flock as eagerly with the same poignant memories, to Indian restaurants named The Far Pavilions, The Jewel In the Crown. . . .
> Raj-mania having become somewhat exhausted, African Safari-mania took its place.[24]

Tourist packages to India are traditionally highly selective, glossing over the complexity of Indian society. On heritage tours, it is customary for places associated with Indian princely lineage and/or the life style of the British Raj to be chosen for visits. The realities, often disturbing, of life for Indians and Anglo-Indians are generally avoided.

In Africa, the safari is an experience, with connotations for host and visitor. Black guides White, in servile role, albeit voluntarily, as driver and game-spotter, allowing, meanwhile, the latter fantasies that he is still in the metaphorical driving seat, shouldering his colonial burden as of old.

The changing political scene in Africa can result in the review of, and alteration to, the presentation of heritage, and commensurate repositioning in the tourism market. A classic and oft-quoted example is the ruins of Zimbabwe, formerly within the confines of White-colonized territory. As heritage writer Patrick Wright has directed, 'let us . . . remember those "timeless" ruins . . . as they burst through layer after layer of European and colonial false "exposition"; how, after all, could the primitive "kaffirs" of Mashonaland ever have built temples of this magnificence – temples, as the "exposition" put it so clearly, which must obviously have had a Whiter, more northern origin?'[25] Tourist patronage in the past might reasonably have expected to have been from Whites from Europe and the Republic of South Africa. Altered political circumstance has radically changed the use to which the ruins have been put by its new guardian, the nation of Zimbabwe, which takes its name from that of the ruins. As icon for Black ascendancy, the ruins have a significance far beyond even the whole Black community of Africa. And as symbols of sophistication, and, by association, power for an indigenous people, Zimbabwe's ruins and Chaco Canyon have much in common.

It can only be imagined how Hong Kong will be packaged for tourism when it ceases to be a colony of the UK in 1997. That a new airport there was considered of sufficient importance by the British for them to endeavour to secure its development with the Chinese in difficult political circumstances in 1991, six years before official transfer of power from the former to the latter, is perhaps a measure of the British perception of the significance of long-distance travel to their projection of the complexion of the Hong Kong of the future.

Perhaps understandably, given its particular history, the colonially derived White society of Australia seems not to care especially for adopting heritage as a vehicle for its tourism industry, appearing to select to concentrate on sun, sand and coral. The White population's preference has appeared to outsiders to have been developing, taking pride in and romanticizing, a cult of 'down to earth-ness': ironically, this is a characteristic it shares, albeit in much different form, with the Aboriginal people of Australia. However, visitors from overseas, culture vultures among them, who are accustomed mostly to seeing old and/or colourful sights on their holidays, may be desperately seeking landmarks in what may appear to them a banal, culturally deserted, landscape. For those who opt to look out back, beyond the outdoor lifeway of the coast and Blue Mountain range, there *is* something interesting to encounter, as the 1969 film *Walkabout* by Nick Roeg exemplified. Traveller and writer Paul Theroux reported the explanation of the word 'walkabout' of an Aborigine, Roy Curtis: ' "It means walking. . . . It means going home." '[26] Arcady, the principal character in Bruce Chatwin's *The Songlines*, said of 'The man who went "Walkabout" '. . . . 'He trod in the footprints of his Ancestor.' The director of the Institute of Aboriginal Development told Paul Theroux, ' "the word has a specific meaning. . . . It is when a person leaves to go into the outback on ceremonial business or family business, to visit sacred sites, to be with the people of his own nation" '.[27]

So, Aboriginals, however much ignored by White Australians whose experience of outback may encompass no more than trips to Ayers Rock (Iluru), Cairns, Darwin, or Alice Springs, have a deeply experienced heritage of their own, closely related to the whole land of Australia. Arguably, Ayers Rock, an Aboriginal sacred site, is an image as readily identified with Australia in the tourist mind as the altogether more modern Sydney Opera House. Writing in *The Guardian*[28] in an article related to an exhibition at the Barbican, London, of art by Aborigines, Tim Hilton reported:

> In Alice they have artists making pictures in the shop windows, and it's obviously manufactured for the tourists. There's plenty of evidence that works are faked and copied.
> Furthermore, the success of some pictures can cause disruption within an aboriginal community, for here are sacred designs that should only be seen by members of a particular group, and only on solemn and private occasions. At the Barbican are paintings by artists who will not disclose their religious meanings.

The tourism industry and the business of art have wrought the culture clash that Hilton describes. The heritage matter of an aboriginal peoples has been colonized by others. A reaction must surely be, 'Is nothing sacred?'

The recent massive changes in the former USSR, so intensely driven by desires for political independence from colonization, were inspired also with an associated desire for restitution of cultural identity of national and/or ethnic groups. That for the more picturesque and colourful areas, tourism, if desired, represented a means of earning economic prosperity was fairly manifest. Preceding events in eastern Europe, for example the tourist rush to Prague, had indicated the potential. The Baltic states are obvious candidates for developing a heritage tourism industry. As an indication that in the West and in the former USSR developing a tourism industry for the former by the latter required recognition that differences in cultural attitudes still pertained, it was necessary to look no further than the memoir of Raisa Gorbachev, even though written before the attempted coup, or to the differences in their impressions of Boris Yeltsin between the peoples of the West and of the former USSR.

A heritage site in 'changing heritage' predicaments because of political events was described by the French newspaper *Libération* in an article reprinted in *The Guardian*.[29] It is a station and associated railway town called 'Granica' (frontier), now in an industrial area of Poland. The area became known informally, because of its early situation, as 'Three Emperor's [sic] Corner'. When the station was no longer in a frontier position, the place's role was gone too. The Poles wondered whether to celebrate the 150th anniversary of the forlorn complex by turning it into an open-air museum.

Meanwhile, in western Europe, the area from which so many early colonizers derived, a 'full circle' situation has developed. New invasion of westernized European countries by immigrants from old colonial territories such as Africa, India and the Far East has been a feature of recent times. France, which has promoted itself as being superiorly alluring, perhaps now wishes it had promoted its attractions less vociferously. Now, immigration is also from newly liberated areas of eastern Europe and the former USSR. We mentioned colonization of rural areas of France in Chapter 1. Here we would just draw attention to the 'heritage situations' that can develop in neo-colonial, touristic environments. In such circumstances, though, it is not always clear who is colonizing and who is indigenous, as an article in *The Daily Telegraph*[30] by Suzanne Lowry indicates. Lowry says:

> It can be startling to the traveller who sits down at a village café, orders a kir and prepares to relish the Gallic ambience to find the peace disturbed by a troop of English mummers in chain mail clanking through the square on their way to re-enact the Battle of Agincourt or Crécy. The Eleanor of Aquitaine Association in Brantome in the Dordogne stages full-dress Medieval fêtes each summer. There are even some Aquitaine separatists (not all of them *anglais*) who would like to see the region return to British rule.

As with the example in Poland, when and where a heritage *presentation* is positioned depends on the attitude of the 'positioner' at the time. And colonialism is not merely a matter of outsiders taking over local culture; it can be attempted in reverse.

If that remark strikes some as outrageous, just examine the main travel-advertisement pages in any mainstream Western newspaper. For example, on a page of *The Daily Telegraph*[31] were exhortations, presumably directed primarily at White, middle-class readers, to visit Egypt, Kenya, Australia, Czechoslovakia, Poland, Hungary, Israel, Greece, Turkey, Cyprus, Malta, Hawaii, Finland, Ecuador, New Zealand, Barbados and South America (and that's just in the top half of the page). With one minor exception (see below), in not a single one of the twelve boxed advertisements containing the invitations is there the hint of a reference to the fact that other people actually live in such places. The whole is couched in terms of an assumed right of foreigners to be invited by third parties to enjoy, and possibly improve, themselves in someone else's country, and to arrive uninvited by the denizens and neither notice nor speak to them. Emphases throughout are on 'YOU', and 'they' are ignored. 'Escape', for example, 'to Breathtakingly Beautiful HAWAII For the Dream Holiday You'll Always Treasure', and don't mention the complex multi-ethnic society that occupies the place (see Chapter 5).

And that minor exception? – an organization which identifies itself only by telephone and fax numbers, offers facilities on Barbados that include, along with a private pool, patio and seaview, a 'cook and maid'. One person or two, presumably some communication with him/her/them would be unavoidable if full value for money was to be extracted. The uninvited guest might even wish to be polite for its own sake. Presumably that would certainly be the case in another situation, culled not from the *The Daily Telegraph* in Britain but, after some search in the interests of fairness, the information leaflet of an American travel firm. Packaged in terms the American market will understand ('Be a pioneer in exploring the "outback" of the U.S.S.R.'), it offers 'Unique trips to Siberia, USSR' (so it will have to reprint for 1992). There you can 'Learn about and experience Native Yakut culture' by staying with 'local Russian families in Yakutsk, an industrial and culture of the region [sic], founded in the 17th century'. While local people are involved, presumably knowingly, in that example, even so, perhaps particularly so, it again illustrates the cultural neo-colonialism implicit in heritage tourism.

The cynic might remark 'Especially so' in this case, for it plays to the American 'dream' of frontier and pushing ever further west, even beyond California, Alaska and Hawaii. With regard to the last, incidentally but very much on the theme of indigenous and colonial, the 'Old Russian Fort' at Waimea on Kauai can remind those who think of frontiers as always to the west of a curious episode in 1815–17. For a short time Russian influence, now represented archaeologically by Fort Elizabeth, preserved and advertised as a tourist attraction, was ascendant on Kauai with a view to claiming that island for the Czar as an *eastern* colonial frontier. Part of the bargain was for Russian resources, in part Aleut Eskimos, led by a German surgeon employee of the Russian-American Company based in Sitka, Alaska, to be used in pursuit of the intra-island imperial ambitions of King Kaumualii of Kauai against his acknowledged sovereign, King Kamehameha. That the attempt failed denies neither its status as 'one of the oddest and most exotic episodes in the history of the Russian-American Company', nor its piquancy in illustrating the ambivalent richness of 'indigenous and colonial' at local level. In this case, richly ambivalent, the end product is that tourists from many parts of the world visit a Russian site in an American state with a native, non-White population on a Pacific island, now hyped under the slogan 'Come for the Beauty . . . Stay for the People'.

In other circumstances the sorts of assumptions and arrogance displayed by the tourist industry in its advertising would be breathtaking; but it is a world which sets its own standards of behaviour. The point, nevertheless, is emphasized here by the fact that, with the exception of the come-on to Malta which appears to be issued by the National Tourist Office, all the invitations on the half-page of *The Daily Telegraph* are issued by private commercial companies, bodies hardly likely to be acting entirely altruistically. Have they asked the 'natives'? Would they presume to invite the world into my home?

We take a lot for granted in most facets of modern life; it is sometimes worth just pausing to examine our assumptions. In the case of those of the travel industry, on the part of both suppliers and, like the authors, of consumers, they can so easily be unconsciously neo-colonial; even before we start to consider heritage issues, 'quality tourism' round the global village must surely involve developing a suitable dialogue with natives as well as Nature.

In this chapter, we have explored in depth such examples as 'the Columbus story' because issues common to many places of the world[32] are raised by them. As we have tried to indicate, the relationship between indigenous and colonial is very complex: it can be two-way or, in either direction, just one-way. It will probably possess a deep time dimension; often, neither indigenous nor colonial are uniracial. This relationship, its suitable presentation to tourists of the globe, requires not just great sensitivity but adequate knowledge. For different audiences, an interpretation needs to be multi-layered. How the indigenous/colonial relationship is presented is, in many ways, now one of the key issues in tourism debate: upon its outcome may depend to a degree where, from now on, people will go, what they will see when there, and with what impressions they will return to base. This heritage debate, therefore, is not just academic; its outcome is fundamental to the future course and conduct of tourism. It may even be more important than that.

East and West

4

Many heritage tourist sites in the world reflect that particularly potent attraction of opposites, the pull-and-putsch lure for one another, of East and West. Rudyard Kipling, doyen poet of British empire, remarked knowingly 'East is East, and West is West, and never the twain shall meet'.[1] For the 'old' countries of western Europe, recognition that there were such civilizations of antiquity in far-off lands must have been strangely disquieting, though nonetheless exciting with the implication that there they would find bounty in forms of knowledge and/or goods. In a range of places around the globe, it has become a part of the culture that locations distant to either east or west be perceived as a kind of fantasyland, wherein exist opportunities, far greater than those at home, of various types. And among them may be a chance of personal fulfilment and/or spiritual enrichment. Tibet was the outstanding *locus* in this last respect for Western hopes and expectations from the later eighteenth century until well into the twentieth century.[2]

The culture of the East, which made a strong impact on such countries as France and Spain, in geographical terms was not only to the east, but to the south as well, in North Africa, notably Egypt, Morocco, Tunisia and Libya. A principal medium for this cultural transmission was the religion of Islam.

Some historical perspective might be helpful before we review aspects of the contemporary tourist industry connected with this East/West relationship. That there was an 'East' is probably one of the most significant cognitive influences of Christianity, at least from the viewpoint of Western Christendom. That there was indeed an 'East' and a 'West' became embedded in European consciousness with the political division and nomenclature of the later Roman Empire some 1,500 years ago.

The major event which first drew West strongly towards East, in the guise of liberator, was the Crusades; which pursuits, holy wars, exercised many men of western Europe, whether by choice or force, for several centuries. The goals on this occasion were sites in the Near East. The principal and most far-reaching development in the creation of a major cross-cultural link between East and West was the opening up of the Silk Route, showing the West for the first time a culture of great antiquity, at once extraordinarily alien yet richly attractive, not least in its worldly goods. Traditional European trading posts with the Orient were Byzantium (Istanbul) and Venice, home city of Marco Polo who in the thirteenth century travelled to China and opened up a trade route between that country and Venice (see Chapter 1 for discussion of the Orient Express train as a tourist attraction). Southern Spain, having undergone Moorish invasion, had for long had an orientation to the Middle East and northern Africa, Islam being turned back only in 1492, the same year that Columbus sailed West to find 'the East' by another route (see also Chapter 3).

In the eighteenth century in Europe, there was a vogue at the higher levels of society for such things as eighteenth-century Chinese wall-papered rooms. In Britain, Chippendale's Chinese furniture was popular; there were Chinese garden buildings also. Pseudo-Indian architecture appeared in Britain in the later eighteenth century. In the late nineteenth century, after Japan had been opened up to the West, Japanese tea gardens were a fashion. A quasi-Indian architectural style was used in India by the Briton Sir Edwin Lutyens earlier this century for New Delhi which he designed with Sir Herbert Baker.

Kipling made relevant comment on the phenomenon of Western designs on the East, opining astringently, 'Asia is not going to be civilized after the methods of the West. There is too much Asia and she is too old'.[3]

The East/West syndrome in society today has come to be symbolic, to the Western world at least, of a First World and Third World disparity, not infrequently demonstrated in the foremost places of the West, those most emblematic to westerners of sophisticated Western culture. In touristic terms, this development, undermining old, graceful images, for those less savoury for traditional tourist visitors, might be seen as potentially disastrous. Invasions from the Third World are, of course, not new to the West, nor inherently bad, but it is the scale of the present-day influx that is the cause for concern to residents and those operating within the traditional tourist industry.

The Gulf War served to highlight the East/West culture clash in contemporary society. Writing before fighting began, Michael Ignatieff offered an explanation of the clash, saying:

> In the Gulf, it is more than armies that face each other in the sands. It is Occident versus Orient, West versus East, Christianity versus Islam, democracy versus authoritarianism, and, last but not least, international law versus piratical nationalism. The moral unanimity that 'our cause' has generated has something to do with the simple criminality of Saddam Hussein's invasion, but much more with the tribal call of ancestral loyalties.[4]

The division between old approaches, carried through to the present, is relevant in assessing the presentation of its heritage by one group to tourists of the other. Ignatieff opined that we think 'in our heart of hearts, that Orientals are culturally incapable of acquiring our heritage. The Western tradition has always seen the Arab world as a lurid nineteenth-century genre painting, full of harem girls, flyblown camels, snakecharmers and thieves.' Perception by East of West may be as partisan as that by West of East can be. In relation to the situation in the Gulf, Ignatieff wrote: 'There is an Occidentalist set of blinkers in the Arab world, just as condescending, just as ignorant as any Western clichés about the Orient.'

The Western attraction to the exoticism of the East has been fundamental to the formulation of many tourism packages, commencing with those to Egypt of Thomas Cook (see Chapter 1). The cultural difference, albeit often experienced on an umbilical cord from safe quarters, is the essence of the visit. The oil or technology affluence of tourists from Eastern venues as far apart as Teheran and Tokyo, and the corresponding poverty of one-way trip immigrants from locations from Tangier to Tashkent, has brought culture clashes on to the home grounds of the West. Notable among such places is Paris, perhaps bearing out, over-well for the comfort of natives and 'traditional Western' tourists, the alleged French belief that a man has two countries, his own and France. For example, a noticeable feature of certain parts of western Europe today, pre-eminent among which is Paris, is a new permeation with Islamic elements. We shall consider the particular situation of Paris further, later in this chapter.

Istanbul, perhaps due to the Eastern side of its character, is still not really geared up to meet the needs of the modern tourist from the West in Western style. The essence of the city is Eastern. Istanbul's principal tourist sites, such as the Roman Hippodrome and Cistern, the Sultan Ahmet and Hagia Sophia Mosques, and the Topkapi Palace, are in

Europe. Across the water from them, in Asia, is the hospital site of the Crimean War, Skutari.

Venice, a city whose wealth was built upon trade between Europe and the East, is, its exotic elements notwithstanding, a European place: Italian with, in the shape of such things as its rival cafés Florian and Quadri in St Mark's Square, Austrian Empire undertones. Venice, a unique historic fabric, is sinking into marsh, not least under the weight of heritage tourism.

Spain's old, very strong, link with the East, through her occupation by the Moors, is set to have a modern equivalent in the form of a Chinese Forbidden City park near Barcelona. The park, planned for the 1992 Olympics in Barcelona, is being created with the active participation of the Chinese. The president of the International Society of Leisure Consultants is reported to have said of the Chinese government that it wishes 'to promote the People's Republic in Europe and considered Barcelona the ideal location'.[5]

Across tracts of the East, Western models are being adopted in the presentation of heritage, not least with the hope that sites may thereby be suited to attract tourists from the West. Hotels, particularly, are subject to such treatment. For example, in Singapore, Raffles Hotel has recently undergone a 'sanitizing' refurbishment. At Potsdam in Germany, formerly East Germany, the palace has rapidly become 'Westernized' through the reburial there of its royal originator Frederick the Great (see also Chapter 1).

Referring to 'the cultural dual carriageway', Rebecca Willis described Budapest to readers of British *Vogue*.[6] Warning 'that Western attitudes to eastern Europe can be dangerously patronising', she described how in Budapest 'while the locals queue patiently outside the Adidas and Reebok shops, the tourists are buying up anything that looks ethnic'.

The present lure of the affluent, libertine, West for peoples of the East, as in eastern Europe, is scarcely surprising. The arrival in western Europe of 'easterners', many of them impoverished, not to say culturally alien, is likely to be disturbing to western visitors and local inhabitants alike. The Mediterranean lands have traditionally been subject to cross-cultural fertilization and perhaps for this reason may be better able to handle new influxes of outsiders. Whereas certain maritime areas, for example the city of Marseilles in France, are accustomed to accommodating East/West cultural mixes, other locations may find such a circumstance more difficult.

Paris, Western model for sophistication and civilization, is certainly accustomed to an East/West dialogue through, amongst other events, the invasion of Egypt by Napoleon, the French colonization of North Africa and Indo-China, and becoming a Jazz Age centre for African cultural expression. It has, however, found a massive arrival on its own doorstep of people who are culturally Eastern, less easy to cope with. Nevertheless, the *pyramide* (see also Chapter 8) by Chinese-American I. M. Pei outside the Louvre, a portion of a French government *grand projet* still in progress, is of a sterile sophistication that was to blend, after suitable pause for reflection on the part of Parisians, into the landscape and to become a popular item on the tourist itinerary.

More ambivalence has been occasioned by areas in the north/northeast of Paris. A Metro trip suddenly becomes a journey through Third World territory; tourists decamped from buses in the Boulevard de Rochechouart to walk up to Montmartre, a place which for many an outsider epitomizes Paris, may find themselves obliged first to cross a zone of North African culture where a street-trader may be resplendent in jellibah rather than jeans. The *bon chic, bon genre* world of the Rue du Foubourg St Honoré is light years away culturally, though only a little distant geographically.

Across the River Seine, where tradition has been to accommodate life styles that are bohemian and colourful, the latest *grand projet*, the construction of a new national library, has, to the embarrassment of state and city, been disturbed by immigrants setting up a tented encampment on the site.

On the Left Bank too, within sight of Notre Dame, a French Roman Catholic religious citadel, is the new Institut du Monde Arabe. The Institut, a monument to cross-cultural links between East and West, is by the leading French architect, Jean Nouvel. In ironic anticipation of the situation of the new national library, in 1991 there was a quasi-tented village feature as a part of the building complex. In the restaurant, eastern-Mediterranean sweetmeats and café arabica are served; yet among its furnishings are those of avant-garde French designer, Philippe Starck. Arab motifs are used in the building, yet Vivaldi's 'Four Seasons' plays in the bookshop. The electronic Far Eastern wizardry of the Médiatèque is dynamically used to present to visitors a multitude of images of Islamic society and its environment. In all, the venture is a brave attempt to explain the mysteries of the East to the West in terms understandable to the latter, yet without the former losing dignity or integrity. Here, the East has sought to speak of itself to the West in a manner to which the West is accustomed.

In seeking to identify the future path of civilization, many commentators in the West are looking to the Japanese way of life for a prototype. An innovative exhibition at London's Victoria & Albert Museum, 'Visions of Japan', devised by Japanese, recently surveyed the past, present and future in that country. Interestingly, the statement was made in the exhibition that, 'In Japan all we do with our heritage is add electricity: kitsch as electronic culture'. Is this eastern view expressive of the future form of the heritage presentations of the world – a world in which there is nothing unusual in an experience's being a simulacrum, virtually real, probably souped-up, 'hyper'?

Our glance at East and West was from the UK. As we indicated at the outset, where you are depends where your East and West are (see mention in Chapter 3 of the Russian fort in Hawaii). As we have sought to show by means of *this* particular look at East and West, regarding one from the other is to be drawn to an exotic entity, different to the norm, and attractive because of that.

Meanwhile, as means for travel across an East/West cultural divide, the Trans-Siberian Express surely has potential for becoming soon a major heritage tourist attraction? To present it as such would provide a good exercise in co-operation for the new political order in the former USSR, and its promotion in that guise could quickly become a contemporary symbol for the new Commonwealth. But maybe even that is already history and the chance to create its new heritage gone.

1   At a Scottish industrial heritage centre, heritage tourists travel by Austrian tram.

2   An Indian's last resort?

3 'A corner of a foreign field . . .' in the World Showcase, Epcot Center, Walt Disney World, Florida.

4 Touring Papua New Guineans play 'cricket' in the UK as a visitor attraction.

5 East/West: the Institut du Monde Arabe, Paris, with 'tents'.

6 A global audience views a presentation of indigenous culture.

7 Building scenery, to see what they should be seeing. Façadism during works on a major heritage item.

8 Re-calling China in Newcastle upon Tyne, UK.

9 Urbane green tourism.

10 A new old-heritage hotel: at Santa Fé, New Mexico, USA.

11 Taurism or tourism? A heritage sight, meat for tourists?

12 Objects about to move? A Venezuelan scene.

13 Heritage homes in an alien landscape.

14 Visitors queue by the Chinese-American-architect-designed pyramid outside the Louvre Museum in France.

15 If it's Luxor it must be Egypt; but it isn't.

16 The glories that were Rome, classically demeaned in a UK shopping mall.

17 Out of place?

18 The same, the whole world over? The advertisement on hoardings in the UK of global products.

The aloha *experience:* *Hawaii*

5

Hawaii is the name for a group of islands at the northern apex of the Polynesian Triangle, the vast scatter of islands in the western Pacific stretching from Hawaii south-east to Easter Island and south-west to New Zealand. The Hawaiian island group is the most isolated archipelago in the world. 'Straddling the Tropic of Cancer . . . isolation has . . . played a fundamental role in the Islands' natural history, the vast oceanic expanse acting as a barrier and filter to plants and animals as well as to man . . . the history of the Hawaiian biota, including man, is one of long-distance dispersal.'[1]

The Hawaiian archipelago is basically the tips of a chain of volcanoes resting on the Pacific Plate. It consists of 132 islands, islets, cays and reefs over some 2,450 km, but 99 per cent of the total land area lies on the eight islands at the eastern end of the chain. Hawaii, the name of the group, is also the name of the largest island ('The Big Island'), comprising nearly twice as much land as the other seven principal islands combined (they are, in order of increasing size, Kaho'olawe, Ni'ihau, Lana'i, Moloka'i, Kauaii, Oahu and Maui). Fundamental to an understanding of them is the concept that they comprise, not just isolated islands, but islands with finite, discretely bounded ecosystems; and that there was for centuries before European contact a dynamic interaction between those ecosystems and the Polynesians who first colonized and inhabited them.

These pioneer settlers arrived in Hawaii towards the middle of the first millennium AD, beginning over 1,500 years of cultural development before their so-called 'discovery' with the arrival of Captain Cook. As a result, it was a 'sophisticated culture that greeted the crews of the *Resolution* and *Discovery* in 1778 and 1779'.[2] The Hawaiians may have seemed uncivilized to the European explorers, but they already possessed as long and as complex a history as post-Roman Europe. One of the many triumphs of twentieth-century archaeology has been to give, literally, substance and intellectual reality to that concept.

Hawaiian culture did not, however, 'freeze' on contact with the outside world just over two centuries ago. It 'continued to evolve and change through the course of the "fatal impact" ', resulting in 'the subsequent development of a modern multi-ethnic society'. It was into that society that we in our turn intruded as tourists in November 1991. We had not previously been to Hawaii and did not know much about the place. The rest of this chapter discusses our immediate reactions to what we saw and were shown, to what we did, and to what we were supposed to think and actually did think during our consciously heritage-oriented *aloha* experiences.

In view of the general theme of this book, to illustrate individuals' differing viewpoints, we present our individual reactions to Hawaii, our two *aloha* experiences, separately.

Aloha experience I: P.B.

Lighting up the sky as the visitor wings his way towards the 50th state of the USA, from airport tower to the rest of the universe, is the single word, *aloha*. Before so much as a foot has been set on the ground, the tourist has begun his or her experience of *aloha*. What will it mean, for him or her as guest, and, as hosts, for the peoples of Hawaii?

Interpretations of *aloha* differ, as we set out to demonstrate by each describing our own. But even the word itself is subject to a variety of interpretations. In *The Pocket Hawaiian Dictionary*, published in 1975, a significant date for Hawaiian cultural heritage as we shall discuss in this chapter, the English translation is 'love, mercy, compassion, pity; greeting; loved one, to love; to greet, hail. Greetings! Good-by!'[3] To the delegates to the Third Global Congress of Heritage Interpretation International at Waikiki, among whose number we were, an uplifting interpretation was provided for *aloha*: 'love, creative force, empathy, compassion'.

A certain easy fluidity is almost a hallmark of things Hawaiian: from the dextrous flow of hula; the ebb and flow of the sea and shore, wind and palm, lava and land; to the gentle, generously accommodating nature of human interaction on the islands of Hawaii.

Natural responsiveness to nature, to human beings in all their complexity, imbues the life of Hawaii and appears inherent, a characteristic that is shared with many peoples with a Pacific heritage. This survival is almost miraculous, given the enormity of the invasion of outside influence.

It is not quite that simple of course. From the *aloha* on the airport tower, and from a variety of earlier pre-conditioning, the visitor is ready for, and wanting, a sublime pre-industrial experience of nature, simple and unsullied. Hawaii appears to change people; certainly, despite all my British inhibitions, this was my experience. The place has power to act as catalyst. The experience of visiting Hawaii alters deeply entrenched attitudes in characters in David Lodge's novel *Paradise News*.[4]

If there is something special about Hawaii, and I, and others, are not just susceptible or over-reacting, then the location of Hawaii, set in a huge sea between superpowers Japan and the USA, for both of whom the island group is an object of desire, and its being inhabited by people of many races and visited by large numbers of tourists, make it extremely interesting to watch. From the point of view of heritage and tourism, this is important enough but if, as it appears to me, Hawaii does buck the trend, has developed a formula for harmonious multi-racial living, then it is worth study.

Though Hawaii is in effect telling a story in direct contradiction to the *raison d'être* of this book, it is gladly included, as a message of hope, in demonstrating that, as far as I can see anyway, tourist and resident with the right approach can get along together.

It would be a drastic over-simplification to suggest that all is sweetness and light and that there are not, and have not been, tensions in the Hawaiian islands. However, the colossal culture clashes that could have been predicted on the basis of roughly comparable situations elsewhere here seem either not to have occurred at all, or to occur only with a very low level of intensity. I wanted to know why. Maybe a reason is that no one cultural group predominates in Hawaii.

By any lights, even the softest ones of the middle of a tropical night, our *lei* greeting, with accompanying kiss, from a lady dressed in a *muu muu*, at the airport, ought to have been a commodified cliché, a tedious routine for the perpetrator and an extreme embarassment for those it was perpetrated upon. Yet, somehow, it wasn't. Despite myself, I was touched. It seemed genuinely from the heart. Could it be, in a country we believed to be absolutely overwhelmed by tourists? We suspended belief and, for the first of many times, realized that our cynicism, borne of the First World, ill-became a Hawaiian situation.

Heritage and Tourism

As we assembled from many parts of the world for the global heritage and tourism congress, it became immediately apparent that its title theme 'Joining Hands for Quality Tourism', together with a logo based on a petroglyph by a Hawaiian native, had not been lightly chosen. As the Program Organizer, Gabe Cherem, was to say in a first-day session, the intention for the Congress was that it should be a means of encouragement to appropriate tourism.

Symbol of the Congress, ubiquitous at its sessions, was the kalo plant. Most interesting in the context of the presentation of the authentic heritage of Hawaii, kalo, which 'sustained life in ancient Hawai'i',[5] is more commonly known by Hawaiian natives as taro. The *Program* continues: 'As tourism has come to replace kalo in Hawai'i as a source of livelihood, it is fitting that this Hawaiian plant serves as a symbol of the Third Global Congress' theme of "Joining Hands for Quality Tourism".' We were to learn that this concept went deep into the heart of the Congress; it imbued all its proceedings in an extraordinary way. A spirit of fellow feeling underlay activities, reaching its culmination in the literal joining of hands at the closing banquet.

The Opening Session of the Congress set the style. Central to the Session was a tripartite presentation, described as 'an interpretation of Hawaiian values as symbolized by the kalo plant' (ibid.). Again, there was, for me, an experience of split-second embarrassment, just as at the airport, before I overcame conditioning. As the week went by, I learnt to mistrust my ingrained mistrust of the integrity of events as they were presented to delegates. I came to believe that in the main what was shown to us as heritage, whether it was actually authentic or not, was generally believed to be so by its portrayers, in many cases with huge passion and conviction.

Clarion call of the Session – to be, I guess, the most spiritually uplifting and stirring of the whole week to delegates, probably of instinctively green persuasion anyway – was the request for Hawaiians to be allowed space by tourists. Pualani Kanahele, self-described as 'born in a hula and chanting tradition', issued to tourists a plea for a relationship of symbiosis: 'give us our space and we will take care of you'. Co-participant with Pualani, and Kia Fronda, a kalo farmer, was John De Fries, working in the business of hotel management and development. He portrayed Hawaii as an experience that gave people the capacity for, he told delegates, 'resonating to your own symbols'.

The stirring of ancient, natural impulses for good, by the mores of First World 'civilization' perhaps suppressed or blunted, is sub-text of many Hawaiian events related to heritage that are presented to tourists. Such themes characterized presentations which we witnessed as part of the activities of the Congress.

Characterizing the Congress was that positive impulse towards friendship to which the events of the Opening Session proved stimulant and inspiration. Throughout its course, natives and visitors, visitors and visitors, were crossing, deliberately, thresholds and boundaries, and establishing new cross-cultural relationships.

Our mid-Congress tour to a State Park on Oahu, at Kahana, proved instructive. Delegates, local sixth-formers from a range of different races, and native Hawaiians from nearby, struggled to put together a *hukiluau*, a native Hawaiian experience. We weren't exactly brilliant at playing our roles of pre-industrial peasants, but as a full-force demonstration of *aloha* the day was superlative. The schoolchildren, from a mass of ethnic groups, had cram-learnt the hula the day before, and danced it for their delegate 'guests'. We were amused, particularly in view of the type of local heritage messages to which tourists to Hawaii are subjected: they had had to learn it specially. We were charmed by the presentation as such. What really bowled us over, however, was the children's unwitting day-long demonstration of multi-ethnic harmony.

The Congress prepared a charter for transmission to the United Nations. It was said in 'The Honolulu Charter', echoing the theme of the Congress, 'We hereby call upon and encourage both private and public groups to join hands in the perpetuation of global diversity and unique place identities – through the application of heritage interpretation principles and practices in all the communities and localities of the world'. Not for the first or last time in Hawaii, at the *hukiluau* at Kahana, we felt we had been privileged to see, expressed in microcosm, such sentiment as this.

In their book[6] published in 1975, Turner and Ash devote considerable attention to *aloha*, giving the strong impression that the spirit of genuine *aloha* was seeping away under a blanket of commodification. They make the astringent comment, 'aloha has become a bad joke'.[7] In 1991, it did not seem that way to me. Despite every influence against its being so, genuine *aloha* seemed in excellent heart.

At a guess, the nadir of *aloha* was the late 1960s and 1970s. Wide-bodied jets increased to a deluge the influx of tourists to Hawaii. Alongside this, flower power, a sort of *aloha*, had a worldwide fashionableness. Few places can have rivalled Hawaii for their drop-out potential and simple-good-lifers from outside appear to have encouraged a native culture of Hawaii to enjoy a new genesis. Nowadays, often a hippy heritage and a native Hawaiian 'Missionary Muu Muu' Victoriana heritage can be found co-existing in inauthentic heritage harmony. A variation on the theme is the segregation that can be seen between somewhat sterile presentations of official native Hawaiian heritage sites, as at the Place of Refuge, close by the 'nature in the raw' shack shelterings of disorientated local native Hawaiians of the present day. Much of the story of other races in Hawaii is given scant attention. The chance for the full, fascinating, multi-cultural heritage experience, that we were fortunate to have at Kahana, has been passed by in favour of a select version. Since the 'real' story is so fascinating, and so significant to the world in general, it is an especial shame that the opportunity to present it is ignored. An interesting exception, the more so since it is in the guise of a collection formed essentially serendipitously, is the group of historic buildings around and including the former Royal Palace in downtown Honolulu. The variety of architectural styles of the Palace and the buildings in its vicinity represent some of the many cultural groups participating in Hawaii's history.

Out and about on the islands, to get the other side of the heritage story, we experienced more, and more, *aloha*; and it was *aloha* on an epic scale.

The essence of *aloha* is that it is a characteristic of human exchange, not an artefact. Native Hawaiian heritage has an inherent fragility because its media of expression are the minds and spirits of the Hawaiian people. Places are imbued with spiritual meaning, rather than endowed with a concrete heritage of fine buildings and objects. Hawaiians are of a perishable wood age, not for example a stone or metal age.

Probably the most salient heritage feature of the contemporary life of Hawaii is Pearl Harbor, serving as metaphor for the large-scale colonization of Hawaii by Japan today. Potential for clash in heritage terms is greatest here because, as was made clear to us in the Opening Session of the Congress, the Hawaiians feel they need their historical landscape to maintain their identity. Hawaiians are agricultural peoples who relate strongly to the land; land-greedy outsiders may be seeking its configuration in another form to realize the land's maximum market potential. The problem is especially acute because the resource itself has such obvious finite limitations. Turner and Ash pessimistically reported: 'In Hawaii, as in many of the Pacific islands, a culture of communal living and free generosity clashes with capitalist business ethics (or non- ethics), and the latter are overwhelmingly the stronger.'[8]

In all my experience at Hawaii, perhaps the most fundamentally disorientating was encountering a situation in which Europe is not important. The context of life in Hawaii and the communities of the Pacific is the two presences of, on the one side, Japan and, on the other, the USA. An article about Pearl Harbor in *The European* after we returned reinforced the point to which I had so rudely awakened in Hawaii. It said 'Europeans are used to the idea that they teach rather than learn: 50 years after Pearl Harbor day, realising this is the thing we need to learn most of all'.[9]

Aloha has survived so far in the modern world and our experience makes me feel extremely optimistic about the long-term future, in Hawaii, of the concept.

When we were back at home in England, we received a letter from a new friend in Hawaii, a man of abounding natural generosity. Of course, his letter concluded with the one word: *aloha*. It was meant, we knew.

Aloha experience II: P.J.F.

It is the 50th anniversary of the Japanese attack on Pearl Harbor, and exactly five weeks to the day since we spent much of a Saturday waiting at Gatwick for our aeroplane to be fixed before setting out for its *c.* 6,000-mile flight to Denver, Colorado. Such is the reality of modern tourism. Snow lay on the ground at Stapleton International Airport where we thankfully changed planes. We arrived in Honolulu five hours late. It was about 1.30 in the morning local time, the temperature was about 75° Fahrenheit, and a smiling Hawaiian lady in traditional costume was waiting for us. She hung *leis* round our necks and the '*aloha* experience' had begun. It persists, for a tape of 'native' Hawaiian music – naive, twangy and marked by its European undertones – strums out its simple melodies as I write. The tape is called 'Hawaii Aloha. The Hawaii of Yesteryear Eternalized in Music'.[10] Thereby hangs part of my tale.

I saw several Hawaiis, a number of different heritages, and a great deal of tourism and some of its effects; though obviously my perceptions were superficial and very much constrained by the nature of my programme. Nevertheless, for the purposes of this book, what I saw and perceived has a certain validity whether or not it is correct in a factual or historic sense: these are my impressions, ill-informed maybe but a reality for me. Although I was only in Hawaii for ten full days, such a period could well be longer than that enjoyed by many tourists who will, nevertheless, have taken away their equally valid impressions. Furthermore, during that time I was exposed to a wide-ranging and rapid succession of cultural and tourist experiences to the extent that I may well have been able to take in more than 'normal' tourists in the same time. Indeed, the privileged nature of quite a lot of my experience almost certainly makes it untypical; and conversely I did not do quite a lot of the things that tourists do or are supposed to do in Hawaii. I did not, for example, visit many of the tourist honey-pots nor did I engage in some of the speciality activities like underwater swimming, sunset cruising or golf.

My programme in fact fell into two distinct parts, as it happens contrasting but complementary in terms of heritage and tourism. For a week I was a participant in a world congress on 'quality' tourism and heritage interpretation, held in one of the tower-block hotels fronting Waikiki beach. Then for four days I toured, ranging from a trip round Honolulu itself on the tourist bus, the 'Waikiki Trolley', to archaeological foot-slogging through jungle and scrub on two of the other islands.

The first part, at one level, could have been anywhere in an American-dominated part of the First World: a standard international hotel (though superbly run) with all modern conveniences. Indeed, for present purposes, its main interest was in its twenty-four-hour exhibition of Japanese mass tourism. The gross visitor expenditure in Hawaii is some $11 billion p.a.[11] So no wonder the place operates round the clock 365 days of the year. Hawaii's major source of income is visitors (nearly 7 million in 1990, as compared to almost 4 million in 1980).

My information was that Hawaii used to be a suburb of Los Angeles but is now a suburb of Tokyo. It seemed to be both, but with the yen winning (as illustrated by the average expenditure per day, $127 by westbound visitors, $589 by Japanese; on the other hand, of some 6.65 million visitors p.a., 4.3 million are from the USA, 1.3 million from Japan). Other places not yet subject to the full flood of Japanese tourism, but either likely or, like London, aspiring to become so, would do well to look at Hawaii, and Waikiki in particular. The income may be potentially high in commercial terms and some benefits well worth having, e.g. unemployment is low (2.6 per cent) with about a quarter of the labour force involved in the visitor industry and four-fifths of the population of just over 1 million being favourably disposed towards tourism. But the price is high too, both in economic terms, for example in rocketing property prices (median price of single-family home on Oahu $270,000) with the consequent social dislocation for local inhabitants (average earnings $21,641 p.a.), and in more subtle ways such as the effect on perceptions and demands of 'heritage'. The name 'Waikiki' itself, for example, refers to the former 'spouting water' of an estuary regarded as a holy place in pre-contact times and still revered in a sense up to the present in that a plaque records its history from marsh to nineteenth-century royal garden and current public park and sports fields.

Much of our hotel's resources were devoted to meeting the needs of yen-based tourism, for example the parallel Japanese breakfast, the expensive clothing and jewellery shops clearly targeted at Japanese consumer-visitors, and the large quantity of booking desks for local trips and attractions with all their information and advertising ver-biage in Japanese. Golf was clearly one of the main purposes of the visit to Hawaii for some but, judging by the continuous queues at the desks, many of these visitors were great consumers of standard, and largely created, tourist provision characterized by a synthetic herita-gism – places like Sea Life Park and the Polynesian Cultural Center, and activities like catamaran-sailing and dinner-cruising into the sun-set on a three-masted 'sailing' ship.

One suspected – a suspicion confirmed on site – that not many were booking for visits to the floating memorial above the sunken US battleship *Arizona* in Pearl Harbor itself (1.5 visitors annually). Already the American newspapers were beginning to discuss the politi-cal and ethical issues raised by the then upcoming half-centennial of what they regarded as the USA's greatest moment of shame (7 December 1941).[12] President Bush has spoken sensitively on the anni-versary at Pearl Harbor itself as I write, diplomatically steering a course between what he knows are the political realities of the late-twentieth-century Pacific, the deep bitterness in his constituency about the event itself and its some 2,400 American deaths, and the icono-graphic power of Pearl Harbor now as heritage. As an event that happened, it can now be appreciated as of historic importance at global level; yet as a symbol it also resonates with numerous other significances across a range from personal experience to strains in national psyches. Since 1941, of course, Hawaii, not without some controversy, has become the fiftieth state of the USA (21 August 1959) and that country's most overt, legalized acquisition in its ambivalent pursuance of what might be called overseas imperialism. That Hawaii was briefly under British rule too (25 February–31 July, 1843), in pursuance, mistaken as it happened in this particular case, of a far from ambivalent imperial policy, adds yet another layer of heritage perception for me.

Japanese tourists were also conspicuously absent from the hotel's main public event each evening, the 'Hawai'ian entertainment' palm-tree-framed beside the swimming pool on the terrace jutting out on to the sand and sea of Waikiki beach. In other words, the lot, cliché-wise. The audience was predominantly middle-class, middle-aged and middle-White. The wiggling bums of the hula-hula performers were to be expected and, though indeed manipulated with considerable dexterity, once seen did not seem to me good repeat material; most of the audience, however, did not share this view, judging by its repeated attendances. But then my view was rapidly acculturated by realizing, from what we were told and indeed shown by our indigenous hosts at the Congress, that this 'hotel hula' was but a commercialized prostitution of the real thing. The native dance, zealously practised and performed by a consciously preservationist minority, is a beautifully sinuous and flowing rhythmic process involving the whole body, not just one bit of it. The arms and hands of the performers are what catch the eye, not their posteriors; and, musically it is the Portuguese-derived (1880s) ukele and Spanish guitar, adopted earlier in the nineteenth-century, that catch the attention as much as the dress. And that did rivet my English eye: indubitably Victorian-style, White-missionary frocks with frilly cuffs and collars rather than the grass (or nowadays sometimes cellophane or plastic) skirts taken over from Micronesian immigrants in the late-nineteenth-century. Indigenous, Hawaiian culture?

Back on the terrace, it was in fact the music which was the biggest surprise to me – in my innocence. In heritage terms, it was marvellously nostalgic, for what I heard was *my* heritage, not that of Polynesia or the Pacific, let alone Hawaii. For the whole sound, its idiom as well as many of the actual numbers, was indelibly locked in the 1950s, my teens, before the whole edifice of crooning and rock-and-roll was sent crashing by the, at the time, startling originality of the Beatles. I suppose that, exactly thirty years on from Elvis Presley's film, *Blue Hawaii* (November 1961), this time-warp stuff *is* now part of Hawaii's heritage too, certainly quite as strong as the more traditio-nal, but actually bogus, guitar-based heritage music associated with the islands in popular perception. This point may seem a diversion, incidental to 'heritage and tourism': it is not, for in the case of Hawaii, as represented by the amazing tourist concentration along Waikiki beach (and I listened in other hotels too), it is precisely the need to entertain the tourist which has created and perpetuated a peculiar but unmistakably 1950s local style of music.

In total contrast to both that and the commercial version of 'Haw-ai'ian music' with its prominent long-drawn out twangs on the steel guitar was the genuine – or so we were led to believe – indigenous music performed for both song and dance by specialist groups for the delegates at the Heritage Interpretation Congress. In broad terms, to me as a non-musicologist it seemed to consist of two distinct traditions, both performed with equal conviction as 'traditional' and part of the Hawaiian musical heritage. One was the basically 'Victorian' big-band sound generally familiar to Western ears from Salvation Army and Colliery Bands, in Hawaii harking back maybe to pre-contact rhythms and sentiments in their lyrics but very recognizably 'European' in their form and sound. The other – and it was but a very small element in all that we heard – *was* indeed different and presumably authentically Hawaiian, even though, like English folk-song for which it may well be equally difficult to demonstrate a continuity of performance, much of it has been consciously revived over recent decades. At its best and simplest it has nothing to do with the descending slurs of slurping guitars, consisting only of a chant accompanied by a beat hand-slapped from a gourd or pot.

But of course music is never simple, and certainly not in a heritage context. 'The rebuilding [sic?] of strong islandwide ethnic identity is one of the most important tasks that the young generation of Hawaiians has before them' begin the programme notes to a compact disc which, intrigued by this musicological dimension to heritage as perceived by the visited as much as by the visitor, I have purchased since my return.[13]

> This identity is a crucial first step in working to solve some of the problems that are now facing the Hawaiian community in today's rapidly changing environment. Traditional as well as modern avenues of cultural expression are being explored . . . to encourage more communication within the Hawaiian community. . . . Keli'i ['Tau'a, a recent recipient of a Master's degree from the Pacific Islands Program at the University of Hawaii'] decided to record an *oli komo* chant, or entrance chant, that was passed on to him through the auspices of Kaui Zuttermeister, one of the few remaining hula instructors. . . . In all its form and variation, chant was a fundamental and essential part of the pre-contact Hawaiian culture, and can be considered the tree from which grew the branch called modern Hawaiian music.

The recording session took place in 1974 'at a very serene and remote group of houses in the North Kona District on the Island of Hawaii' where 'The pāhoehoe lava walls of the main living room provided excellent acoustics and a natural recording environment'. The music on the resultant disc ranges from Keli'i's pre-contact chant through

'*Aloha* Ka Manini' with its memorable couplet 'Āhole i'a piko lihaliha/Poi 'uala kāohi pu'u' ('The belly portion of the Ahole fish is rich and fat/It goes slowly down the throat with sweet potato poi') to 'Blue Hawaiian Moonlight' with its steel guitars and soupy vocals. Regardless of the eclecticism in this musical mish-mash, the result 'reveals previously unapproached standards of musicianship and recording technique in the field of Hawaiian music' to the end, presumably, of contributing to the overt objective, i.e. ethnic identity as a means to political rights.

The task continues, overtly as, for example, in the high-profile Native Hawaiian Advisory Council which 'provides water rights advice and related legal services to the Hawaiian community, especially the *makaainana* who have survived by *malana aina* [lovingly working the land] . . . we work to empower other Hawaiians to increase their ability to recognise and effectively assert their legal rights and thereby perpetuate our cultural heritage'. Such legal assertion and cultural perpetuation could well, *inter alia*, affect tourism since hotels, for example, cannot proliferate without plentiful and secure water supplies: a clear clash there, Hawaiian-style, of a sort familiar throughout much of the world.

Without a great deal of subtlety, the hidden agenda of political objectives through the definition of ethnic identity was also displayed to the Congress in a series of magnificent evening occasions. Delightful, hospitable and interesting though these were, my problem was that, in a tedious academic way, I entertained serious doubts about the authenticity in a scientific, anthropological sense of the music and dance presented to us as part of 'the' Hawaiian heritage. Of course, at one level, it was and is 'heritage' *sensu* traditional, coming from earlier times, but clearly much of it was of either or both a nineteenth-century and modern (1960s) revivalist nature. Furthermore, while one could not be but swayed by the enthusiastic pleasure with which we were entertained, a nagging uncomfortableness remained in my mind that, naively and perhaps unconsciously on the part of our hosts, we were being gently brainwashed. Apart from the question of cultural continuity, after all, Hawaiians of pure Polynesian stock now comprise but a very small minority of even the 31 per cent of the 'mixed race, primarily part-Hawaiian' component of the Hawaiian population (otherwise 24 per cent Caucasian, 23 per cent Japanese, most of the rest being of incomer stock from China, South-East Asia and the Pacific islands). Yet here we were being shown as *the* Hawaiian heritage a scenario, itself many layered and in a scientific sense corrupt, consisting exclusively of Polynesiana (with unacknowledged European and Christian elements). What about the heritage of the great majority of the population, or indeed the essence of the population of the Hawaiian islands now, its multi-ethnicity? We were in fact implicitly being invited to participate silently in a heritage conspiracy.

The point was made, perhaps unconsciously, by one Congress occasion that was in contradistinction to the others. It answered my question above: 'What about the others' heritage?' We had enjoyed the generosity of a 'Welcoming Lu'au' at Sea Life Park complete with stunning performances of Hawaiian, i.e. Polynesian-style, music and dance (though disturbed for this participant by the proximity of captive sea-creatures and the *Essex*, Nantucket, a $^5/_8$-size replica of a whaling ship reconstructed in 1964, the original having sunk on 20 November 1820, after being rammed by an 85-foot sperm whale near Easter Island: wrong vibes). We had also absorbed a lively 'Quality Tourism Showcase', again with messages that 'Hawaiian' heritage equals 'Polynesian' ethnicity and culture. The unanswered question about others' heritage came from the third occasion, the 'Folklife Hawai'i Showcase': here were the Japanese, the Chinese, the Filipinos, the Samoans, the Puerto Ricans, the Malays, the Laotians and the Koreans, and even, overtly at last, a nod in the direction of European traditions. Unstated but glaringly obvious was the message: those residents of Polynesian extraction enjoy a heritage, indeed *the* 'true' Hawaiian heritage; everybody else has 'folklife', by implication a sort of second-division conglomerate of crafts and traditions like making dolls and bamboo balls.

Politically and sociologically, such a message is of course dynamite; philosophically and academically, it raises profound questions fundamental to heritage and its interpretation. Indeed, Hawaii as perceived by this tourist begs not simply the question 'Who owns the Hawaiian heritage?' but 'What *is* the Hawaiian heritage?' The smiling and apparently innocent answer we were given to the latter question at our Congress was 'indigenously Polynesian', given even greater precision if one noted the definition adopted at another conference that 'Native Hawaiians [are] those who trace their ancestry prior to 1778 A.D. , in Hawai'i'.[14] My reaction was that such an answer was simple, one-sided, scientifically unacceptable, politically loaded and deadly: surprising to this naive visitor to the *aloha* experience but, of course, only too familiar elsewhere (see also Chapter 3).

I made some notes at the time to this effect and discussed my impressions with some of our hosts. Without in any way backing away from the concept of a distinctive indigenous heritage of Hawaii, i.e. stemming from an unquestioned aboriginal culture, some were prepared to acknowledge that its manifestation at the Congress was the result of a consciously cultivated process, presented in its best light for our benefit. Knowing by then that the *aloha* principle involved more, much more, than merely putting flowers round guests' necks, I also asked whether the practice of it denied its adherents the capacity for mutual and self criticism. There was some grudging agreement on the point, though with the important caveat that *aloha* practice involves talking about problems, not avoiding them in trying all the time to be 'nice', and in particular talking about interpersonal problems. Asking gods and the like for help comes afterwards, and ideally is mutual, for example within a family or between friends. It sounded very much like the process Westerners have had to rediscover, using professional counsellors to implement it.

On the heritage issue, I found some confirmation of my *in situ* perception in 1991 of three elements making up 'heritage Hawai'i'. At base, a genuine aboriginal Polynesian culture exists. It survived into the nineteenth century, despite the massive effects of contact and colonization, but was greatly weakened and eventually virtually disappeared as a dynamic independent element in the life of Hawaii. It was swamped by the 'missionary effect', a Victorianization process not only replacing indigenous culture but thriving as a major influence in the creation of a White, European, Christianity-based, culture melding with other new elements from Asia in particular, brought in by successive groups of immigrant labour. They were needed for the sugar-cane plantations imposed extensively on the landscape by the new White capitalist landowners (their imported employees were the equivalent of the negroid labour force imported into the Caribbean and the southern USA for the same purpose).

The third element results from another colonization, the largely White, middle-class takeover and its encouragement of the remnants of indigenous culture, rapidly merging in the 1960s with a politically conscious revival of things Hawaiian. The CD referred to above is but one example of the results of that process. Others are various Western-style institutions and societies, with committees and the like, consciously preservationist in outlook and well-meaning in intent. Such may be open to the criticism that the attraction of the remnants of Hawaiin life style may have been as much their quaintness, their 'other-worldliness', as the scientific and social interest of authentic cultural values.

A factor in this last development could perhaps be distinguished as a genuine fourth cultural element. The Hawaiian renaissance of the 1960s was not merely White-inspired but also represented a genuine upsurge of Hawaiian consciousness, bound up with the emergence of a relatively few well-educated indigenous Hawaiians and their articulation of concern about socio-economic inequalities. Questions about 'Why are we disadvantaged in our homeland?' quickly became the more fundamental 'Who *are* we?', prompting a 'back to our roots' movement and, in part the re-creation of cultural activities from eighteenth- and nineteenth-century descriptions in a still-continuing quest to establish ethnic identity. In other words, immediately beneath the surface of our colourful and pleasurable heritage-based entertainment lay local political objectives; yet what we were really looking at was not merely a local issue, of course, but a manifestation in Hawaii of a global phenomenon, the attempt by minorities, often ethnic minorities, to establish a political presence through the re-creation of a group identity significantly based on cultural revival. Such may seem deep waters for heritage and tourism along Waikiki beach; but the surf there is part of the same sea everywhere lapping the global village.

In a curious way, the other, apparently totally different, part of my *aloha* experience also proved familiar. Of course, as experienced it *was* different, new and exciting: casually to island-hop a couple of hundred miles in half an hour, to plunge into dense jungle and across both *pāhoehoe* and *a'ā* lava, and actually to achieve a personal ambition by standing in the middle of ancient landscapes long familiar from academic papers and books excellently synthesized in Kirch[15]). All this was the stuff of real field archaeology in 'romantic' mode. Of course the temperature (*c.* 85° F) and vegetation – and lack of it on barren volcanic flows – was unfamiliar to an archaeologist better versed in European, and particularly British, fieldwork; so too were many of the details of the archaeological field evidence and some of the terrain (though the cattle-grazed pasture of the ex-volcanic Kohala District was topographically very like my native Cheviot country). The cultural and historic contexts of the field evidence were also outside my ken at the start, though my tuition was excellent. For I was privileged, being taken to Kauaii and 'the Big Island' by fellow professional archaeologists engaged in 'rescue archaeology'. This context, the occasion for the work, was all too familiar and soon, despite the to me alien elements, the whole quickly fell into a well-known scenario. Though this is not the place to expand on the archaeology as such, interestingly for present purposes those days in the field demonstrated a very close connection between general issues of heritage and tourism already raised and their particular manifestation in Hawaii in contexts other than Waikiki beach.

Essentially, large areas of the Hawaiian islands, and particularly their leeward sides, were formerly under intensive cultivation. Remains of 'ancient fields', sometimes part of extensive organized landscapes complete with rectilinear frameworks, sophisticated irrigation systems, settlements, temples, burial sites and tracks, survive across swathes of countryside, on west-facing slopes, along river valleys and around estuaries in particular. Current research is dedicated to locating and mapping them, to elucidating their deep chronology and typologies, and to modelling their uses. The whole may be pure archaeology, of global significance in an academic sense; in another perspective, it is authentic Hawaiian heritage, marvellously if fortuitously preserved in a way which puts it on a par with any of the very best of analogous survivals that I have so far seen anywhere in the world.

Yet, we heard nothing of this at the Congress, tunnel-visioned as we were into a perception of heritage as conceived by our delightful but scientifically uneducated hosts. Regrettable though that may be, it is worth emphasizing why, as the perceived and presented heritage whiled away the Congress's evening hours, I made my plans to visit the 'ancient landscapes' on Kauaii and 'The Big Island'. I was taken to three such landscapes because the two on Kauaii had been recently discovered and surveyed and that on Hawaii was being worked at the time. This was not for reasons of research or gentle antiquarian enquiry. My colleagues were there on developer-funded projects, recording and assessing areas of landscape for possible selective pres ervation of archaeological sites in advance of golf-courses, hotels and holiday/retirement homes.

'Heritage and tourism in 'the global village"? Little Englander that I am, I had forgotten this book in my excitement and pleasure at being on an island in the middle of the Pacific; but as I stood in the middle of that remarkably preserved, rectilinear relict landscape overlooking Kealakekua Bay, its title came back to me as something peculiarly but sadly apt to where I was. I was surrounded by a huge tract of authentic Hawaiian heritage, its very landscape, known locally but not appar- ently perceived generally in those terms. Furthermore, such protection as it enjoyed came from the normal provisions of a state of the USA rather than indigenous stewardship; yet, albeit non-indigenous myself, as a student of early agriculture and historic landscapes worldwide, I was surrounded by the raw material of my trade and, therefore, by what in a sense was my heritage too.

To be honest, since the place was already known to me as a gem in my academic field, I would have gone there anyway but I was actually there on that particular day with my particular colleagues because of tourism. The development threat to this landscape may have been commercially motivated but the perceived opportunity for development was tourism-led. And what better use for a scrub-covered, stone-littered and bumpy chunk of agriculturally redundant real estate than another international hotel or two and yet another championship-class golf course for Japanese visitors from the west? Plus some housing development for incomers from the east? – indeed, while we're at it, why not make it a global village, with room, designs and attractions for all comers? It would be a super place for a Hawaiian Heritage Centre to pull the tourists in: pity we would not have much to put in it, but perhaps we could get by with a 'History of Golf' display, hula-hula on the hour and continuous piped 'genuine' Hawaiian music.

Our instant reactions to Hawaii are doubtless superficial and ill-informed; but they are genuine tourist impressions and, in that limited context, have, we hope, some first-hand validity. Some of the main points arising are taken up in Chapter 11. Meanwhile, readers should be aware that there is, of course, a huge bibliography of Hawaiiana, scholarly, scientific and popular, which we have scarcely used for our purposes here. We would draw attention in particular to *1988 Statewide Tourism Impact Core Survey* (August 1989), 'one of the four components of the Tourism Impact Management System (TIMS), a system for the continuous monitoring of the impact of tourism on the economic, social and physical environment of the residents of Hawaii'.[16] It is directly relevant to our essays, though it does not focus on our heritage concerns, and is immeasurably more authoritative. Two-thirds of those questioned for it said that 'they felt most visitors were sincerely interested in Hawaii's culture and people'. We are happily of the same opinion as that majority.

6 *Urbane and streetwise*

Each town is an assemblage of heritage; some cities are among the greatest heritage sites in the world.

Tourists flock to towns and cities, almost invariably as points to take off from or arrive at, often as residential centres and frequently as tourist attractions in their own right. Paris and London are outstanding examples where 'heritage', as much assembled from the rest of the world as indigenous, is very much the tourist bait; but throughout the world, many a little town by world standards tries to float *its* own little bit of bait upon the sea of tourist consumerism.

Mérida in Venezuela, for example, is 'Full of history, hospitality and progress. . . . A region of important tourist activity [which] wakes up towards a splendid future of gratifications' where the 'Round night' includes 'multiple trails which procede the most ephemeral, but also the most deserving dose of joy . . . with abundant grudges of mountains, terraces of heights, immoderate rivers to couple the yearnings of furtive love'.[1] Aigues-Mortes (its name from the Latin, *aquae mortuae*, 'dead water', not 'fevered corpses' as one Franglais tourist explained to another), where essential fieldwork for this chapter involved a genuine tourist rip-off dinner, really has an authentic claim on the attention of the cultural tourist but makes no attempt to belie the vibes of its etymology as it looks out over the western reaches of the Parc Naturel Régional de Camargue in southern France, 'erect in a melancholy landscape of ponds, sea marshes, and salt pans'.[2] More modestly, with a lot to be pleasantly modest about, a roadside plaque outside a locally important market town in Northumberland merely enjoins the car-driver intent on diverting along the bypass to 'Visit Historic Morpeth'.[3]

'History' in this context used to be delved into and paraded largely as a matter of local interest and pride, and this is still the case in the many

Morpeths of the world; but now motivation appears to be more consciously concerned with projecting and marketing whatever history happens to have bestowed. This may take the form of a central role in significant historical events, as at Potsdam, Boston and Singapore, the accidental survival of a historic streetscape as in Mdina, Malta, or of a particular old building such as the Roman amphitheatre still in use in Nîmes, the centre of tauromachy, or the magnificently improbable Gothic town hall in Springfield, Illinois. Or it can be rather less obvious and even creaking somewhat in its creativity: with its halo of religious numinosity, one of the great cathedrals of the Christian world, and a World Heritage designation to boot, does Canterbury, England, really need its 'Rupert Bear Trail' as well? 'Urban heritage', manifestly eclectic and elastic, has been sharpened as an economic tool, for towns, as always, need their trade.

Tourists, however, do not see themselves merely as trade tokens. They want quite a lot of a town, and this is where the clashes of interest can begin to develop. In the first place, a city or town has to *seem* to be attractive from a distance in order to attract the attention of the potential visitor. While the serious scholar will go wherever his or her original sources in art gallery, museum or archives lie, no one essentially bent on leisure will willingly go somewhere perceived as being 'worse' than domestic circumstances. For the same reasons, it is difficult to take a positive decision to go somewhere if the attraction to make one do so is not clearly defined. Furthermore, there's not much point in going to a town that no one back home has heard of: where are the social-status Brownie points in visiting 'anywheresville' (unless you can elevate it over suburban sherry to *the* undiscovered place where everybody will be touring two years hence)? Here we are, of course, thinking of the destinations of mass tourism, places brought within reach of large numbers of people through the financial advantages of large-group travel. Setting off to 'explore', for example, the towns of rural France on a bicycle or 'middle America' (*sensu* the midwest states of the USA) by car, is quite a different matter. The element of *not* knowing the specifics is a major part of the hoped-for experience in such cases, in contrast to the expected experience to be garnered by going to, say, Montpellier in eastern Languedoc, France.

Let us stay with Montpellier for a moment, for it illustrates a number of general points about urban heritage and tourism. Montpellier, though perhaps not yet a major tourist attraction in its own right, has many assets, not least an airport as a good destination from which to visit the southern French coast and a direct motorway connection north to Paris and south-west to Barcelona. It is also very much in the Mediterranean climatic zone, a fact not irrelevant to the character of its history, the nature of its heritage, or the economic potential of its future as seen by itself in terms of lead player in an emergent high-tech European sun-belt. One result – and we have to be highly selective – is a visually striking culture clash in the urban matrix, in the city's streetscape and architecture, a clash newly-created and worth going a long way to see.

Le vieux Montpellier is architecturally typical of many provincial French cities and towns, yet idiosyncratic. Unlike many others, for example, it did not originate in Roman times but in the tenth century AD, and furthermore it was in Spanish hands for almost a century and a half before 1349 when it was sold to the French king. Crowded around a hilltop, it consists of a network of sinuous, sloping, urban lanes, interspersed with small 'squares' of varied shape flanked by high, stone buildings. Many are medieval in origin, the barrel-roofs of their vaults often now tantalizingly glimpsed through the windows of smart *boutiques* and hair *salons*. Some enjoyed major conversion and much rebuilding in the sixteenth to eighteenth centuries when new façades, characteristically marked by imposing baroque and classical double-leaf doorways, effectively hid the cool light-wells and open courts of the fashionable *hôtels*, grandiose town houses of substantial citizens.

A good example, not least because it houses the collections of the local archaeological society and is therefore (sometimes) accessible, is the Hôtel des Trésoriers de France in the eponymous *rue*. A private residence in the fifteenth century, it was an official *hôtel* of the Treasurers of France in the seventeenth century when it was considerably enhanced, finally becoming a museum in the twentieth century. Many *hôtels* remain private residences but the hungry visitor can sneak cultural snacks by peering through intimidating doors left ajar. The courtyards of others can legitimately be entered, and in some cases the buildings too, since they serve various official functions and, for a quick internal inspection in the interests of science, a little act as *le fou anglais* wandering into the wrong room neither caused surprise nor demanded much dramatic talent. The proper tourist is, of course, properly catered for: as Michelin rather primly recommends, he or she can take part '*aux visites organisées par le Bureau Municipal de Tourisme sous la conduite d'une guide-conférencière*'.[4] Our fieldwork did not extend thus far.

Musty, antique and very, very private is the ambience of these dwellings, set in a context of a very public street life focusing on the tables and chairs of the pavement cafés. What a contrast is Antigone! Post-modernist, neo-fascist, eclectic classical, trad-brutalist and very public architecture on the grand scale, this massive urban regeneration project proclaims the new Montpellier down by the river. 'We are part of the grand European mainstream stemming from Greece and Rome, arranging the cityscape with a touch of the Versailles to suit our purpose and create an image of ourselves. We include the Hôtel de la Région in our grand design but we are more than French in our aspirations. Here is tradition, order, change and ambition on a Euro-scale' – our interpretation, in our words. The President of Montpellier district actually wrote 'Une Europe forte est le gage de sécurité et d'avenir pour nos enfants'.[5] The vision might work politically and economically; but meanwhile Montpellier has created a major urban monument in its own right, a freak of pre-fabricated late-twentieth century heritage architecture about which no information leaflet existed on site in 1991.

It is likely that Antigone will rapidly become a tourist attraction, as is doubtless also intended. Brand-new and bulky, it creates a powerful image, the more visual in impact precisely because of the contrast with the typical French historic architecture on the hill above. Which place is the heritage? Which heritage is in place?

Urban centres can have the power to pull in resources and create something new, something which is a great local achievement and yet becomes of far more than local significance. In the case of Glasgow, Scotland, it is the Burrell Museum. It serves the purpose of simul-taneously enhancing the image of Glasgow while being successful despite preconceptions of the place. It draws in the tourists and, becoming identified with its city, becomes part of its heritage. At the same time, as so often, a curious ambivalence is at play. Glasgow's pride in so successfully housing, displaying and marketing a windfall collection must be tempered at times by thoughts of the magpie mentality which assembled it and the methods by which so much of the material was wrenched from its cultural context (see Chapter 9). Yet, as a tourist honey-pot, the clean lines of its modern building melding into the rusticity of a post-industrial city, the Burrell is eminently successful.

The city and town, both as an idea and as a physical agglomeration, is clearly one of the most important legacies of the past to the present – a truism, but of central relevance to modern tourism. Tourist brochures and the like stress, of course, many urban attractions other than heritage: shopping, in particular, and cities as convenient places from which to travel to other attractions are often mentioned. But, in homing in on such features, the tourist industry is in fact merely concentrating on certain functions of cities and towns which have been characteristic of urban centres throughout the ages – indeed, those very characteristics which, in assemblages of, say, three or more, define urbanism and distinguish it from other modes of human settlement.

Of a town, 'shopping', more grandiosely trade, is a prime function. Some towns were founded specifically as trade centres, others acquired urban status as a result of their being in the right place at the right time for the exchange of commodities; others died because trade moved elsewhere. Similarly, being in the right place to serve as the node in a communications network is also an urban trait. Modern tourism wings its way to places with such attributes and in so doing reinforces those very urban functions. Hence the modern urban scramble to acquire an international airport and to promote new marketing ventures. Vitoria in northern Spain exemplifies the scramble (see Chapter 7). Montpellier, instanced above, is also promoting an additional attraction: with its new airport open, it is developing 'le Marché Paysan à Antigone qui accueille des dizaines de producteurs de produits régionaux'. Newcastle upon Tyne, already with a thriving regional 'shopping culture' (cf. Hong Kong below) and a mini-international role for 'shopping tourism' in northern England, southern Scotland and western Norway, is doing things the other way round. Its Metro rail system was recently extended to its relatively minor international airport, and it is now expanding the latter.

All this is, however, small beer compared to the existing situations in many cities in, for example, South-East Asia. All the tourist promotions for places such as Hong Kong ('where shopping has reached the status of a national sport'), Singapore (see also Chapter 10), Kuala Lumpur, Manila and Bangkok emphasize, again and again, their merits as shopping and communications centres, the emphasis always being on indigenous products ('exotic' for would-be Western tourists) and convenience for visits to holiday and heritage attractions in the region. Thus is the historical urban function perpetuated in the age of global tourism; yet, as always, clashes occur behind the good intentions and the colourful bazaars. For at one and the same time, developments to meet tourist requirements physically change the nature of historic cities and, more insidiously, tourism inevitably modulates, and can prostitute, indigenous life ways and cultures.

The general thrust of the argument here can be applied across the whole range of urban functions. Clearly they include a number of centralized activities. Government, administration, justice, banking, religion, commemoration and museums, leisure and entertainment, creative and performing arts including festivals: these are just some of the main ones. An obvious result in heritage terms is that cities and towns tend to accrete large, impressive and long-lasting buildings. Such were originally put up for practical reasons, though often with a touch of urban status-seeking too, and now, even when redundant, form significant parts of the ambience and image of the place. Tourists love them; and so does the tourist industry. Every such building has to be (made) special and therefore worth visiting and memorable: each becomes 'unique', the 'tallest', 'longest', 'smallest', 'oldest', 'best-loved', 'best example of . . .' or, at worst, 'the outstandingly typical'.[6] Ordinariness is anathema; the absolute rules.

Large hotels, so characteristic of cities and towns (though not confined to them), are often part of the urban heritage, functionally if the town has been or is a meeting-place, and also architecturally for any one of a host of reasons. They too come to acquire absolute values: La Mamounia, Marrakech, is 'incredible', though the Royal Monasour, Casablanca, is, more modestly, just 'One of the finest hotels in all of North Africa'. Similarly with all sorts of other buildings: in Germany, Speyer Cathedral is 'the largest and most imposing of the High Romanesque period' in that country, while Zons has 'the best preserved medieval [sic] fortifications'. The Kek Lok Si Temple and the Million Buddhas Precious Pagoda is Penang's 'largest and most elaborate temple complex', while Cathedral Square, Helsinki, contains 'a collection of the Baltic's loveliest buildings'. Sadly, however, Dubrovnik, 'a poem in stone', is no longer 'perfectly preserved with its ancient battlements', though presumably Rio de Janeiro's Carnival will continue to be 'the most extravagant of them all'. The 'mostest syndrome' extends from individual historic buildings and traditional events to, of course, whole cities. India 'can boast the remains of ruined cities from virtually every epoch of human history'; Jaisalmer, a still-inhabited medieval desert town, is 'perhaps the most spectacular', while Kausambi is 'one of the oldest – and most impressive'. In Europe, which 'no place in the world can equal . . . for its concentrated diversity of cultures, sights, people and history', Sofia, Bulgaria's capital, 'Steeped in several thousand years of rich history', is 'the greatest city' on the continent; Bruges is 'Europe's most perfectly preserved medieval town' (with 'the best chocolates in the world'), Lucerne is 'the most photographed city' in Switzerland, and Venice is 'the world's most romantic city'. Who needs history when hype brags it bestest?

The borrowing of images from another culture or age can be another facet of promotion now but it is not of course a new phenomenon. Witness the examples of the plan of the city of Washington D.C., the paintings of the Pre-Raphaelites, the architectural 'designs' of British architect Quinlan Terry and the many style 'revivals' through time. Nevertheless, the post-modern period has been characterized by the simultaneous assemblage of cultural images, as demonstrated, for example, by the many constituents from many cultures of our Western meals (see also Chapter 10); and the same phenomenon can be seen in the urban fabric. Our architecture, most acutely our shopping malls; the myriad moving pictures of the television screen; all serve to indicate how cultural images are pulled in from the four corners of the globe on a scale as never before. We *see* presentations of alien cultures/ heritages daily in our home country (see also Chapter 11); in our (the authors') urban context, we can not only see but actually go into an English village, a Greek restaurant, a Roman forum – all fake of course.

Public monuments have frequently been used, particularly in the nineteenth century, for making statements of power/authority/ superiority/subjugation, or partisan politics. The connotations of the chosen images are of course key. Many 'new' towns and cities throughout the world have sought to stamp authority and instant age, to obtain an immediate 'stand-in' simulated culture, via colonization of the classical images of Greece or Rome. A specific link among the more general ones is that between law (and order) and Rome: thus the classical appearance of many city and town halls, law courts, etc. City Fathers who wish to appear as enlightened Medici go for a link with the style of Florence. Byzantine architecture perhaps has more mixed metaphors. An area richly exemplary of this use of cultural images is the West Riding of Yorkshire in the UK. A reason for cultivating a Greek association was explained by Valentine Cunningham when reviewing a book on arts patrons. He said, 'When the city of Munich labelled its galleries after the Athenian house of painting Pinakotheke, it was claiming the kind of kinship that has empowered the makers of Western civilisation at their noblest moments of self-valuation'.[7] The Greek style is especially popular in the United States in architecture and in town and city nomenclature; Philadelphia is an example of the former, Athens (featuring as a name in the USA) the latter. The amusement, albeit semi-fond, that so many of these alien images evoke, indicates how resistant a society may be to such transplants. Most of us can easily conjure up a remembrance of such cultural white elephants in the landscape. It is surely no accident that a good number of buildings in this category are accorded the designation of folly.

The practice of pulling down a historic monument which was a visitor landmark in its original location and re-erecting it elsewhere, can produce a strange cultural juxtaposition (see also Chapter 7), for example the rebuilding of a decontextualized London Bridge over a stretch of desert in Lake Havasu City, Arizona. Even though a historic landscape and the traditions associated with it may remain stationery on their home ground, a potential exists for alteration through attention from outside. Because Brigitte Bardot and others concluded that the Palio, the 'oldest horse race in the world', was dangerous and cruel, staging of the Siena event, 'an umbilical link between each citizen and the city's heritage', was threatened.[8] In the event, the summer 1991 Palio was postponed though only 'because the rival jockeys refused to line up for the start'.[9] An earlier report in *The European*[10] had quoted Siena's mayor as saying: 'We are not going to let publicity-seekers take away an important part of our tradition'; and reporter Tony Rocca continued, 'The Palio is a genuine medieval pageant – and definitely not staged for tourists'.[11]

Nevertheless, towns develop now to gain a competitive edge in, or just to keep up with, the tourist market; tourism itself forces urban places to change to meet its needs. Either way, urban development and reconstruction carries with it interesting heritage implications. Conflicts and ambivalences here arise basically from one of the main characteristics of a successful town or city: its very dynamism. Discounting new towns deliberately created this century (see below), the fact that a town exists today says something about its power at least to survive; in many cases, growth and expansion may well be the hallmarks of its history over recent centuries. By surviving, a town necessarily has to be continually rebuilding upon itself; by rebuilding, its chances of surviving, indeed of being prosperous, increase. Yet, by definition, such vital work is essentially destructive, altering, removing, destroying that which was there already. And that which was there is the town's archaeology before renewal; just as the act of renewal itself produces structures which themselves in time become archaeology.

In Montpellier, Antigone is as much that city's archaeology of the future as was Nîmes's amphitheatre its archaeology of the future in Roman times, an archaeology which has now come to pass. Even more aptly, in Nîmes, the point is made in La Place de la Maison Carrée where, cheek by jowl, Norman Foster's shiny new steel-and-glass cube faces the dull-sounding 'Square House', actually 2,000 years old and the best-preserved of all Roman temples still standing. So the very dynamic which enables the Nîmeses of this world to last for 2,000 years produces a tension in heritage terms between the old and the new; and that tension can so easily be exacerbated by the understandable belief that, to ensure survival, the old *must* give way to the new, that the new has priority.

In the age of mass tourism, that belief has to be challenged, if only on practical and economic grounds. For what is it that tourism thrives on? And how many towns and cities now can afford not to tempt the tourist with their heritage, either standing as part of a living urban community, as briefly touched on above, or as ruins of former communities, at best visible as monuments? Paradoxically, as so often the case in heritage matters, it is precisely those cities which lost their momentum to renew themselves and lay down and died which now provide such magnets for the world tourist industry: think of Chaco, Ch'ang-an, Leptis Magna, Macchu Picchu, Mohenjo-Daro, Petra, Ephesus, Troy and Zimbabwe. More dramatically, think of Pompeii and Herculaneum; more modestly, think of the 'ghost towns' of the north American frontier, places like Jerome near Flagstaff, Arizona, and Dyea, Alaska (see Chapter 3); and, in the English countryside, greenfield sites of former urban status like Old Sarum, the grassy banked forerunner of Salisbury, and Wroxeter, precursor of Shrewsbury as Roman Viroconium, now superficially marked mainly by a bit of bath-house wall.

But there is a further question. It is not too difficult to make the argument that obviously important, often visually impressive, standing structures should be preserved, partly as sites for visitors to see, partly as icons of local pride. This applies whether it be a 5,000-year-old megalithic complex, as at Tarxien in the suburbs of Valletta, Malta, Chartres cathedral, or the early-twentieth-century Post Office in Fayetteville, Arkansas. The values may be relative: 'oldness' itself is an example but the argument is based on an absolute: either you keep the building or you lose it. If it is knocked down, it has gone and no reconstruction, however well-done or well-motivated, can replace the authenticity of the original. Berlin, rather belatedly accepting the fact that, like it or not, its Wall *is* its heritage, is facing this problem now: it is rebuilding a short stretch of it as a tourist attraction. But even the original, the obvious heritage of major standing structures and buildings, is only part of the story. A fuller understanding of urban history can only come from a much more holistic attitude towards the archaeological products of the processes of urban change itself.

Two examples will suffice to make the point. Major buildings may well be genuinely important historically – as architecture, as monuments to corporate or individual achievement, as the *locus* of significant events, as icons. They cannot, however, represent more than a part of what has happened in a city or town. That applies, of course, even if all types of evidence were wholly taken into account, but nevertheless, taking buildings alone, a range of other types, non-monumental in intent maybe, say important things about an urban settlement and its society. Artisan houses of the nineteenth century are a case in point for they may well represent an important developmental stage in a city's growth and prosperity.

The city of Bath, England, now a World Heritage Site, was in the 1960s understandably fixated on its Georgian heritage of great terraces and urban streetscape; but obliterated were hundreds of less-grand contemporary and Victorian houses which represented not just another level of society but also, quite as much as the grand houses, an important phase in the growth and prosperity of the City's history. Pushed towards its limits, the argument could demand preservation of even less distinguished buildings, such as those in the downtown slum area of Tucson, Arizona, cleared in the 1970s. But at least that town saw the development of a systematic examination of the area and its buried archaeology before it was redeveloped, a locally important example of a process which has, sometimes on a huge and continuing scale, especially in Europe and Japan, led to the emergence over the last generation of 'urban archaeology' as part of the mainstream of the discipline. One of its aims, obviously, is to help preserve the monumental and obvious buildings: that is common sense, if only to meet tourist needs; but as a message it does not go far enough and many have failed to realize this. For scientific reasons, even if there is nothing for the tourist to see, at least record the other buildings before destruction so that archives as well as preserved buildings can provide the basis for urban history. Scientific and ethical questions apart, if that is not done, increasingly history will become distorted and 'the heritage' narrowed to the visible and maintained, the great and the good.

Clearly, however, dichotomies exist here: maybe broad-based historicity is not required either by town politicians or by tourists, provided they can see selected bits of monumental history preserved as heritage. One such typical selection was shown to one of us (P.J.F.) on a standard day-tour of Caracas, Venezuela. In a pseudo-vernacular restaurant he enjoyed a 'traditional' tourist lunch. Either side of it he saw 'old' Caracas around Plaza Bolívar with its eponymous equestrian statue, shipped in bits from Munich and rescued from the sea-bottom after the vessel carrying it sank on Los Roques; the Casa Natal, Simón Bolívar's birthplace, and the adjacent Museo Bolívariano; the seventeenth-century Cathedral with the Bolívar family chapel; the Capitol, home of the National Congress, with the *Salón Elíptico* where the Declaration of Independence is kept beneath overarching ceiling murals of the battle of Carabobo; and (accidentally) the changing of the guard at the National War Memorial, its classical aura inevitably taking thoughts back to colonial Spain's Roman provincial history. Its many statues included that to 'La Nación a Los Precursores de La Independencia', the whole to Western eyes having the general ambience of an up-market garden centre. He also saw, but they were not pointed out, the extensive shanty-town outer suburbs historically characteristic of so many cities but very definitely not part of their tourist heritage.

Similar tours experienced in London and Paris by boat, and Malta and Los Angeles by mini-bus, suggest that all such are essentially the same and shared by millions of people every year. What a paradox if, all over the world, tourists are travelling to visit cities and towns that are different and yet, unless they make the effort to eschew the tourist tour and 'do their own thing', everywhere everyone is being fed the same soup – 'heritage' minestrone: the contents differ in detail but the concoction is still minestrone. As one travel brochure rather surprisingly asked, making the point that its tours induced 'delightful confusion: a half-remembered kaleidoscope', 'Did we feed the ducks in Geneva or Lausanne?'[12]

Of course, the details of cities and of what is drawn to the attention of passing tourists *do* differ. In terms of perception and experience, there is indeed a lot of difference, for example, between a Buddhist temple and a Catholic cathedral; but both are *religious* buildings. So, probably inevitably, a perception of urbanity selected for tourist purposes concentrates on the architecturally obvious, famous names and local/national patriotism. Understandably, every urban place needs its local heroes for its own self-esteem; better still if it can glow with pride at an association with someone of national or greater standing. Nevertheless, such figures tend to be inflated in significance to meet the needs of the 'mostest' type of tourism – who after all wants to visit the home or museum of a nobody? – while, at this level of mini-bus heritage tourism, interesting but controversial issues such as social variety, ethnic diversity, and social and ethnic deprivation are clearly not part of urban heritage. Pity: such are among the traits which make cities different and dynamic as well as interesting. Witness Caracas, Kabul, Los Angeles, Sarajevo alone in the early months of 1992. Ten minutes debussed in some exotic but carefully 'touristified' Chinatown or 'Latin quarter' in a Western city, waiting in readiness for the regular arrivals of the tourist coach, is not quite urban authenticity. To take a 'safe' alternative, in Paris try walking not only with all the other tourists along the Champs Elysées but also through the 'North African' quarter south-east of Montmartre to sense something of one sort of diversity inherent in one contemporary urban society very much as the result of historical processes. Every true urban visitor, but not the safely packaged mini-bussed or group-coached tourist, will be able to think of his or her own analogue to that, and ponder on the growing dichotomy between processed heritage and historical process.

A tourism which truly faced up to providing 'quality' would address such matters, not simply pretend they do not exist by glossing over them with alternatives – in the case of Montmartre, 'les Folies' – or ignoring them altogether. Maybe the average tourist does not want to know; but maybe the average tourist should be made to become acquainted with urban reality, which is after all rather more a product of history than a soft-focus, sanitized heritage alone. That is a moot point: can, or should, a service industry take its consumers down a particular, possibly doctrinaire, even élitist, route? Does tourism have an educational role? If not, fine, let's just enjoy ourselves and confine our perceptions of heritage to pleasantries; but if it does, – and many tourists do travel for self-education – then perhaps the tourist menu, the very concept of urban heritage indeed, should be broadened. In a curiously vivid way, the sociologies of contemporary urban societies are arguably as much 'historical', and can certainly be made as interesting in presentation, as any old building or patriotic tomb.

This would certainly appear to be the case in Belfast, Northern Ireland, a city described as the scene 'of the world's longest running urban conflict'. In 1992, 'several thousand' tourists are expected. 'Many come . . . as part of legitimate community, political or social service groups' because Belfast 'is still one of the safer places in which to see urban warfare and its effects first hand'. 'Welcome to West Belfast', says the tourist map provided by Sinn Fein, the political wing of the Provisional Irish Republican Army; 'the bloody landmarks . . . are on the holiday map', said the sub-head of the article reporting this example of 'political tourism', 'serving an existing demand', maybe, but providing for less than 1 per cent of Belfast's tourist trade.[13]

Annapolis in Maryland, USA, provides a rather different illustration of socio-urban heritage. There, a public interpretive programme based on town excavations has been running since 1981. It was first designed for visitors and then 'various local audiences, including the city's African-American comunities', a phrase incorporating the vital point that a city's population is not just uni-dimensional in its heritage perceptions but contains many minorities, ethnic and otherwise, each with its own current needs of several pasts. The programme's success has stemmed from carefully controlled presentation. One of the basic principles is 'any particular interpretive moment must be a unique event, tied explicitly to its place, its time, its interpreter, and its audience'. Two of the basic beliefs are that 'an effective archeological interpretation must acknowledge the contemporary social world that is its platform . . . site tours best serve the interests of their audiences when they encourage visitors to keep the present in mind as they think about the past'.[14]

These are the antidotes to twee-ness, nostalgia and cliché. Further, such an approach to visitors can offer, indeed involve them in, participation in rather than a mere passive consumption of heritage: in Annapolis at the Main Street site, 'among other things, a tour about tourism given to tourists . . . was focussed on ceramic evidence of the segmentation of daily life in the 18th century and suggested that one contemporary product of this way of thinking is a division between work time and leisure time that allows for vacations and tourism, the very activities that brought most visitors to the . . . site'. Using in this case 'the activity of tourism as a tie between past and present', it was possible to expand from the particular of 'potsherds, strata and builders' trenches' to the more general such as, here, 'the early history of capitalism'. As a result, 'visitors were engaged with the interpretation rather than making themselves into human cameras'. That must have been particularly so – for how do you photograph an idea? – when the tour discussed ways 'in which Annapolitans have subtly used the city's history, and in particular stories about George Washington, to guide contemporary visitor behaviour . . . [suggesting] that all interpretations of the past are the products of contemporary needs and interests'. Such a suggestion is of course anathema to and the exact opposite of most site interpretation, whether delivered by signage, a leaflet or a human guide; it is not what is delivered and, to be fair, it is almost certainly not what most tourists want. But if their perfectly legitimate expectation is 'to know', and the guide's function is to enlighten, is it unavoidable that both parties perform only within a framework of unilaterally passing and receiving 'information' as if the past was known, dead and solidified rather than party to a dialogue driven by contemporaneity?

The Annapolis tour 'closed by suggesting to visitors that the next time they visited an interpreted historic site they could ask [themselves] just what [the interpretation's] version of the past wanted to get them to do'. Such an approach to urban heritage, however, raises at least three questions. First, it answers positively the query about whether tourism has an educational function. Second, questioning as well as questing tourists within an educational situation could overload the intellectual and presentational abilities of far too many guides, trained if at all only to act as talking set-piece guidebooks rather than teachers. And third, a presentation along Annapolitan lines is far more difficult to conceptualize and deliver than the minimalist approach of many tour operators with their set-piece and cliché-loaded versions of highly selective and unquestioning heritage. Perhaps their product meets the need of the segments of the mass market they package into their coaches, mini-buses and boats; just as the more cerebral packages offered by the more up-market operators aim at more discerning – or just richer – tourists. But it still seems legitimate to query whether mass heritagism *has* to be as it is; it *could* be different and it *should* be both more informed and more informative.

There is a related problem of perception, touched on in both the Annapolis and Tucson examples above. Standing structures, whatever their social or architectural status, are only the tip of the cultural iceberg in urban circumstances. The other nine-tenths of the archaeological cake, to change the metaphor, lie buried in layers below the icing of the visible, but only superficial, streetscapes and buildings. The phenomenon of archaeological urban stratigraphy is of course the product of the dynamism which produces and perpetuates an urban settlement: a city buries its past as it survives and develops, sometimes assisted by natural forces such as flood deposits and volcanic ash. Occasionally, like conquest, they can be terminal, as at Pompeii, but burial is still the result. The 'dead city' tells of the Middle East are probably the best-known archaeological sites illustrating the principle of urban stratigraphic accumulation; but exactly the same process has resulted in prehistoric but still-living cities like Jericho seeming to be built on mounds. Even in Europe there are many similar examples: deserted tells in the Balkans, for example, and extant cities and towns, like Paris and Oxford, sitting on metres of deposit – human rubbish, if you like, but crucial scientific evidence from another point of view. So here is another sort of 'culture clash', again between the old and new in one sense but rather more fundamentally between the perceptions, the culture, of scientist and developer.

The relevance of this to heritage and tourism is at least twofold. In the first place, the acquisition or non-acquisition of information from the buried urban archaeology can radically affect the history not only of a particular town but our understanding of the whole process of urbanism within which that particular place has developed. On the general point, it is almost entirely through archaeology that the origins and development of the urban process as a world phenomenon have been studied, in effect by synthesis from site-by-site examination at places such as Jericho, Athens and Teotihuacán; similarly in any one region or period, such as Anatolia in the fifth to fourth millennia BC or western Europe in the second half of the first millennium AD, it is from the archaeological evidence that both trends and particular detail come.

Maybe this does not immediately matter to the tourists who switch their gaze from guidebook to monument as they stand in front of the preserved heritage structure they have come to see or been guided to look at; maybe it does not even particularly matter that, perhaps in advance of development to construct a new tourist hotel, the origins of a particular town have been pushed back a thousand years by study of the buried archaeology there. This can easily happen: Aylesbury, an apparently medieval foundation in Buckinghamshire, England, is a recently attested example, now with pre-Roman origins. But whether it matters in touristic terms or not, such changes in knowledge matter a lot in other respects and ultimately underpin the various frameworks in which tourist interpretation, however well informed or trite, is presented. Nevertheless, there are dissonances here, in theory, practice, perception, preservation and presentation.

One particular place where such dissonances occur together is the urban cemetery, an especially characteristic feature of the city or large town. Until recently, few people visited them except out of need, their image of gloom and spookiness, dreariness and death, reinforced by a thousand pictures on television and cinema screen: that cemetery in 1940s Vienna, for example, with which the film *The Third Man* so vividly opens and closes. Yet now they loom increasingly large in late-twentieth-century affairs, not least in relation to heritage and tourism. Death becomes greener as urban cemeteries are seen not just as places for human peace and quiet in ever noisier, more hassling cities, but also as oases for wildlife and plants; and this happens just when those very cemeteries now best endowed ecologically through disuse and lack of maintenance are seen in another perspective as 'ripe for development' precisely because they are 'wasteland' in urban places where un-built-on land is in short supply and valuable.

More pertinent to the man-made urban heritage, cemeteries have come to be seen as 'valuable' in quite other senses. These other values of perception add to the tension and open clashes in battles for their future. Attitudes to the dead are, curiously in a less religious Western world, becoming more respectful, motivated perhaps more by atavistic ancestor worship than established religion; and some particular dead persons buried in one place are awaited for reburial elsewhere. Two empty tombs in the National Pantheon, Caracas, for example, await the remains of Venezuelan founding fathers, Francisco de Miranda from Spain and Antonio José de Sucre from Colombia. Some people were famous when buried, others have become famous since death; either way, their graves or tombs now have become places of pilgrimage, for reasons of piety, inspiration, exploitation or just fun. Particular individuals apart, a cemetery overall is also a marvellous scientific resource, its inscriptions revealing masses of information about the history of the city. Family names, of course, fashions in Christian names, marriage alliances, and patterns of mortality (age at death, who was buried where, etc.): these and other aspects of city life, for example aspects of 'indigenous and colonial' in the brief, inscribed biographies of immigrants, foreign servants and careerist expatriates, are all there. Inscriptions are characteristically in such quantity that they lend themselves to the 'god' of the late twentieth century, the number-crunching computer, for the purposes of historical research. And then there is the architecture of the tombs, the art of the crosses and gravestones, and the craft of the stonemason and metalworker, a combination which says much about the community and the place of religion in it, as well as of nameable individuals.

Found all over the world, because so many cities expanded so hugely in the nineteenth century, these memorials are now a hundred or more years old, far enough away in time for them to have become 'historic' and for us to be able to appreciate them as 'heritage'. So, urban cemeteries, places of the dead, take on a new lease of life as tourist attractions. Some are promoted as such. Glasgow's Necropolis is an outstanding example in terms of its excellent visitor trail and funer-eally dramatic situation and architecture. Macabre though this may sound, the cemetery is 'new' as a tourist facility only because it contains memorials to our immediate forebears, for we as tourists have, after all, been visiting the places of the remote dead as a staple of our traveller's fare since tourism began. Is there so much difference in travelling to see the Chinese Emperor's terracotta army, the tombs at Mycenae and Marx's grave in Highgate? One might ponder, however, whether a difference in kind, rather than one merely of degree, has visited the urban cemetery when, as at Père-Lachaise in Paris, respond-ing to its perhaps primary contemporary role as a major tourist attraction, electric scooters are available for hire 'to allow foot-sore visitors to get round the 109-acre site – the largest in the French capital'.[15] But then there are so many people to *see*: Colette, Molière, Proust, Balzac and Simone Signoret among the natives, and among the foreigners American rock star Jim Morrison of *The Doors* and Oscar Wilde from Ireland. The cynic may well remark 'Trust the French to come up with this response to tourism'; but, equally, trust the French to provide quiet and unobnoxious *electric* scooters.

The instance vividly exemplifies one facet of the impact of tourism on urban heritage. Even as recently as twenty years ago, few would have thought of cemeteries as major tourist attractions, let alone of the need to cater for tourists by providing them with scooters of any sort in such traditionally sombre surroundings. This cemetery example, however, serving as representative here of so many other aspects of historic urbanity like public gardens, waterfronts, canals and bridges, makes a far more important point than that of physical impact. It shows that, just as a town or city has to change to stay alive, so that place's heritage, the significances and values that we attach to bits and pieces of its surviving fabric and to former residents, must change also. And that process of evolution demands an awareness on the citizens' part of good academic information coming from discovery, research and reassessment, quite as much as of perceptions deriving from standard histories, visitor surveys, tourist projections and the like.

One of us (P.J.F.) was seriously threatened with being put in the stocks when he levelled a charge of 'hypocrisy' at the leaders of one small town, rather complacent about its thousand-year-old history and its endowment of standing half-timbered buildings. As he saw it, their pride in their town's history and heritage was false while they allowed its buried archaeology to be ripped apart in redevelopment; they looked at their preserved buildings and their civic celebrations of an anniversary of a local battle, and were considerably annoyed. This was a case of complete misunderstanding on both sides, for each was using different criteria to form different perceptions of what that town's past consisted of and by what it should be represented; but the town turned out to have Roman origins all the same, which made it more interesting to some, even though nothing Roman is to be seen, while in no way detracting from visitors' superficial appreciation of the pretty buildings.

Twenty years later, when he (P.J.F.) stood with others at the main cross-roads in the centre of Quibor, a small and 'obviously' Spanish colonial foundation in Venezuela, he thought of that little British town. In front of him was an archaeological excavation, a proud example of pioneer urban archaeology in that country; it clearly demonstrated pre-Hispanic occupation features. On the other side of of the road, the town square was ablaze, visually and aurally, with civic *fiesta*, welcoming in 'traditional' style the largest group of cultural tourists ever to visit there. The group was made up of several hundred members of the World Archaeological Congress and their many hosts. Whose heritage was available to whom? At that moment in that little town the past and present, the heritage on display and perceptions of it, were multi-layered in a particularly ambivalent but vivid way.

In essence, so far, too much tourist attention is being concentrated upon too little of the whole world collection of urban heritage and the significant historical processes of which it is, at one and the same time, product and witness. For many, many reasons, some of which we have tried to indicate, the tourist is not being allowed the opportunity to see visually, and 'see' in the sense of 'perceive intellectually', all that he, or she, might. Towns and cities are actually much more interesting than the tourist is often allowed to appreciate – and there is no need for the visitor's experience of *urbanitas* to be effectively short-changed. Tourism may thrive, but tourists are constrained. Selection and ignorance inhibit the quality of the urban heritage itself; they bottle the potential of the experience of an urban visit both for the individual and for our better collective appreciation of urbanity as a very remarkable world phenomenon.

7 *The rural scene*

The majority of the world's population lives in the country; yet a high proportion of those setting out to be tourists live in urban circumstances: cities, towns and suburbs. Furthermore, almost by definition, they move from urban outskirts to other urban outskirts as they fly between their main destinations as global tourists. Much of the time, they fly over water, though the height of intercontinental flights is such that this matters little in terms of external terrestrial perceptions. If anything, cloudscapes rather than landscapes catch the eye as each and every passenger is wrapped in a sort of depersonalized and timeless airborne package, culturally neutralized into marginal differences of sartorial style, plasticized food and audio-visual menu.

Even when the land below can be seen, at most it may be noticed as a bit of countryside, a glimpse of a rural scene; it scarcely registers as landscape, an artefact to be perceived and interpreted where Man has marked its surface, often influencing its vegetation and shaping its superficial form. For the tourist, essentially the travel is the means to an end of visiting something rather than part of the 'experience', the tour, which has been saved for, anticipated and paid for in advance. Yet in many parts of the world, the landscape itself, however viewed, is as much part of the heritage as the more obvious monuments and sites to which the air-conditioned coach whisks the ex-pressurized passenger on landing. And while many of the tourist meccas are indeed urban, like Paris, Athens, San Francisco and Mecca itself, a great number of the sites to which the urban-based hordes make an exodus now exist in rural surroundings, though such may not always have been the case.

Immediately a number of major heritage-management issues present themselves. How, for example, is it best to present a rural attraction to an audience largely soaked in urban life ways? Is there indeed a 'best' way, taking 'best' to mean ideal from the historical point of view; or can the 'best' only be a lowest common denominator, a pap of cultural compromise, given the multi-ethnic origins and wildly different educational levels of visitors likely at a major rural site? To what extent, in any case, are such major sites representative of former rural life ways? Furthermore, how can the essential rural nature of a country site be preserved when tourist needs require the trappings of suburbia or town centre – large parks for cars and coaches, cafés and conveniences, good access roads well-lit and clearly signposted, and nearby hotels? Interpretively, how do you cope with a site which, now ruins in a desert or overgrown by jungle, was once 'urban', at least by the standards of its day?

And what about time? 'Wilderness' is described as 'primeval', 'landscape' as 'timeless', 'scenery' as 'untouched', 'countryside' as 'unchanging'. Yet, of course, the essence of that greater part of the globe's landmass which is rural is precisely that it has changed and is changing all the time. Nature has always attended to that, and so has Man since his emergence, always extending and increasing the impact of his presence. Even in pre-farming times, his activities were far from environmentally neutral wherever he (or she) hunted and collected and furthermore, in his own mind anyway, he created a cultural landscape, likely to have been along the lines shown to Western scientists by indigenous peoples in Australasia, Africa and the Americas. Such peoples, then and now, enjoyed different concepts of time from those of many modern societies, and now tourists come to their destinations all over the world with their own cultural chronologies. The obvious example is that 'medieval' to the European is 'prehistoric' to the North American, but many others visit with different concepts of time past or with fixed points unrelated to the date of birth, itself 'floating' by a year or two, of a Jewish carpenter's son some 2,000 years ago.

Above all, perhaps, but depending on your standpoint, there is the question of the integrity of the site, 'the resource' as academically based heritage managers conceptualize it: how can its scientific value be preserved, in the form of physically existing components above and below ground, while meeting the reasonable needs of possibly hundreds of thousands of tourists of whom the great majority may well have travelled thousands of miles to be there?

Two of the few certainties in this complex are that each tourist, however much packaged, comes as an individual with individual expectations; and that there is no portmanteau solution, each site being individual too. Ideally, in addition each visit, each 'experience', should also be a unique occasion, particular not just to site and visitors but also to the moment in time at which it occurs. To create such a sense is difficult, especially if the laggards of the group in front are still leaving and the chatter of the next group to arrive impinges on what should be a developing relationship between tourists and a perhaps increasingly harassed guide. Nevertheless, at the levels of both strategy and detail, and at many points in between, much has by now been learnt about the inter-relationship of rural heritage and tourism: it is possible to discuss what seems to be 'good' and 'bad' practice in terms of professional management. That said, however, among the many variables in operation at any one site, or indeed throughout a heritage institution at, say, national level, much will depend, irrespective of the nature of the site itself, on the motivation of management and the resources available to it.

We will now look at some specific examples and then turn to a few themes. We begin with mini-case-studies of two rural World Heritage Sites. Both are in the UK, indeed only some 80 km apart and not far from where we live; but any whiff of parochialism is, we hope, offset by the fact that we know both well, by their world status, and by the way in which they bring to the fore many of the issues common to rural heritage sites throughout the world. They lack an overt racial or ethnic dimension (that is, as a management issue), since they 'belong to' and are managed and interpreted by organizations and people native to England; though in fact neither was English in inspiration, yet another example of a heritage paradox. Ethnicity has already been discussed in Chapters 3 and 5 and is touched on again later in this chapter.

The sites are: Fountains Abbey and Studley Royal, North Yorkshire, and Hadrian's Wall, crossing northern England through the counties of Tyne and Wear, Northumberland and Cumbria.

Fountains Abbey and Studley Royal

The extensive ruins, now carefully consolidated 'as found', of the large, originally early-twelfth-century Cistercian Abbey lie across a valley bottom. In themselves, they constitute an outstanding monument, 'the loveliest of England's ruins'.[1] In addition, however, part of that loveliness stems from their present context, a landscape and tenurial context which is quite unlike their medieval surroundings. The Abbey was dissolved in 1539 and in the eighteenth century its valley was landscaped into one of the outstanding gardens in England. This combination of visual delight accreted over nearly a millennium, part accidentally but also very much deliberately, irresistibly justifies the World Heritage designation now; but, despite the authentic historicity of the complex, its mid-twentieth-century management history might have led elsewhere.

In recent decades, Studley Royal, the estate including the landscaped gardens, experienced difficulties of maintenance and management style, reflecting its ownership by local authorities while they themselves were undergoing change. Ownership passed in the mid-1980s to the National Trust, a body which has subsequently successfully undertaken major restoration works, not least of the water gardens. It has also initiated a positive management programme for the many individual structures, such as temples, for the woodlands which are visually such a crucial part of the man-made 'natural' scenery, and for the increasingly large number of visitors (200,000 in 1990). The Abbey ruins themselves are the responsibility of the Historic Buildings and Monuments Commission for England ('English Heritage') as a Property in Care. Perhaps idiosyncratically English, the shooting rights over the estate are privately owned – and exercised, much to the disquiet of visitors.

In 1991, therefore, this World Heritage Site exhibits characteristics typical of many large rural heritage complexes throughout the world. Its history is long and diverse, its academic interest considerable. It is extremely costly to maintain and manage, and great demands are made by it on conservation and other professional skills. It enjoys, if that is the word, numerous different official designations, and its management is split between two national bodies, both statutory but one an arm of government and the other a charity relying on voluntary support. Local interest, official and personal, in the place is intense; a private interest in one of its functions, shooting, itself a sort of heritage activity, is much valued, of great monetary value, and overtly exercised. And meanwhile the tourists pour in in ever larger numbers.

This last fact has forced the Trust to take radical action: the commissioning of a new multi-million-pound visitor centre. For this to happen, and for its benefits then to be reaped, a huge effort has had to be made, ranging from the purchase of non-heritage land for car parks, a new road and the centre itself, widespread public consultation, a highly detailed programme of archaeological mitigation, and a fundamental redesign of visitor access to the estate and the Abbey. Yet one suspects that, once all is complete and functioning in 1992, the vehicles will arrive in their thousands, the people in their hundreds of thousands, and perhaps but one in a thousand will pause to wonder at what has been done for them, indeed quite specifically for them. The site itself needed none of this; it is the phenomenon itself, contemporary tourism, and its physical impact upon the heritage, which demanded it. Simultaneously the heritage tourists themselves implied that their expectations, growing as fast as their numbers, required ever better paths, toilet facilities and eating places.

Pondering this phenomenon as exemplified at Fountains, feeding upon itself as it drags the trappings of suburbia into the rural scene, a useful question would seem to be: should it be otherwise? Should not the individual visitor, the thronging tourists, be blissfully unaware of the managerial and financial infrastructure making their experience care-free? – and, furthermore, making it inconsequential in the sense that the visit carries no consequential responsibilities for the site? Indeed, does not the tourist have the *right* to expect that it should be thus? Whatever the answers, the tensions in the running and the presentation of this major rural site, so typical of others, are clearly there – though perhaps not to the tourist. Yet clashes of interest, of policy, of culture, lurk round every manicured lawn and bosky grove: public access and private sport; the expense of conservation of the historic resource competing with the expense of providing for tourist needs and expectations; the mundane and the aesthetic. On a global scale, Fountains may be just down the road from where we write, but its significances, for management, heritage and tourism, are far from parochial.

Hadrian's Wall

Exactly the same applies to Hadrian's Wall: rural heritage local to us but vibrant with tensions and clashes as in many another rural heritage area. It hardly needed its World Heritage Site designation (1987), and even now (1992), locally, this status has hardly been recognized and certainly not yet taken suitably into account. But it is not the Wall itself which has been enhanced by world designation, a fact which immediately takes us to one of its problems in terms of heritage and tourism: ignorance. The Wall is well known; it is not known well.

Among many reasons for this is that it is *believed* to be known well, thereby inhibiting enquiry and encouraging the recycling of populist cliché and myth. Much of the information and thinking resulting from recent research is not yet published and is certainly not yet in the 'popular' syntheses and guidebooks. People tend not to read them anyway. Furthermore, the bulk of tourists who 'do the Wall' do so differentially, congregating at one or two 'visual hotspots' for half an hour while ignoring the other 99 per cent of the frontier both spatially and intellectually.

Yet nowadays the Wall is undoubtedly a major tourist attraction with perhaps more than a quarter of a million visitors each year from a worldwide customer band (as most of it is of open access, it is impossible to count them: one of its management problems). And it has always attracted visitors, a significant minority of them scholars and writers; so it has an extensive literature. Daniel Defoe, for example, 'conscious of an English heritage', wrote about it in prose described as 'achieving the most satisfactory mode of literary tourism'.[2] He 'was tempted greatly . . . to trace the famous Picts Wall, built by the Romans, or rather rebuilt by them . . . and I did go to several places in the fields through which it passed, where I saw the remains of it, some almost lost, some plain to be seen'.

Nearly three hundred years ago, then, Defoe had already raised some of the fundamental issues which still concern the managers, presenters and walkers of the Wall. Who built it? How should it be preserved? What should it look like and what sort of access should be available to whom? How should it be interpreted and for whom? Such questions are common to many examples of rural heritage, whether of world status or not; but the World Heritage label seems to increase pressure and expectation.

In the first place, 'Who *did* build the Wall?' exemplifies a question fairly basic to all tourist heritage sites. Presenters need at least to know that, academically to put the site into some sort of cultural and chronological context if they so wish to do, and pragmatically because it is one of those elementary pieces of information that even the casual visitor tends to want to know. In the case of Hadrian's Wall, it was not built by the Picts, that is certain; though many a Briton, together with other indigenes of late prehistoric Europe, doubtless actually laboured on its construction under Roman military supervision once Hadrian had ordered a wall to be built in AD 122. But, for long, scholarship decreed that it was the Wall of Severus, Emperor from AD 193 to 211, and now, by one of those curious twists of academic interpretation afforded by further research, Hadrian's Wall is indeed recognized to have been extensively rebuilt by him. Much of the authentically Roman wall that we see now is actually Severan rather than Hadrianic. It was, however, altered, knocked down, repaired and robbed by many others over the 1,700 years after Severus, but most of them are anonymous. Some would probably like to remain so.

Among them would doubtless be the Commissioners who were responsible in 1750–1 for obliterating miles of the Wall beneath the Military Way, a new strategic road linking Newcastle and Carlisle in the wake of the 1745 rebellion. Theirs was a destructive compromise, their main concern being to avoid offending, or having to pay compensation to, the local landowners; so they literally took the line of least resistance *along* an existing boundary originally designed to prevent passage at right angles to it. What an ironic fate for what had been in its day the strongest-built frontier system outside China.

One known latter-day builder, however, was John Clayton of Chesters, a Roman fort on the Wall where his house was built in the *vici* (suburbs). Local estate-owner, long lasting Town Clerk of Newcastle upon Tyne and antiquary, he was motivated by the continuing destruction of the Wall in the early decades of the nineteenth century to buy up and rebuild parts of it. He was particularly successful and active along the stretches either side of what has come to be the modern honeypot site on the Wall, Housesteads fort. As a result, another rich irony is that much of the actual Wall seen by most of today's tourists is neither the Picts', nor Hadrian's nor Severus', but Clayton's, not seventeen but one and a half centuries old.

Despite Clayton, the Wall in the late twentieth century is in an extremely varied state, more so than when Defoe commented on its condition some two hundred years ago. None of it, after all, had been restored in his day, whereas now, at one extreme, great management and conservation skill goes into maintaining impressive lengths with good public access. Elsewhere, at the other extreme, some lengths do not exist. In between, some parts which were once there are no longer visible at or above ground level; which is not quite the same thing as saying that they do not exist, though to all intents and purposes that is the effect as far as tourists are concerned. One American tourist is supposed to have demanded his money back because the Wall is not standing to its full height. Why, others may well ask, can we not see it if it is there? Why don't the lazy archaeologists get off their backsides and uncover it?

There are several answers to such questions: one is that a particular length of buried Wall, or an unexcavated turret, for example, is deliberately *not* being excavated now, is quite consciously being preserved untouched underground, so that next century or later archaeologists with different questions from ours will be able to have access to 'pure' evidence from which to try to answer them. Intellectually, this is a perfectly proper argument and one in keeping with a 'green' approach seeking to perpetuate the life of a finite resource, which informs a lot of heritage conservation. Just try telling it, however, to an impatient and enthusiastic tourist who has come 3,000 miles to the site and paid a lot of money to do so. 'I want to see my heritage now' is also a cogent, if more emotional, argument, and one in keeping with

the demand-and-supply character of modern tourism and its consu-
merist considerations.

So here is another clash, more strictly two. One is philosophical: as a
general principle, should we have it all now or, knowingly denying
ourselves, reserve some 'new' heritage for our successors? The other is
more practical: if we make as much heritage as possible available now,
are we prepared to accept that we will be destroying its academic
context in the process of exposing it to the wear and tear of weather
and tourism? A sequential question is: are we prepared to pay for both
the process of scientific examination and public presentation?

One of the difficulties with Hadrian's Wall is that perception of it
generally does not accord with the reality. It was and is a very complex
structure. The Wall itself was originally built to different specifications
and in different materials over some 118 km from the River Tyne to
the Solway Firth. It is but one part of an extremely sophisticated
frontier defence system which itself was radically adapted several
times during its three hundred or so years' use in the Roman period
alone, never mind its subsequent history. The frontier has extent in
depth north–south as well as length east–west; it is long-lived and
structurally complicated. It exists in a living landscape, urban and
rural. Surprisingly perhaps, this range of qualities was recognized in its
World Heritage designation, the official title of which is the Hadrian's
Wall Military Zone. Uniquely, this Zone has no drawn boundaries on
a map: it is a concept that has been designated, not a place or a
monument and very definitely not just the Wall itself. Furthermore, it
is the landscape context of the military zone which is recognized in the
designation quite as much as the plethora of Roman sites and structures which are strewn over it.

Interestingly, pre- and post-Roman elements in that landscape, and
features of any date which have still to be discovered, are presumably
also included in the designation. The former have, after all, contributed to that landscape, not only in being visible components of it now
but as representative of activities with landscape consequences. A
prehistoric settlement, for example, implies land-clearance, tree-felling
and farming, all affecting the ecology and almost certainly a factor in
creating the present, much appreciated wild and barren scenery of the
most visited parts of the tourists' 'Wall country'. Similarly, the pattern
of attractive stone field walls across the moors which give such
character to this landscape must also be included even though they are
not only 'late' – mainly nineteenth-century enclosure of the 'waste' –
but positively contributed to the degradation of the Wall by often
being built of stone from it.

So there are problems of perception as well as protection and presentation, problems which are exacerbated by the large number of institutions with an official or self-given interest in the Wall area. They range from UNESCO and its World Heritage Committee to the councils of the parishes in the Wall area, from tourist and commercial bodies to local amenity and conservation groups. So management of the Wall area, itself complicated enough in size, content and concept, is made more difficult by the ramshackle organizational structure which, like the complexity of the landscape itself, has accreted over the years. Consultation and co-ordination, involving annually hundreds of meetings and many thousands of 'committee hours', are a major demand on management time, trying to make the machinery for looking after the Wall work rather than looking after the Wall itself. This is a not untypical situation with regard to the organizational infrastructure 'looking after' the heritage that tourists expect to see.

Hadrian's Wall, then, exemplifies for present purposes far more than local concern. Much that it represents, and a lot that can be said about it, not least the questions it raises, are of general application. Should a World Heritage Site, for example, be almost entirely in private ownership? If not, what are the alternatives? – in this case, the state's buying up a fairly large chunk of northern England? Should the management of such a World Site be centralized, and if so how? Or is it adequate to dissipate considerable effort in and through the clumsy, unintegrated, largely *ad hoc* arrangements that prevailed at the time of designation?

On a different tack, should the interpretation of the Wall be militaristic, glorifying the glory that was Rome, or be 'soft' and 'green', quietly down-grading militarism, stressing ecological impacts and landscape history, and relating the whole, in keeping with worldwide moral and political concern, to contemporary issues of ethnic interests in imperial circumstances (see Chapter 3)? And what, if any, is the role of the local individual, the Claytons of this world, in the presentation of a World Heritage Site? – mere 'human interest', or does it actually matter whether the tourist knows whether he or she is looking at the real thing or a much later restoration? The cynic and some parts of the tourist industry have a ready answer to that question, an answer which can doubtless be explained, if not ethically justified, on pragmatic grounds.

But the ethical question obstinately remains: while a whole service industry could be sustained on the basis of a fraud, euphemistically a parsimony with the truth, should it be? There is too a practical question hanging on the ethical one: given an upmarket trend in some parts of the tourist demand, can the quality expectation behind it ultimately be satisfied if the difference between the genuine and the restored is not explained? The answer is surely 'no'.

As do many other heritage sites, Hadrian's Wall begs another question, that of access in relation to contemporary use. Here it comes in several guises: we select one particular facet as exemplar. The Wall itself is long; it crosses an island from sea to sea; it passes in part through apparently wild and empty, though in fact farmed, landscape. In other words, it is ideal for serious walking, providing an interesting environment, some physical challenge and a clearly defined objective – to walk from one end to the other – which, if attained, can allow a legitimate sense of personal achievement within a historical tradition of 'walking the Wall' going back at least to Defoe in the early eighteenth century. Should therefore ramblers, people whose prime interest is in recreational walking *per se* rather than cultural tourism, be encouraged to use a prime scientific resource, also designated a World Heritage Site, as their playing field? To be specific, is it appropriate to create a long-distance trail under official auspices along the Wall, thereby deliberately promoting a new and potentially mass use? And this on top of, and distinct from, the existing mass tourism of the casual walker to specific spots along the Wall. If the answer is that such promotion is indeed inappropriate, as many non-ramblers believe to be the case, then what is the philosophical rationale for distinguishing between historically motivated but casual visitor and serious walker deliberately choosing to tackle the challenge of a trail which, incidentally, also happens to be a world-class archaeological landscape? Both make demands, of management, of facilities and in wear and tear, though their demands are different, in incidence, pattern and type. Why, therefore, add to the problems by creating a new use? – the resource is under enough stress already, not least from hundreds of thousands of tourists' feet walking along it each year. Here, as at many other archaeological sites, both famous and less well known, a high level of tourism can be very damaging physically; 'saving' heritage for the public to visit can in fact easily lead to over-use and severe deterioration.

At one level, as occurs in many countries, the incompatibility appears to be when organizations with admirable objectives come into conflict at one site. In the case of Hadrian's Wall, the Countryside Commission is charged with improving access to the countryside and the creation of long-distance trails has been one of its successful mechanisms for so doing; but the Roman frontier itself is protected principally by two other organizations, English Heritage and the National Trust. Both are very much in the business of encouraging access but they give a priority to conservation where conflict occurs. However, behind this characteristic organizational clash lies a more fundamental issue.

This concerns strategy, irrespective of organizational objectives. The strategic question, especially relevant to rural heritage, concerns the extent to which we pursue now policies which are essentially exploitive or custodial. In the case of Hadrian's Wall, most of the custodial work in the past two decades has actually been necessitated by increasing exploitation of it as a tourist resource. Adding to such exploitation is not compatible with a conservation-based strategy. In practical terms, then, the question becomes a simple one of deciding whether we want to pass on to the twenty-first century as much as possible of a 'real' Roman wall and its attributes or an increasingly non-Roman and modern one.

Debate on this issue is sharpened because it takes place in a Britain of the early 1990s where the more general question of 'access' is rapidly becoming a significant political matter. Access to Hadrian's Wall is a facet of access to heritage and the countryside, and indeed of 'freedom of information' as much as 'freedom to roam'. Where can I go? What can I see? are questions begging others. Who owns the past? elides into Where are the boundaries of heritage? – in both physical and ideological senses. It is the pressure of tourism as much as anything which forces those questions to be asked, and which will force answers to be given. Tourism may regard itself a 'good thing' but, good or bad, such values raise issues, not just of economics, but of politics and ideologies too. The one thing it is not is neutral.

All over the world, modern development threatens to impinge on heritage sites whether they are designated or not; and this applies to World Heritages Sites too. Hadrian's Wall illustrates the point in typical fashion. An application to drill an exploratory bore-hole for hydrocarbons in the designated Zone was made in 1991 and was approved by the Planning Authority. The Secretary of State for the Environment intervened, referring the application to a Public Inquiry. There, the international company making the application stressed its sense of environmental responsibility, its legal obligation to prospect after seismic reconnaissance if the data suggested the presence of hydrocarbons, and the short time required for the operation. The Planning Authority, supporting the application and defending its decision, stressed that, should gas or oil be found, it would not approve a subsequent application to exploit either. The opposition ranged widely from the owner of the nearest house concerned about his view, through the local and district councils concerned about various impacts, to representatives of national and international bodies arguing that such a development on a World Heritage Site was simply wrong in principle. The Secretary of State's decision is awaited.

Whatever it may be, the case raises the whole question of externally driven demands on World Heritage Sites. What, for example, is the standing of such designation at state level, especially when, as in the case of the UK and 117 other countries, they are signatory to the 1972 UNESCO World Heritage Convention? In Britain, the designation has no formal statutory force, though it is coming to be seen as 'a material factor' in planning considerations. Formalities apart, is it possible to accommodate such activities as oil-drilling within the concept of a World Heritage Site and, at practical level, within 'quiet', normal use of the rural scene? Such a development, directly impacting on heritage by, for example, damaging archaeological sites, could well also impact on tourism.

On the whole tourists do not travel expecting to be greeted by modern industrial development, and cultural tourists in particular will resent and then avoid contemporary intrusions into the quality of the personal experience they are seeking. So, focused on Hadrian's Wall – and it could be any one of a number of other major cultural zones in the landscape – is a combination of high principle and medium-term pragmatism which the public inquiry articulated. This process itself lubricated the 'culture clash', here as elsewhere, between proposed exploitation, of a cultural as well as natural resource, and a novel, in many respects highly successful, universal concept of World Heritage still trying to establish itself in the 'real' world of commercial fossil-fuel exploitation, planning and competing land-use proposals.[3]

Threats to the rural heritage loom large in those two examples, threats which come in many guises. One person's heritage threat is, however, a normal and desirable development to another, often the person living in the countryside. The tension, often the clash, is quite unavoidable, not least because most of the world which is not under water is rural and that major part of the globe is in use, changing and being developed, all the time. The best that can be done – and it should be the norm – is for knowledge and understanding to inform decisions about rural developments so that heritage considerations are as much taken into account as are other practical matters like geology, rights-of-way and engineering constraints. Such can mitigate the clash and, given time and resources, archaeological recording can at least make some recompense for the physical and scientific loss that land-use change so often involves. Ultimately such a process can play back to the tourist, for a better understanding of the landscape can lead to better presentation and interpretation of the rural scene which he or she is visiting. Yet of course the irony is that it is the infrastructure and consequences of tourism itself which so often threaten and despoil that very scene and its ambient qualities which attract the tourist in the first place.

'[T]he spirit of Helios, to whom Zeos had given the whole island, wafted through the lemon trees', wrote Helga Hegewisch, in classically elegiac vein, of Rhodes in the Mediterranean.[4] 'Then came the age of mass tourism – and after that nothing was the same'. She voiced a familiar lament, but none the less a realistic reaction from many parts of the world. What went wrong? Old houses were modernized and painted white to look 'traditional', new villas crept up the mountainside, a foreign community of 'writers, artists and assorted expatriates' moved in, *emigrés* returned, bars 'abandoned *retsina* wine, served fashionable cocktails and even warm beer for the British clientele'. The details may vary from place to place but this list is both indicative and symptomatic of physical and social changes brought about both for and by tourism in small communities whether in seaside settlements like this (Lindos), rural villages, or farms and homesteads scattered across the landscape.

Often, as in this example, no one intends the results described, though another irony is that the writer helped begin the development she deplores: 'The old 17th-century Arabo-Turkish houses . . . (we bought ours for a song and cleaned it up) were empty and run down'. For how many places around the world does that little personal saga hold good? – we set out to please ourselves, a dozen others do the same independently, and together we have inadvertently opened the flood gates to tourism and a demeaning of the heritage, social as well as physical, that we actually set out to savour. And what happened here? 'We formed a Greek Heritage Society. . . . Culture was in, ecology ruled. And yet for a long while it was not OK with the people . . . who wanted no gratuitous, paternalistic advice'. Then came political change and 'Buses loaded with tourists . . . will be banned. The amphitheatre will be restored [and] there will be a new square, graced by a restored St Stefano church on its old foundations.' Maybe that *dénouement* will take place but, whether it does or not, this story of one locality has a classical simplicity and global resonance in its applicability to a thousand places and their experience of heritage and tourism beside the sea and across the rural scene.

It would find echoes on many an island in the Pacific; it is obviously reflected in Hawaii (see Chapter 5); those who know the Isles of Scilly off England's south-west coast will recognize it too. What about inland? A striking example comes from *Le Causse Méjean* in Lozère, southern France. It also is already in a larger tourist area, and contains its own tourist honeypots like Aven Armand, 'La merveille souterraine', a vast and spectacular cave in the limestone which dominates the area. The *Causse* itself is one of several plateaux c. 900–1,000 m above sea level. It is now but sparsely inhabited: 449 people in 1975 in 57 hamlets, small villages and single farms, scattered over 33,000 hectares; *c.* 1,613 inhabitants in 1911. Flocks of shepherded sheep graze much of its wide-open space which is virtually treeless except for modern coniferous plantations. Thin soils, relics of massive erosion, characterize much of the plateau except in locally extensive dolines which are cultivated for cereals. The nature of the area's agriculture is perhaps indicated by the fact that as recently as the late 1930s at least 117 pairs of oxen provided the traction-power; by 1972, they had been replaced by 89 tractors. By any standards the *Causse* is an isolated area difficult to make a living in; yet, after obvious depopulation and emigration, according to themselves it is the most dynamic members of the community who remain and it is their attitudes which, in a rural heritage and tourist context, are noteworthy.

In 1970 'Le Méjean' Association was formed by the Caussenards themselves (cf. the incomers' initiative on Lindos described above). One of its first achievements was to compile and publish *Le Causse Méjean. Elévage Tourisme.*[5] The approach to heritage and tourism was clearly thought out from the start and has been consistently followed. It was implicit in the organization's full title: Le Méjean Association Caussenarde pour l'Accueil et le Développement Culturel. In practice, three main objects have been pursued: to maintain control of their own cultural heritage and its use; to promote appropriate, i.e. low-key, environmentally and culturally friendly, tourism and welcome individual tourists, while making it quite clear what the local rules of visitor behaviour were; and to endeavour within a vibrant rural community to keep indigenous young people on their parents' farms by basic improvements in living standards financed, in however small a way, by income from tourism as well as traditional sources.

The sort of tourism encouraged is walking, bicycling and horse-riding, botanizing (but plant-collecting is forbidden), bird-watching (vultures, eagles and hawks are visible and protected, but watch out for the locals' shooting smaller birds) and visiting archaeological sites. Some ancient monuments have been restored: the dolmens de la Marque and de Pierre-Plate are cases in point. Heritage pride of place, in terms of both group identity and promotion of gentle tourism, goes to the architecture, distinctively vernacular and picturesque, and currently ranging from the completely ruinous to the almost chi-chi restoration of many a second home. Numerous hamlets now consist of one working farm and several 'done-up' but usually empty farm houses.

You are welcomed to the show-piece village, Hyelzas, with a most helpful information board which tells you of the local *gîtes*, *produits*, sites to see and walks, all carefully colour-coded and way-marked. The significant words for our purposes, however, are in *small* lettering at the bottom: 'Nous sommes très sensibles aux soins que vous prenez pour respecter notre village. Merci' ('We are well aware of the trouble you are taking to respect our village. Thank you)'. No threat, no order, not even a request: just a quiet recognition of the mutual trust implicit in your being there visiting someone else's home, someone who is glad you are there and realizes the constraints you accept on your behaviour.

Hyelzas was 'un vieux village qui se mourait et dont les ruines faisaient peur, tellement cela ressemblait un village dévasté'.[6] Today, it is nothing of the sort: 'tout revit. . . . Le village s'aggrandit et prospère, heureux village, dont nous sommes fiers'. Local initiative under local control has brought this about; a new cheese factory is as crucial as the restoration and opening to the public of a splendid 'maison caussenarde d'autrefois', a seventeenth-century farmhouse simply presented in its own right and extended into a most informative 'musée de la vie rurale'. No gimmicks, no hype, simply 'une maison de pays' which 'attire chaque année un bon nombre de visiteurs'. Even the lady at the entrance was uncertain how many 'un bon nombre' was: slack management, no doubt, to many elsewhere in the heritage business, driven by concepts of target numbers, budget forecasts and the 'visitor take', but here one felt that the place would be there and open, for its own sake and as emblem of Caussenard pride and goodwill, whether or not anyone turned up.

As you leave the village a roadside board bids you 'Au revoir' and goes on to express the hope that you are satisfied with 'votre accueil et nos présentations'. 'We wish you a pleasant journey, thank you for your visit and good-bye'. A poster outside a small café and gift shop not far away, the acme of commercialism thereabouts, said it all, politely: 'Le Causse Méjean vous propose . . .' – and beneath was a map with a number of suggested attractions and activities. 'Respectez la nature, nos moutons, notre agriculture, vous serez nos amis' ('Respect Nature, our sheep, our farming, you will be our friends'). Unlike so many corporate good wishes, impersonal and probably insincere, this one read and sounded genuine. It expressed the ethos of the community, not just the genius of the place. Equally, quietly and with good manners, it made quite clear that tourism, as conceived and practised on the *Causse Méjean*, consists of a bond, a partnership of mutual respect. This two-way relationship is emphasized by an addition to the above suggestion: 'Dans le respect de l'Agriculture un tourisme que "se mérite" ' – in other words, tourism has to be seen to be worthwhile by the local community in the light of its acceptance of responsibilities rather than the assumption of rights. Doubtless some visitors abuse the implicit trust on which the welcome to stay in *our* homeland is based, and it would be easy to fear that such a policy will prove too naive and impractical in the face of human inconsiderateness and tourist rapacity. But here is a model for rural tourism which so far appears to have been successful. It encourages the sort of tourism the locality can both provide and benefit from while remaining true to its natural environment, social and economic basis, and cultural heritage; in creating its own sort of tourism, it defines its own type of visitor and experience, and can be reasonably confident of satisfying the former with the latter; and, arguably most importantly, it seems to result in a symbiosis of heritage and rural tourism which gives a sense of identity, purpose and achievement to the local community.

Not too far away from Le Méjean is Simiane-la-Rotonde, *un village perché* high on a hilltop which 'has escaped the worst ravages of the tourist industry'.[7] Here, however, in contrast to Lindos which fell to such ravages by mistake, and Le Méjean which has escaped by intent, rusticity seems to have persisted through good fortune and inertia. 'More houses here lie derelict than have been sold off, simply because they are so large'; 'we are higher up and much less fashionable' than the Provence of Peter Mayle and other expatriate writers, another cause of deterioration to the rural scene as far as the residents, articulate and otherwise, are concerned. But this article puts its finger on another, more fundamental point which is common to much of the world. That world cannot feed itself; yet, 'The major problem for most of rural France is that farming has become uneconomic and country life is now a struggle for survival'. It would be idle to pretend that it has ever been otherwise for most people trying to earn a livelihood from the land.

As in France, so it is now in many rural areas elsewhere, and not just in the 'developed' world of North America and Europe. Rural poverty and the consequential drift to towns and cities is a global characteristic, as familiar in South America as in South-East Asia, India and Africa, even though the relative strengths of the various reasons for the phenomenon vary from area to area. Though that phenomenon is probably more important than heritage and tourism, it has a direct bearing on both in several ways. It produces, for example, the empty village houses snapped up by incomers on urban salaries, and this engenders social disintegration. It produces unwanted farm complexes which are then converted *in situ* into museum farms, as is the case at Hyzelas, or, carefully selected as typical, dismembered and transported for re-erection in folk and agricultural museums, often in cities. Skansen, Stockholm, with Delsbo farmstead from Hälsingland province the equivalent of the Caussenard *maison de pays*, is the prototype, influential in creating similar open-air establishments, now great tourist attractions, in many cities such as Copenhagen for Denmark, Arnhem for The Netherlands and Belfast for Northern Ireland. The Irish National Heritage Park near Wexford, where you are enjoined to 'See 9000 Years of Ireland's Past', is an interesting hybrid, not a genuine folk museum, for its buildings are not displaced originals, yet created with academic care and avoidance of the careless pastiche of the normal commercial theme park.

Rural buildings, however, old or new heritage, involve a wider range than those of peasants and farm labourers only. Large buildings, sometimes industrial, sometimes domestic, sometimes institutional, often of considerable historic and architectural interest, also stand empty, adrift now from their economic bases in formerly viable rural communities. Vacant country houses are commonplace, formerly rooted in successful farming in, for example, Poland and Germany, Tuscany in Italy, Malta, Ireland on both sides of the border and throughout England, Scotland and Wales. So, too, are industrial buildings now redundant for similar reasons: it is often forgotten in pursuance of bucolic dreams that, historically, a great deal of industry was and still is carried on in the country. Odd consequences can follow from such redundancy. Bliss Mill, built in 1873 at Chipping Norton, Oxfordshire, was 'a model rural showpiece'; it is now so again, but differently as 'An outstanding restoration of a unique Victorian tweed mill' converted into forty-four luxury apartments and duplexes 'in some of the best of English countryside, yet within easy reach of major motorways'.[8] How different reads the prose about another piece of redundant industrial plant concerned with one of the commonest of rural activities, recorded because it was making way for a new installation, that of a sewer plant: 'The plant site area is situated at an abandoned sawmill complex less than 50 years old. . . . The investigations discovered no prehistoric sites and historic artefacts were all related to the sawmill or railroad complex. No further archaeological work was recommended.'[9] The historic rural scene can be, we perceive, not only industrial; it can also be recent, in that case of the 1940s, though given the heritagization of the Second World War that should not be surprising. 'It was like driving into the Second World War', said a planning officer of his reaction to visiting a 1937 aerodrome in rural Wiltshire; '[it] is considered in aviation archaeology to be a model showpiece, a unique period example tastefully finished in good stone'.[10] As the past closes in on the present, and the heritage net widens, so is provision made for the rural tourist of the future.

Rather more grandiosely in architectural terms, Taplow Court, not very far west of London and a fashionable place for Edwardian society, fell from grace, belonged to an electronics company in the 1960s and has now become 'the property of a Buddhist organisation called Nichiren Shoshu'. Nichiren was a thirteenth-century Japanese religious teacher. Late in 1991, the owners organized an exhibition of ceramics in the house illustrating 'how the English factories of Worcester, Wedgewood, Derby, Spode, Minton *et al.* were inspired by the porcelains of Japan'.[11] Whose rural heritage are we glimpsing here? Yet, whatever the visitors made of the occasion, a direct link connects it, the house, the rural economy and the globalization of heritage. And that link can manifest itself in other ways too: Minto House near Hawick in southern Scotland, completed in 1814 as the family seat of the Earls of Minto, vacated some fifty years ago and subsequently a girls' school, is now yet another derelict country house – but one with a future. It has been sold, like Taplow Court, to a Far Eastern buyer, and is to be demolished stone by stone for rebuilding in Japan.[12] These two examples must suffice just to hint at the cultural cross-currents that arise in many lands from the presence of empty, re-usable houses in anyone's country.

Empty and deliberately abandoned farmhouses were already a feature of the mountain villages in Galicia in the 1970s. Being replaced by rectangular constructions of breeze block and concrete, they were round or oval in plan, of drystone construction, and thatched. Internally, they were divided in two, with cattle kept on the downhill side divided by a wooden partition from the all-purpose family room uphill centred around an open hearth. Furnished simply with box beds, rudimentary seats and a cauldron hanging over the fire, the interior was aromatically rich, lightless and impregnated with smoke. No wonder the occupants preferred the unadorned functionalism of the new houses; but touristically and scientifically their old homes were much to be preferred by visitors. They were of course pictures-que, photogenically quaint and 'interesting'; but much more import-antly they represented the end point of a long, pan-European tradition. Here it had evolved into an oval regional type of the 'long-house', that form of multi-purpose building housing family and beast under the same roof which European farmers had been occupying since they first began cultivating crops some 7,000 years ago. Its equivalents, regionally adapted, have been recorded into this century in, for example, Brittany, Norway, Holland, Ireland and the Western Isles of Scotland. Earlier English versions, known from archaeological excavation of medieval settlements, influenced early colonists of the eastern American seaboard, just as, at about the same time, the idea of the plough (technically the ard), and specific types of cultivation implement originating in Roman provincial times, crossed from Spain to what is now Venezuela in the wake of Columbus and the conquistadores.

In that little academic résumé we are dealing with two of the fundamentals of rural life: what people lived in and how they cultivated the soil. The approach may be archaeological and ethnographic on a comparative basis, but the subject matter is deep, functional tradition, truly rural heritage – even though the serious scholar would not use that much demeaned word in this context. Such material things, and the ideas unconsciously enshrined in them by their peasant makers, are silent testimony to the strong cultural undercurrents crucial to the dialogue between past and present, between traditional artefacts not necessarily old in themselves and modern minds trying to understand not just what happened in former times but also how we have arrived in present circumstances. Similar arguments could be made with different examples in other fields from different parts of the world, for example the spread of metalworking techniques in China and India or the traditions of floristic exploitation in and around the Pacific. Such basic developments, interconnections and traditions do not, however, leave great monuments; they are not brought about by 'events' or 'great men'. In a sense, certainly a touristic sense, they are not therefore memorable and indeed barely presentable, for they cannot be tied down to one place, person or particular time. Interpretively, this presents us with a real dilemma, particularly as the history mentioned in the above examples is actually towards the more 'exciting' end of the otherwise overwhelmingly undramatic range of the rural scene, everywhere and throughout time.

Is the rural heritage then bound to be a closed book to mass tourism? Beyond a certain point in complexity, and beyond the point of local interest afforded by the 'this is what people did here up to early this century, and probably much earlier than that' presentation, the answer is probably 'yes'; and particularly for the urban tourist in a hurry. Let us return to Galicia and examine its current tourism advertisement:[13]

> Try Galicia for a spell. We've been welcoming guests for
> centuries. The first major tourist centre in history was in Galicia.
> Medieval pilgrims walked from as far away as Poland to pray at

the shrine of St. James the Apostle in Santiago de Compostela.
. . . Today's visitors come to Galicia to play as well as pray, to
marvel at its soft green beauty, its lilting language, its mild
climate and bountiful estuaries. Revealing Galicia's Celtic roots,
music is played on the bagpipe, while legends populate the
mountains with meigas, playful witches. If you want to be
charmed, this is the place to come.

Ignoring the mistakes of fact in what is actually quite good tourist-
speak, where, however, is the serious heritage in that verbiage? Is the
Tourist Office really so unaware of the marvellously varied and significant heritage of Galicia that it has no better idea than to trot out
bagpipes and witches? Perhaps it does not want to know; perhaps the
potential tourists to a wonderful part of the world's countryside don't
want to know either. It might be said that they will both be much the
poorer, but does it matter that they don't know? Ignorance, after all,
can be bliss, and maybe that has to be the way of the world in its
appreciation of the greater part of the rural heritage. 'OK, so they
grew corn and ate it. So what?' The words of one visitor to a historical
farming presentation may sum it up neatly: the dilemma and a common reaction. The answer to his question – 'They survived' – is hardly
the stuff of great tourism; and yet, in that insistent paradox of
heritagism, it is actually the stuff of rural life throughout history, and
continues to be today for most people earning their livelihood from
the soil. But try telling that to the man in the baseball cap who never
grew corn and eats it only as flakes from a packet effortlessly grabbed
off a supermarket shelf.

That most people most of the time have just lived on, and off, the land,
however, is, fortunately from the tourist point of view, not the only
facet of rural heritage. There are other pegs from which to dangle
'interest'. Take Vietnam, for example, and like good tourists just
ignore the all too familiar observation that 'Half a century of continuous war has left a country chiefly preoccupied with the drudgery of
mere survival'.[14] Yet it is that fact of war which provides material for
tourist excursions which 'are edifying but not uplifting', an interesting
point considering that the 1990 advertising slogan was 'Vietnamese
Smile is Tourists' Joy and Hope' and that American war-veterans form
a large proportion of visitors. North-west of Saigon is Cu-Chi where
tourists, in 'an area once white-zoned by American defoliants', crawl
along some 250 km of guerilla tunnels 60 cm deep and 45 cm wide.
'Our guide points out ventilation shafts, booby traps once filled with
poisoned stakes and narrowing passages designed to choke off larger
pursuers. The place stinks of not-so-distant violence and we emerge to
a landscape pocked with bomb craters.'

Clearly, if you want to be charmed, this is the place to come; or you might consider the Chernobyl area. 'A travel agent in Kiev appears to be serious about offering guided tours of the region of Chernobyl, site of the world's worst nuclear accident. It takes in the dead town . . ., villages where radioactive waste is buried, and the sarcophagus of the damaged reactor at the atomic plant'.[15] Both those examples, each offering a somewhat more gruesome aspect of the rural heritage to tourists than accords with most perceptions of it, seriously re-emphasize how the tourable past is catching up with the present (the last American marines left Saigon on 30 April 1975; the Chernobyl disaster seems only yesterday). The Vietnam experience also makes the important point that warfare is another way of catching the tourist's attention in the countryside. What you do with it is another matter, but from battles of classical antiquity, through the many civil wars which, in touristic terms, so many landscapes have so helpfully seen, to the variously motivated visiting of the battlefields and cemeteries of the twentieth century, there is plentiful scope for numerous forms of military tourism. Since even now the interpretation and presentation of battles in, for example, the English and American civil wars can be contentious, much sensitivity is needed in interpreting more recent international conflicts. Chauvinism is an easy way out, playing to a local audience which is likely to be predisposed to hear the message, but can be offensive to visitors from elsewhere. It is probably impossible to be neutral about Vietnam to a contemporary audience – or even about Kuwait, 1991; and as for countless places in the former Yugoslavian countryside. . . . The one thing certain there is that perception of heritage itself, never mind its interpretation, will continue to be highly charged and contentious for a very long time.

Just as current events change perceptions, and therefore 'meanings', of rural heritage despite the overall impression it may give of stasis, so do new discoveries. This may be in the form of documentation – some long-lost manuscript or map for example – but it is the archaeological discoveries which catch the attention of the media. The ambivalence here is that they always seem to take people by surprise; whereas such discoveries are normal, not because archaeologists are clever but because a great many people have been doing things in the countryside for a very long time, and even more are now disturbing the earth's surface and, therefore, the results of our ancestors' activities. Nevertheless, some discoveries of a newsworthy sort do come from research: the discovery of a new pyramid in Egypt was one such, and it made good copy ('Exclusive: The face unearthed after 3,000 years') even though it was, predictably, 'the result of years of painstaking detective work'.[16] The same newspaper also claimed,[17] less credibly,

'First "motorway" found in Irish bog', referring to the discovery of a network of timber trackways preserved in peat from as much as 5,500 years ago. Without in any way diminishing the importance of the discovery in helping to understand the Irish countryside and the achievement of prehistoric European communities, it actually follows the patient recording of similar features in Denmark, Holland and, most notably, in Somerset, England, during the 1960s and 1970s, for which similar journalistic claims were made. Nevertheless, here we have examples of major discoveries illuminating the development of landscape itself which, paradoxically, by their very nature are unavailable for tourists to see except briefly at the time of their discovery and, rarely and only after expensive conservation, in small bits preserved in museums.

The same problems of preservation and public access were illustrated by three other archaeological discoveries in totally different fields which hit the international headlines in the autumn of 1991 (nothing special about the time – any period would produce equivalents). They concerned discoveries of the sort which the media and the tourist industry love, though in these cases they are academically important too; such correlation does not always occur. Two cases concerned caves and cave paintings, the other was a corpse (see Chapter 9); all three were widely reported so, with one exception, specific references are unnecessary. One cave was near Marseilles (see Chapter 11), piquancy being given to its discovery, and accessibility, by the fact that its entrance is now, as a result of a rise in sea level over the past 10,000 years, some 37 m underwater; hence the cave's unknown existence until 1991, its discovery by a diver and the excellent state of preservation of the Palaeolithic paintings above water level at the back.

Parallels with the art at Lascaux were drawn, but at first glance there is not much scope for mass tourism in this discovery. In view of the effect of such tourism on the Palaeolithic paintings at Lascaux, perhaps that is as well. Though the temptation has been resisted so far, a new entrance could of course be blasted through the rock from above and behind; it is a technique used elsewhere, though any such decision demands a careful judgement about the relative merits of, on the one hand, conservation from scientific and aesthetic points of view and, on the other, public access in the sense of making it available to large numbers of people. The pragmatic solution at Lascaux, where tourist numbers had seriously degraded the art, was to build a surrogate when the original was closed in the interests of conservation. Interestingly, Lascaux 2 was provided by the local community out of self-interest: faced by a significant loss to the local rural economy by the closure of the original, it met the threat with an extremely well-done substitute painted cave which has been so successful as tourist bait that it has become an attraction in its own right. Would-be paying customers are advised to arrive early if they wish to gain entry that day.

The problem with the other cave discovery, the Zubialde cave near the Basque town of Vitoria in northern Spain, is not so much access as authenticity, a favourite angle in popular perceptions of the ancient past. Again containing ostensibly Palaeolithic paintings some 15,000 years old, the cave's newsworthiness lay in the doubt expressed by some scholars about whether the art was actually only a few weeks old, i.e. a superb forgery. Newsworthy or not, that so far remains the situation in academic terms, mainly because no further publication has followed and no access has been possible for other scholars.

They, understandably, wish to make their own judgement about a discovery which, if authentic, would undoubtedly be of great scientific significance. Beyond academic concerns, which are nevertheless fundamental to the whole question of the cave's future, the discovery is of considerable tourist potential and great economic relevance.

On one side of the equation was the academic debate. Local experts authenticated the discovery: a much respected professor at the University of Vitoria was quoted as saying, 'All tests to find falsification in this cave have proved negative' (not quite the same as tests proving the paintings positively to be genuine); while experts elsewhere expressed doubts on the basis necessarily of photographs, their reservations summed up by the remark[18] that we are looking at 'either the discovery of a previously unknown style of cave painting or an innaccurate copy. . . . They fear that wishful thinking may provide the Basque country with a bogus tourist attraction'. The other side of the equation was also neatly expressed by the newspaper: is the artist a forger 'whose contribution to science may be less than his contribution to tourism in the Basque country?' In other words, here as is usual elsewhere in the world, heritage interpretation depends absolutely on scientific research and academic judgement: authenticity is all. If the paintings *are* genuine, 'The Council of Alava province is proposing to build a full-scale replica beside the original cave . . . [which] will never be opened to the public . . . [because] the breath of visitors would be enough to destroy the delicate environmental conditions that have kept them intact for millennia'. So, either way the tourist loses: if the discovery is authentic, he or she will see only a copy; if it is a forgery, he or she will see only a forgery. Perhaps that will not matter all that much, for both will be interesting and few tourists could tell the difference anyway. On the other hand, either way Vitoria, which has a new airport, seems to have a tourist attraction only 20 km away in its surrounding countryside, and the city, Asturias and the Basques need tourists.

The paintings, however, have now 'been conclusively proved to be fakes'.[19]

8 *In the museum direction*

The cultural heritage numbers among its components millions of objects. People travel locally and globally to see these in museums; the tourist industry is in part founded on providing the mechanism to enable people to do just this, to take tourists to the objects, to move in the museum direction.

Yet museums themselves appear and disappear as a volatile component of the cultural scene; and the objects constituting the supposedly contained cultural heritage themselves move, frequently, for many reasons and often controversially.

Here we discuss, initially, some aspects of museums and collections, and then the concept of 'the moving object' (Chapter 9), within the context of heritage and tourism. In seeking out some general issues, we have looked in particular for examples of 'culture clash' and 'cultural transformation'. Much of the material is culled from current newspapers rather than the museological literature, since the public interest in all this is itself a matter of significance and the same issues are raised many times over in many parts of the world as matters of report in the media; the value of much of that material for our purposes here is, we hope, like little flashes of light playing over and reflected from the museum idea, not so much intrinsic as exemplary.

In itself, the idea of a 'museum' is a curious one. The word is from the Greek, *mouseion* , 'seat of the Muses', the nine goddesses in Greek and Roman mythology who were the daughters of Zeus and Mnemosyne, 'inspirers of poetry, music, drama, etc.'. How then did the museum come to be defined as a 'building used for storing and exhibition of objects illustrating antiquities, natural history, arts, etc.'?[1] Where is the inspiration, where the divine muse, in that? A whole library, and a whole subject, museology, have been created trying to answer that question and to implement the numerous answers, while simultaneously the idea has spread around the world, even into societies to which the very concept of a special building to store and exhibit cultural and natural objects is not native As a result of the nearly worldwide expansion of this idea, museum buildings now range from a shack to the most prestigious of (at the time) contemporary, purpose-built architectural creations. The Burrell, Glasgow, comes to mind, though hardly *avant-garde* like Rogers's and Piano's Pompidou Centre, Paris, Arata Isozaki's Museum of Contemporary Art, Los Angeles, California, and Stirling and Wilford's Staatsgalerie, Stuttgart, Germany.

Perhaps architects need museums rather than vice versa, for a museum does not have to be in a great building, or even in a building at all. Many museums, after all, grind along in unsuitable, even highly undesirable, buildings, often converted from original uses such as factory, palace, barn, church, penitentiary, railway station and lunatic asylum. Others, being essentially of the open air, need no showpiece building at all.

In the instance provided in Paris by the vastly conceived and hugely implemented 'Projet Grand Louvre', how stunningly clever it was to build the, in some ways, least important part first, the new entrance. To engage one of the world's great contemporary architects to design it, and to proceed with his apparently absurd proposal not just to enter the Louvre from underground but to do so through a pyramid, and a glass one at that, right in the middle of that vast courtyard enclosed by the superb architecture of one of Europe's great historic royal palaces – to do all that can only be admired as the triumph of artistic sensitivity over common sense. It is often good practice to 'get your retaliation in first', and that seems to have happened here: Mr Disney's executives, if they have any soul at all, can only look in despair at I. M. Pei's pyramidal *coup*, 'au cour même de Paris' and not beyond outer suburbia. The pyramid is, however, only the most iconographic part of the work completed in phase 1, 1983–9, and in train and projected in phase 2, 1989–96. Both phases will result not only in significant additions to the understanding of the Louvre and its context from the extensive archaeological excavations which preceded and continue hand in hand with the work, not only in a superbly restored and renovated great building, but also in what in many respects will be a new museum. Great museums, like great cities – and Paris is both – constantly renew themselves.

Many a city and town would in fact regard its urban status as incomplete without a museum, preferably nowadays a new or refurbished one, almost regardless of the quality of its collection; it should be housed in an iconographic building. Museum buildings are one of the more powerful statements that a place can make about itself and about how it would wish others to see it; witness Nîmes in 1992, with the new Foster Médiatèque nearing completion overlooking La Maison Carrée (see also Chapter 6). A demand for new museum buildings will continue too, and not only for prestige purposes. War, for example, is a terrible razer of museums, presumably because of their iconographic values, and it is presumably precisely for the same reason rather than simple functionalism or a pure love of scholarship that one of the priorities for postwar winners and losers is to rebuild the old museum or build a new one. The national museum in Bucharest, for example, was destroyed in the brief civil war in Romania recently; on the international front, the greatest Islamic collection in the world was removed to northern Iraq from the Kuwait museum before the building which had housed it was destroyed during the 1991 Gulf War. The collection has already returned to Kuwait, awaiting the rebuilding of the museum.

Paradoxically, war also creates museums — or at least creates the occasion for creating a museum. The Imperial War Museum in London is a case in point at the international level; practically every military unit seems to have its own too, promoting self-proclaimed instant heritage after every incident and over the years pulling in to base camps everywhere bits of the opposition's hardware from distant lands. The global distribution of Iraqi military souvenirs from 1991 would, for example, already be quite an interesting museological and heritage study in its own right. The ambivalences in the thought were picked up by a journalist contemplating another theatre of war, Afghanistan, 'littered with the debris of broken conquerors from antiquity to the Soviet army's rout'.[2] As he said, the War Museum in Kabul ought to be impressive but now it sees few tourists for, in effect, the whole country is a war museum with 'the Salang highway, strewn with Soviet armour that Afghan guerillas have rendered into abstract metal art'. Anyway, an army general arranged for the vintage tanks in the real War Museum to be removed for a foreign collector, an instance of a more general point discussed in Chapter 9.

Leftovers of war as museum matter continue to crop up all over a world inclined to bellicosity and material self-justification thereafter. Commercial exploitation and even remorse are, however not un-known in postwar museological reactions. Eden Camp in North Yorkshire, England, for example, housed German and Italian pri-soners of war from 1942 to 1948. Through the enterprise of a local millionaire who originally planned a crisp factory on the site, it 'now sells itself as the only modern history theme museum of its type in the world'.[3] Set in twenty-nine huts guarded by barbed wire and watch towers, it 'deals with the social, political and military history of the [Second World] war' and apparently attracts 200,000 visitors a year paying £3 a head to experience, among other things, 'the conditions in which prisoners lived'. Presumably that is not, however, what in any realistic sense tourists visiting another postwar museum would wish to do. Not that there is any need for them to do so, as we cross into a different zone of sensibility where the remains, the context and the contemporary relevance of the memories deny the need for any sort of Eden treatment.

The Konzentrationslager at Dachau was the first concentration camp in Nazi Germany; the power of its name fifty and more years later vitiates any need for further exposition by us. It is, however, now a museum. 'The misery, brutality and degradation seem to have got into the buildings, objects, even the trees on the site; they seep out of every document and photograph in the museum. . . . The unspeakable crimes and cruelties of the past confront us in the present'.[4] However appalling the reasons for its existence, it is the sort of museum the world needs, not for synthetic tourist entertainment or nationalistic revenge or even to engender remorse alone. Next to it now is a Carmelite convent. 'The tourist suddenly finds himself in a different world', a world saying, with one of the Sisters, 'it is important that everything doesn't stand still at the cruelty of the past . . . what happened at the camp should not be the end'. The convent was founded in the belief that 'what was needed was atonement, the redemption of evil by love . . . for the past, for the present and the future'. The very word 'tourism' seems tawdry in such a context, while the concept of 'museum' is enhanced. When human kind is battling, not with its past but with it own nature, then 'heritage' too takes on a different dimension. Perhaps it is precisely because of that inherent nature that, as an expression of itself, humanity's quest for its heritage through tourism seldom approaches the experiential depths, in many senses, of Dachau.

To cite such high-flown motives is not to deny that economic consider-ations, such as a wish to attract the tourists back, may play a role in postwar situations. Indeed, war or not, the major revamping of an existing museum or the building of a new one may be undertaken specifically to create a new tourist attraction or provide a needed tourist facility. The remarkable museum-plus construction at la Villette (see also Chapter 11) in north-east Paris, fits in here.[5] Not that symbolic functions are far away either, and la Villette has social and political functions very much bound up with policies of urban re-newal, the imaging of *la gloire* as a French national concept. The contrapuntal dissonance with Mickey Mouse (see also Chapter 10) not far away can only add to the cross-cultural vibrancy of Paris, surely already the museum capital of the global village.

Some of the best new museum buildings *as museums* are, however, not grandiose structures but relatively small buildings appropriate to their setting, for example an archaeological site or national park. Tourists will have their individual favourites in this category, personally satisfying places rather than world-renowned buildings; among examples we think of are the museum-cum-information centres at Pecos and Chaco, both in New Mexico.

If a museum's function is to store and exhibit objects – and clearly we would add 'and to stimulate and educate the viewer' – the range of objects embraced is almost limitless. So are the conjuctions that can be engineered, and clearly all sorts of culture clash can thus be created, both deliberately and inadvertently. The 'purity' of a collection – confined to the pottery of one potter, for example, or the objects from one archaeological site – can be a limited but perfectly legitimate objective, satisfactory to curator and visitor. More stimulating in a way can be the dissonances and harmonies, visual and cerebral, set in motion by the compilation of an artificial assemblage – of the 'these are what I like' variety, for example – or by the housing of a collection in a curious context. The Museum of Mankind (some title!), with its superb displays of global material culture, of desert nomads and Polynesian islanders, Eskimos and Africans, in rooms at the back of Burlington House off Piccadilly in London's West End, is one case in point; another is the almost entirely White-colonial material and completely furnished rooms of the American Museum at Claverton Manor (see also Chapter 2), a modest Georgian former residence just outside Bath, England, its manicured garden beauty set off with 'a replica of a Tepee' within an institutional objective of 'a desire to increase Anglo-American understanding'. The great collection of Attic vases sitting on glass shelves within a replica Roman villa overlooking the Pacific at Malibu (the J. P. Getty Museum) might well be cited as both decontextualized and inappropriately recontextualized; yet others would find the creation of that situation entirely justified by the stimulation afforded by it.

Indeed, some apparently inappropriate museum contexts can jolt the viewer in their unexpectedness. One of the most vivid objects one of us has ever seen – and remembered, for the incident was fifteen years ago – was a sherd of blue glass displayed, alone and without pretension, in a temporary exhibition case at the University Museum in Tucson, Arizona. It had been found in a mid-nineteenth-century context in the downtown excavations. It was Chinese. Also on display were sherds of English porcelain from the same context. Only connect . . .

On other occasions, the viewer may well be jolted by neither the object nor its display context but by the medium of presentation; on first experiencing an audio-visual presentation, for example, or one of the increasingly available 'hands-on' facilities in, for example, a science display or archaeological excavation. Again to personalize, for that is what much tourism is actually about, one of us will always recall a first experience of holograms, vivid in themselves and doubly so for being, so inappropriately, of objects from the whole of the prehistory and history of the Ukraine and displayed, in their absence, in a redundant church in York.[6] Of course the real point about any museum collection is that it takes whatever material it consists of out of one reality and bestows on it another life. What we see, and how we see it, in a museum can never be as it was seen originally; holography merely emphasizes that point. Apart from the museum context itself being different, we are different; so, in a sense, the concept of the museum is based upon a fallacy.

Some objects involved in this mute intellectual conspiracy are too large to go into a building; they may be a large structure themselves. Some very large chunks of masonry, such as *stelae* from Central America, monoliths from Egypt, and marbles from Athens, nevertheless do find their way into museum buildings, along with tiny *objets d'art* such as Roman gems set in precious metal. In fact, whether moved yet or not, a high proportion of the cultural heritage has a potential to be moved, sideways, upwards or downwards on site, short distances, say to a local museum, and round the world to wherever economic supremacy can be expressed by the acquisition of someone else's indigenous heritage. Meanwhile, as we have seen, many new museums have appeared, and others have closed; some have been refurbished and enlarged, others have moved. As we have already suggested, despite their cultivated image of stability and permanence, museums as a phenomenon are actually unstable.

Further, for many objects, especially those caught up in the inter-national market for art and antiquities, one move is seldom the end of the story: many objects move several times, often for reasons which have little to do with heritage or tourism in the normal senses. So, one of the characteristics of cultural heritage is that, far from its possessing that locational stability which is often thought to be one of its attrac-tions, and one of the *raisons d'être* of the museum, a significant proportion of it is constantly on the move. Such is the character of human nature in particular – though Nature can be influential too –

that 'the moving object', both in and without museums, seems to be the norm rather than unusual (see Chapter 9). Though holography offers a medium both to limit the movement of objects and to increase their availability to different audiences, its impact is likely to be in the public domain rather than in the world of private collection. Possessing the real thing, not its image, is, for many, including museum curators, the whole point of collecting; and the discerning exhibition-visitor is very likely to want to see that real thing too. Among other consequences, this can make it difficult for even the keenest cultural tourist to keep up with the game, again especially with well-known objects. Many have experienced that peculiar disappoint-ment of arriving at a chosen place to see a particular object only to find that its container, the museum, has moved (or is closed) or that the object itself has been removed. We need to look at why this happens.

Despite the enormous range of artefacts involved here, all share common factors from the point of view of heritage and tourism. In the first place, if obviously, they have been retrieved; we know they exist and we probably know something about them: a trite point maybe, but worth remembering when you think of the presumably much greater number that have existed and been destroyed or have yet to come again into existence by being retrieved and making their mark on our consciousness. Despite museums' self-promulgated aura of material omniscience, they only contain a fraction of what has been made, and that will always be the case. Scholars study, and tourists are shown, but fragments of a past which we can never recover; we can only create 'new' pasts and they, by definition, are contemporary, formed in our minds and imaginations from those fragments. This can be a sobering thought to museums already groaning from artefactual overload; they should nevertheless accept it. It would be unwise to be didactic on the strength of a fragmentary data base.

Second, if again obviously, artefacts were all made at some time in the past, be it yesterday or 100,000 years ago. It is important to us, for a whole host of reasons not always scholarly, that we know when that date was. Most were made in one place, within a cultural setting of which, to varying extents, they are representative. The way in which they were made, for example, and their function(s), can convey to us archaeological and perhaps historical information. In other words, all artefacts have a context and a scientific potential; and this is as important to the tourist experience as it is to academia, for a legitimate tourist expectation is to be afforded authentic information almost as much as it is to be confronted by the authentic object. While some-times such authentic information simply cannot be provided because it does not exist, it remains a mystery why many a museum, perhaps hung up on aesthetic ecstasy or simply incompetent, chooses not to provide such information.

Most of the issues arising from the movement of a cultural object in the past, and currently, stem from the loss of context and the subsequent use of such artefacts in contexts for which they were not intended, for example as prized items in a museum or private collection. This process tends to reduce scientific value while adding other values such as the aesthetic and pecuniary. On the other hand, while that may be generally true, authenticity is of crucial importance in cultural trading, often adding several noughts to monetary value. Nevertheless, even this shifts emphasis from academic and scientific potential for its own sake into a function of subsequent 'added value'.

Indeed, while we are here much concerned with curation and the physical movement of objects, it could be argued that of far greater general significance is the movement in the perceived significance, the 'value', of the object through time. The object remains the same (more or less, but its travels can of course harm it) whether or not it is moved; it is perceptions of it which move. They both decrease and enhance its desirability, as interpretation and fashion change around it in societies removed, always in time and often in place, from its original context. After all, such changing perceptions and evaluations happen whether or not the object itself is moved, though the movement of an object such as a Chinese bronze to an American midwest museum is often the trigger to re-evaluation of its significance for a new band of viewers in and from a different cultural context. But equally, the arrival of floods of tourists to see something *in situ* can also lead to local re-assessment of the object which perhaps up to that time had been seen as mundane. The sites and material culture of Roman provincial life in what is now western Turkey, for example, were not particularly valued by the local population until recently when it was realized that things Roman, rather than prehistoric, Islamic or Ottoman, were what brought the tourists in.

Archaeology and anthropology hold dear the concept that an artefact possesses 'meaning' and such a premise cannot lightly be dismissed; but in addition to its original 'meaning' or, more likely, 'meanings' in the originating society, the student of heritage, and especially heritage in a tourist context, needs to recognize the shifting 'meanings' of the object in recent and contemporary times. Further he or she should acknowledge the existence, and the significance of that existence, of a range of perceptions, and therefore of 'meanings' in the viewing audience. 'Relative values' is now a cliché but, provided its sense is not limited to monetary considerations, the phrase encapsulates the concept, fundamental to interpretation and presentation, of 'meaning' not only changing through time; it also expresses the idea that 'meaning' changes every time an individual, from what is likely to be an increasingly diverse constituency of *voyeurs*, looks and reacts. Clearly, didacticism is out, as it always was the easy way out through mono-model explanation, though firm and informed guidance towards a range of 'meanings' is much to be desired. So, however static an object, in terms of its significance through time and across contemporary perceptions, it might as well be jumping up and down. The concept of 'the moving object' embraces the flickering movement of meaning across its surface just as much as changing its physical location. Yet of course the very act of labelling an artefact in a museum, of in fact giving it a meaning, tends in practice to fix that meaning in time, or rather for some considerable length of time judging by the infrequency with which redisplay, reinterpretation, is undertaken in the general run of museum practice. Nor is the excuse of limited resources entirely plausible; 'once labelled, forever true' seems still to be deeply ingrained in the museological psyche.

Now let us consider some of the issues when an object does take a trip from its own context into another, by definition different, situation. This is a fairly basic consideration for the museum curator and the antiquities dealer. It may travel alone, a prized 'capture' moving into a new context of public gallery or private collection; or it may move with other objects, originally from the same context, such as a collection of ethnographic material from a Pacific island, or its companions may be a diverse assemblage. Such may have been brought together by extraneous circumstances such as an expedition through different cultures or as a 'collection' homogenized only through being the result of an individual's collecting activity. Whatever the reason and the mechanism for the move, a culture clash ranging from the mild to the dramatic is inevitable as the object settles into a new context. Why it is there, and how it is presented, for example, can immediately set off visual, intellectual and cultural vibrations. So too can the building housing it, from the approach, setting and architecture to the interior design and décor. Hence our beginning this chapter by considering the museum as a building, and continuing with some thoughts on collections and objects; now we look at some examples of museums proper, i.e. of buildings and objects together.

The Burrell at Glasgow is an outstanding example, for both building and collection, the setting and the style, vibrate with all sorts of resonances. The building itself is, of course, new, in angular, vaguely

Scandinavian-modernist idiom fronted by a decontextualized but genuine medieval Gothic entrance; its setting is suburban parkland. The collection is irritatingly ambivalent but not, on the whole, a thing of beauty. The objects travelled as an ensemble for their present display, but most had already seen their major journeys in moving as unrelated individual pieces from many parts of the world into Mr Burrell's private collection. Such public and private assemblages constitute new groupings for which it is most unlikely that they were made. Individual items in such groupings give off new vibes in their new context; collectively, a message different from the sum of the individual 'meanings' is created. The present Burrell Museum provides an outstanding yet typical example: a lot of the material in it is not only unrelated culturally or in any other way, except in demonstrating the eclecticism and basic lack of taste of the collector; but a lot of the items are individually second-rate – and that is being kind.

Further, many of the antiquities, as distinct from the 'art', are displayed without adequate contextual information, presumably because the nature of the act of acquisition was in many cases not conducive to the establishment of authentic data about origin. Of a provincial Roman glass bottle, 'Egypt, First Century AD' exemplifies a minimalist approach to contextual requirements in the same way that, had we bought it from its secondary context in a secondhand furniture and antiquities shop in Bungay, Suffolk, a Roman jar could have been labelled in a hypothetical antiquities cabinet 'East Anglia, First Century AD'. This sort of thing requires only a little cash and a jackdaw mentality – and a certain obliviousness to the implications, practical and ethical, of such antiquarian junk when it lacks a proper context.

Had that Bungay jar, which had probably only moved a few miles and through two pairs of hands, been accompanied by an exact provenance, such as which grave or which layer on exactly which part of which site it had come from, and associated with what, then it would have been of value to us as archaeologists. As it was – and we did not buy it – its main value, like so much of the archaeological material in Mr Burrell's collection, is as 'art'; and claims there, given the mass-produced nature of such things as Roman pots and phials, tend to the tenuous. So really all it is saying is: 'Look, I had enough money to be in Egypt and pick up nice little objects like this'. In other words, it represents a mini-ego-trip. The Burrell's Rodin sculptures, which had been removed when we last went to see them (see above, p. 108), essentially fall into the same category, though clearly they are also meant to carry a message of further enhancement along the lines of 'And I had enough money and good taste to buy these too'. But a major difference is that a Rodin is good enough as art to see off and indeed set off the neighbours; common-or-garden domestic Roman things merely lower the tone if the possessed object is intended to impress.

However, *collectively*, cultural hotch-potches like the Burrell Collection also convey a message, a new one deriving from the assemblage as a whole. Maybe this is personal, as in the Burrell case, or it may be institutional as in a great museum; but whatever it is, it is a creation with a 'meaning' different from the sum of the small voices of all the individual items in the collection. Here, the exterior and interior of the building, the fittings, the style of presentation and the like, all contribute quite as much as those 'small voices'; indeed the latter may well be drowned by the clamour of the architecture, the exhibition design, or the pre-selected, dominant interpretive theme. A 1986 exhibition in the National Museum of Scotland serves to exemplify the point: it consisted of a well-chosen assemblage of British prehistoric artefacts, including some fine individual pieces indeed but basically from the range of items that can be seen in many a provincial museum any day of the week. The whole was aggressively presented under the title 'Symbols of Power' in a monothematic interpretation which, however challenging, however 'right', is nevertheless only one of several models available for understanding the third and second millennia BC in Britain. An exhibition has to 'shout' to bring in the thousands of visitors, many of whom perhaps would not normally go into a museum or gallery. Perhaps you can do this with an exhibition but perhaps should not with a permanent display; but if the tourist numbers mount, then maybe the means justifies the end. At least that argument can be made, and it is, increasingly.

There are other ends too. A distinguished museum curator, Frank Willett, made an interesting museological comparison in what he called 'two case studies of reaction to colonialism'.[7] The *locus* of one study was Scotland, perhaps to the surprise of some global villagers who would not necessarily think of that country as having a 'colonial' problem in the presentation of its past. They should visit the National Trust for Scotland's Visitor Centre at Culloden! Anyway, the Scots' defeat there led, in Willett's words, 'to the suppression of Scottish culture' (by the English of course). Now,

> In terms of heritage awareness, Scottish national feeling . . .
> manifests itself in a great efflorescence of new museums . . . many
> supported primarily by government agencies that aim to promote
> employment and tourism rather than the heritage as such . . .
> [yet] every Scottish town and village seems to want to express its

own historical and cultural identity by establishing a museum of its own . . . Scotland has . . . twice as many museums per capita as for the UK as a whole!

In that context the 'Symbols of Power' exhibition can be seen in another perspective; though all-British in scope, it possessed a hidden agenda in addition to its particular hierarchical theme. It was also saying, by showing a range of material objects, including some outstanding individual items from Scotland in the context of comparable material from Britain and Europe, that the Scottish prehistoric heritage was at least the equal of others', not least that of the English – a very proper and 'ex-colonial' thing to do in a museum context. Ex-colonial was also the context of Willett's other case study, of museums and heritage in Nigeria. There the first permanent museum building, at Jos, was opened as recently as 1952, and the Nigerian Museum in Lagos five years later (compare with Scotland where the first public museum was opened 150 years earlier and the first national museum in 1851). Despite many vicissitudes, Nigerian 'museums serve a sense of heritage translated from tribal and regional settings to a national stage'; while a touring exhibition of sculptural antiquities from the national collections 'resulted in a striking recognition of black African achievement among both black and white Americans, and later among Europeans as well'.

One of the conclusions from Willett's comparison is particularly relevant here. 'Nigerians of different languages, cultures, religions, and allegiances can begin to appreciate how the past has made them one as well as many peoples. The Scottish experience has been very different. . . . Through their museums and primarily at local level, Scots are now recovering and re-expressing the history and culture of Scotland . . . [and thereby] throwing off the English cultural yoke.' In being vehicles for the formation, delineation and expression of cultural identity, museums clearly have a crucial function, as clearly needed in the 'old' countries as in the 'new'. But, in making the generalization, we should note Willett's real message: even where countries can be labelled the same in one respect, be it 'ex-colonial', 'Third World', 'post-industrial' or whatever, each is different in other respects, not least in its own historical experience and its own perception of what that experience 'means', both to itself and to others. That is a major factor to be taken account of anywhere in defining museum functions, deciding what to collect and to keep, and in designing displays and exhibitions.

Another example tends to bear out that generalization 'Europe's Celtic past' (a rather dubious phrase in itself), wrote David Keys, '. . .

is being resurrected as a symbol of imminent European economic and cultural unification'.[8] He quotes a Welsh Tourist Board spokesperson as saying 'I wanted to show that we had a single European market 2,000 years ago'. The medium was 'dozens of special events, from exhibitions . . . to . . . historical re-enactments', the former consisting of 'two Celtic exhibitions'. Fundamental to them, of course, was archaeological material, both that moved from within what is now Wales into the permanent collections of the Welsh National Museum in Cardiff and that moved temporarily into Wales from elsewhere for the exhibitions. As in the 'Symbols of Power' exhibition in Edinburgh, the material was presented within the context of a strong theme, in the Welsh case a contemporary political one. The original 'Celtic' objects, whatever their original purpose or the niceties of their academic interpretation, were overtly being used as the vehicle for propaganda.

Similarly, it was no coincidence that, also in 1991, 'some 2,300 "Celtic" objects from 200 museums in 22 countries, insured for £91m', were moved into a great assemblage in Venice's Palazzo Grassi for an exhibition titled 'I Celti'[9] (see also Chapter 11). Meanwhile, in contrapuntal distinction from the new, politically opportunist, collective message of that great assemblage, consider the Gundestrup cauldron. One of the outstanding objects to have survived from the reality of late-prehistoric cultural achievement as distinct from the no-no fantasy of a homogeneous Celtic Europe, the cauldron is richly decorated in figured and symbolic silver. Now, so one academic argues, some of the motifs should be interpreted in terms of Indian shamanistic inspiration. So, while the object itself is prestigiously moved from exhibition to exhibition, and given different meanings by organizers and viewers, so its academic interpretation also moves, shifting appreciation of its cultural significance from continent to continent. Scholars and tourists are left to wonder whether the Gundestrup cauldron's value as heritage lies in its prototypical 'Europeanness', in its message of multi-ethnicity rather than racial homogeneity 2,000 years ago, or in its artistic essence as an early 'global product'. Perhaps that, rather than insisting on one received 'meaning', is how it should be.

Once the concept of multiple meanings has been grasped, then further purposes can be envisaged. This is particularly so in one of the museum's oldest functions, in some cases the original one in the minds of its founders: education. Oddly, perhaps, the pressure is coming from teachers who want to use museum material, expertise and facilities, rather than the teachers responding to proselytizing by the museums in the educational world; but in any case, many curators, perhaps under political and financial pressure to justify their position, 'were looking for new uses for their collections' anyway.[10] Certainly such is the case in Britain where the implementation of a National Curriculum in primary and secondary schooling has palpably increased the demand for the 'museum experience'.[11] The *Independent* article (Note 10) was in itself an indication of the new importance of museums in formal education. It quoted the Director of the 1990 'Museum of the Year' in Britain, the Museum of Science and Industry, University of Manchester, as saying: 'Museums have moved from being passive providers, delivering the same thing to any kind of visitor, to a much more active response to the interests and needs of very varied groups of people'; but then proceeded to miss half the point by expanding: 'Of course, that applies to all the museum's visitors, from families with toddlers to pensioners' – as if age and visiting-group structure were the only criteria separating out the Director's 'very varied groups of people'. The sociological structure in any large community, as in the Manchesters of the world, is of course far more complex than that indicated, embracing potential museum needs among people with, for example, all sorts of handicap – medical, economic, educational, linguistic – and numerous cultural requirements. Local ethnic considerations, for example, could well be a prime demand in making appropriate museum provision. Such ethnic provision should, however, surely include 'local indigenous' – a new permanent exhibition we saw recently was admirably explained in half a dozen leaflets in languages of Asia and India, but there was nothing in English, let alone the local dialect. It seemed implicit élitism – 'Whites can understand anyway' – and reverse ethnicity seems to have clouded the curatorial thinking in that case. And then, what about all the other visitors? In their various ways, they all have 'special needs' too, whether they arrive from Liverpool down the road or Liverpool Bay, Northwest Territories, Canada, and whether they come singly to study or in a happy band of tourists with a half-hour slot in which to whizz around. That's not funny: one pack of tourists was given all of five minutes to 'do' the museum in Victoria, Gozo, off Malta, and that was only because one of us insisted it be included at all.

The critical visitor may be aware of some of these nuances of management, function and interpretation, and be able to take them into account in seeking what he or she came for; the mass-tourist, with half an hour to 'do' a museum, has not time, and possibly no sensitivities, to react through discerning and judgemental filters. In the circumstances, 'Just tell me what I'm looking at. Tell me what it means' are reasonable requests. The casual tourist to the Burrell at least sees the Egyptian glass, the architectural pieces wrenched from their physical, never mind their cultural, contexts, and passes through, ever questing but probably seldom questioning how or why such objects came to be there in the first place. For his and her delectation? Perhaps such is sufficient answer if that is, in fact, the result.

Such idiosyncratic collections as Burrell's, meeting touristic needs at one level, exist in many parts of the world, especially now in the USA and Japan. The Malibu manifestation of the J. Paul Getty cultural empire is an example. But in Japan similar assemblages may be in corporate hands rather than in public-sector museums.[12] The great collections in the former follow the long-lived collecting tradition in European culture: we go out, we acquire and we bring back; we move the objects, possibly to our greater glory. While this may seem to the Western mind a 'natural' thing to do, such activity is of course acculturated and not necessarily common to *Homo sapiens*. As Malraux wrote in 1949, 'to the Asiatic's thinking an art collection is as preposterous as would be [to a Western audience] a concert in which the audience had to listen to an ill-assorted miscellany of pieces performed without a break'.[13] However, change is on the way in Tokyo in the form of the Edo–Tokyo Museum initiative, driven by the Governor and his deputy who reportedly 'recognised the need for the museum on travels abroad'.[14] And interestingly, a man called Hirochi Takeuchi, who had served in the role of managing director at the Long Term Credit Bank, was reported to have written: 'The reason France is so highly respected around the world, even though it has done some terrible things in the past is because it has Paris. . . . There is little in Japan to inspire sighs of admiration overseas.'[15]

For commercial purposes, cultural cross-currents can now, apparently, be totally ignored as in the advertisement (Franklin Mint Limited) exhorting the naive collector to 'Take a trip through time. To Genghis Khan's China and Queen Victoria's India, Tibet and Fiji and Rome. When you build a treasure trove of Great Historic Coins of the World.' Such eclecticism through time as well as space smacks of charlatism – or the collecting policy of one of the great museums of the world. Behind such nonsense, however, lurks one of the mainsprings which moves objects around the world, sometimes into museums but often not: the desirability of the object itself, especially when about to be installed in a new, personalized context, irrespective of original context in culture, place or time.

Some objects were of course meant to be moved, and they provide museums with something of a conundrum. If mobility was their *raison d'être* in the first place, it can never have been intended they should end up static and indoors as in many transport museums. Their very presence in a museum is therefore a contradiction of sorts. Some such mobile museum items run around outside as intended: the National

Tramway Museum at Crich, near Matlock, England, is a good example of that; and there, 'the past awaits you' on pages 1 and 2 of its brochure and you are enjoined to let it 'catch up with you' on page 3. Comparable items are indoors at the National Railway Museum at the tourist-rich city of York, though they are allowed out from time to time to steam around the countryside. They also invoke nostalgia and wonder at applied technologies as motives for collecting and tourists' visiting.

Even more 'dead' in such situations are objects intended to go even faster, like Concorde 001 in the Air Museum at Yeovilton, near Ilchester, in Somerset, and the vast assemblages of space technology on site near NASA's launch-pad in a Florida otherwise dominated as a tourist mecca by Mickey Mouse and friends. In the National Air and Space Museum, Washington D.C., the competition comes from more conventional establishments of cultural tourism of the sort common in most capital cities. No one could reasonably deny that such objects, after a lifetime's moving, are appropriately located, when early-twentieth-century locomotives are curated in York and mid-twentieth-century space-craft are available to the public in the USA. Furthermore, both attract tourists, adding significantly to the critical tourist mass and boosting the local economies of York and Washington. But matters of this kind are not always as straightforward.

Where should what be in a case like this?[16] The CSS *Alabama* was a ship; it still is, though it might as well not be in a sense for, now a wreck, it is inaccessible except to the few. It is, however, also now 'historic', with accretions of multi-cultural symbolisms as well as of the results of over a century's inundation. It was built in Liverpool, fought in the American Civil War under the flag of the Confederacy, and sank off France. In recent times, the wreck has been located by French divers and explored with funding from a group set up by a Texan. Liverpudlians wanted to join in the diving, for they saw the wreck as part of their heritage too. Objects retrieved from the wreck are likely to go on a world tour before being put on permanent display at a Cherbourg museum. Meanwhile, the *Alabama* Trust formed in Liverpool is appealing for funds to finance the building of a replica *Alabama* to go on show in Liverpool 'as a tourist attraction'. The replica would be made in Indonesia. The museum-object concept merges there with the 'moving-object' concept (see Chapter 9) and both elide quite nicely with heritages, tourism and some sort of global cross-culturalism.

That example also makes the point that heritage objects, whatever their nature, can be recent and still be emotive; and there too, as is quite often the case, shades of adventure, mystery, possibly even skulduggery, add spice to the story that can be told about an object when it reaches the point of display. The tons of precious-metal objects looted from 'primitive' and, more to the point, non-Christian, cultures in Central and northern South America, by Spaniards in particular, is part of one such 'adventure' story (though some would now see it differently: see Chapters 1 and 3). Another part is the loss of some of the booty as ships sank for one reason or another around the Caribbean. But it is the third part of the story which gives real zip to an already glamorous tale: the stirring adventures, compound of patience, research, bravery, endurance, serendipity and a certain roguishness, of modern high-tech buccaneers who, in our own time, have found the wrecks and re-looted the loot. Fortunes have been lost and made, often with scant attention to the canons of underwater archaeology or the requirements of local, national or international law.

The apotheosis of the process is exemplified in a 'Spanish Treasure' museum at Key West, Florida, a blatantly commercial operation glorifying the story's adventurous and treasure-seeking aspects. It is a popular tourist facility with a good story line and authentic material; but if the thrice-moved objects are the real thing, don't ask about the constructional details of the ships they came from or, in some cases, where the wrecks are located. There is a clear clash here between all sorts of interests; and while the argument could be sustained that the treasure-seeking activities would have gone on anyway, for the sake of finding and selling any *objets trouvés*, perhaps there would have been no museum if there had been no tourists or no hope of attracting tourists by opening such a museum. Even so, one of the main issues is not clear-cut: is it better to have this sort of private-enterprise museum, where at least some material is viewable which would almost certainly otherwise not be available in the public domain, or no museum at all?

Museums are wonderful, frustrating, stimulating, irritating, hideous things, patronizing, serendipitous, dull as ditchwater and curiously exciting, tunnel-visioned yet potentially visionary. The real magic is that any one of them can be all of those simultaneously. What a brilliant concept that can embrace everything from culture to micro-liths, butter-pats to Concorde, dinosaurs to art; and to collect them from the smallest of localities or the whole world, including under the sea; for anybody and everybody. And it is such an elastic concept too: what is a museum and what is not?

Just look at the variety in one area: it could be almost anywhere, but it happens to be Alberta, Canada, where a special edition of *Alberta Past*[17] brought a lot of heritage information together to promote a 'Take an Historic Alberta Break' campaign under the sponsorship of the Friends of Head-Smashed-in Buffalo Jump Society. Our annotated list from it is selective, biased towards advertised attractions that are or could be museums or have museum-like functions:

Andrew Wolf Winery ('100 year old French vats in castle-like winery'); Alliance and District Museum (local history); Astotin Interpretive Centre (in Elk Island National Park, with Ukrainian pioneer home, bison park, etc.); Battle River Pioneer Museum ('artefacts, history, wildlife, minerals and antique machinery'); Brooks Museum; Centennial Museum, Canmore (mining and heritage); Donalda and District Museum (local history and archaeology, Canada's lamp capital with over 750 kerosene lamps); Drumheller Dinosaur and Fossil Museum; Edmonton Telephone Historical Information Centre (experience fibre optics, etc.); End of Steel Heritage Museum and Park ('best little museum in the Peace'); Etizkom Museum; Fort Calgary Interpretive Centre (birthplace of Calgary with 'outline of the original Fort'); Fort Museum; Fort Normandeau Interpretive Centre (with reconstructed fort); Fort Saskatchewan Museum and Historic Site (early-twentieth-century buildings, North West Mounted Police fort, pioneers, agricultural); Fort Whoop-Up Interpretive Centre (replica fort, whiskey trading post); Glenbow Museum; Head-Smashed-In Interpretive Centre (at a World Heritage Site); Historical Museum at Shandro (Ukrainian pioneer history); Iddesleigh Museum; Irvine Museum; Luxton Museum ('extraordinary heritage of the Indians'); Markerville Creamery Museum ('the only restored creamery in Alberta', established by 34 Icelandic farmers 1897, working till 1972, restored to represent 1932 by Icelandic Society); Medicine Hat Museum; Musée Heritage Museum (Indians, Métis, Missionaries, Pioneers); National Porcelain Warehouse (includes Clay Products Interpretive Centre); Nose Creek Valley Museum (regional history, life style of early residents); Olympic Hall of Fame; Peace River Museum and Archives (local history, fur trade); Provincial Museum of Alberta ('wildlife, geology, Indian culture and social history'); Redcliff Museum; Red Deer Archives (documentary and photographic history); Red Deer and District Museum (local history); Remington-Alberta Carriage Collection ('fascinating world of horse drawn transportation'); Reynolds-Alberta Museum (transportation and agriculture); Rocky Mountain House Interpretive Centre ('explorers, natives and the voyageurs'); Rutherford House, Edmonton (tea and croquet at Edwardian mansion home of Alberta's first premier); Sir Alexander Galt Museum ('finest small community museum in Canada'); South Peace Centennial Museum (agricultural); Stony Plain Multicultural Centre (local handicrafts, history); Ukrainian Cultural Heritage Village (Ukrainian pioneer settlement of east central Alberta, 1892–1930); University of Alberta Paleontology Museum; Vista 33 (view gallery and museum, artefacts and telecommunications); Wainwright Museum (in original CNR railway station, local history, oil industry, buffalo park and military camp); Waterton Heritage Centre Patrimoine (art, artefacts, tales, photos); Wetaskiwin and District Museum (pioneer gallery, native culture, local history); Whyte Museum of the Canadian Rockies (art, heritage, archives). No wonder the slogan is 'Alberta: culture and multiculturalism'.

That little collection does not just contain the history of Alberta. With a range, and names, like that, they *are* the history of Alberta, particularly when you think of the effort that has gone into creating them in pioneer country, and the pride with which they are presented to hoped-for 'Partners in Alberta's Heritage'. The impression is, however, that they would still be there, collecting their kerosene lamps and 'Indian flints', even if no tourist arrived; for, re-packaged though they may have been for the purposes of encouraging tourism, their true inspiration, function and future lie in their local communities in a multi-ethnic state. Though by definition museums contain surviving fragments from earlier times, these museums, and probably the great majority of museums in the world, are really saying, not 'This is what we were', but 'This is who we are'. And that applies as much to the French Government and J. Paul Getty as to the Icelandic Society in 'historic and idyllic Markerville . . . 20 minutes west of Highway 2 from the Penhold turnoff'. Museums collectively may well give off confusing vibes; but a good one knows 'where it's at', and provides good directions.

The 'moving object' **9**

Here, elaborating on a theme already touched on in Chapters 3 and 8, we shall look at what happens when a heritage object or objects move(s) from one cultural context in the world to another. We wish to concentrate on the idea that cultural objects, in all their bewildering variety, are characteristically on the move; and to look at some of the implications of this phenomenon for heritage and tourism. Not perhaps the first word that comes to mind in that context, 'loot' is nevertheless our starting point, for it seems to constitute quite a large element of the 'moving-object' story.[1]

A typical context for the 'moving object' as loot is: 'The Spanish navy has stepped up patrols against treasure-hunters searching for a giant hoard of gold and silver in the estuary of Vigo, Galicia.'[2] It is a familiar story, with counterparts through the centuries all round the world; in this case, with connections to many countries and close to the plot of Anthony Price's thriller, *War Game* (1976). With the elements of gold and silver, some facts and a lot of speculation and hope, this example centres on the return under the escort of twenty French ships in 1702 of the seventeen galleons of the Spanish 'Fleet of Gold' from the Indies 'after three years in the new empire laden with gold and other precious metals'. The British fleet attacked it in Vigo Bay, capturing thirteen ships and sinking others. At that stage, 'loot' intended for the Spanish imperial coffers had already been moved from the indigenous cultures of Central and South America and was being further dispersed into the Iberian peninsula, into Britain as booty from the battle, and to the bottom of the sea. An attempt to recover the unknown amount of loot in that temporary sub-marine context was made as early as the day of the battle, 22 October, the first organized expedition for that purpose being eighteen years later.

Since then 'other attempts have been made by Spanish, British, French, Italian, North American and Swedish groups'. Now, 'Every year people come to hunt for the treasure, and there will be a lot more interest generated during the Columbus celebrations' (see Chapter 3). The authorities 'fear the damage that could be caused by treasure-hunters' and it is their 'pirate expeditions' which have occasioned the increased patrols. Meanwhile, authorized work has located fourteen sunken galleons, and the 'official Fifth Columbus Centenary diving team is searching for the . . . *Santo Cristo de Maracaibo* – the most prized of all the ships . . . the British were unloading booty when it sank'. There could be a lot more 'moving objects' soon. With unconscious irony, right beside the article in *The European* appeared one of Spain's tourist advertisements for 1992 extolling its heritage, 'your walk through history', in travel-speak phrases such as 'full of precious jewels' and 'moments you'll always treasure'. The imagery of 'loot' is powerfully embedded in heritage and tourism.

Of course 'loot' is a favourite word among adventure-story writers and journalists (or at least headline writers), but, despite its clichéd nature, the word seems appropriate here. For one thing, like the word 'corpse' it immediately strikes a chord in the cacophony competing for public interest, and that is where much mass tourism originates. Perhaps a definition is nevertheless required: we mean by 'loot' an object or objects of cultural value acquired by illegal or dubious means and moved from one context to another with a view to financial gain. *Movement* from one place to another is crucial to the definition.

The 'gain' could, however, primarily be aesthetic or in status. It could be on the part of the real looters, carefully at several stages removed from the action but initiating the process by letting it be known that they would be interested in acquiring certain specific objects or types of material. The looting of museums at Herculaneum and Corinth, for example, or the removal of tanks from the Kabul War Museum (above p. 104), assuredly did not represent random burglaries by petty thieves: the robbers knew there was a market for their loot if they were successful.

Many places elsewhere in the world have been subject to similar depredations for a long time, their cultural material moving off to new lives elsewhere, often in private collections. The movement continues and much evidence, by the nature of the phenomenon often circumstantial, suggests its increasing extent, frequency and monetary scale. Overall, this phenomenon is a major loss to scholarship in that the bulk of the material never surfaces properly in moving into private collections; in moving to such destinations it is also a loss to the general public and, therefore, to the tourist.

Curiously, perhaps, most of the 'heritage-loot' story concerns straight-forward pillage and theft in normal, illegal terms, yet numerous cases of cultural objects moving in our already familiar military context come readily to hand. 'War', or more generally military circumstances, seem to loom large where 'loot' is concerned. At the mega-end of the range is, for example, the whole question of cultural property 'looted' by and from Nazi Germany during and at the end of the Second World War; at the other extremity are individual objects rifled from the graves of the war dead or military decorations of the brave auctioned by impecunious widows amidst great public chest-baring by the popu-lar press. Interestingly, both the examples used here involve objects moving across not just national boundaries but from continent to continent; and both involve in our own times the movement of material from contexts in which it was not indigenous anyway. Nor is race far away from either, and while gain is certainly a motive in each case, personal monetary profit seems to mix with gains and losses, of status for example, at an institutional level too. And as in adventure stories, also present are elements of danger, mystery and skulduggery. All this for 'old' objects at one level; but of course, monetary value apart, it is also occasioned by their enhanced symbolic value as icons in contemporary society.

In itself, 'Nazi loot' is a huge subject. We have just picked out some strands in the story, mainly from current newspaper reportage. This is not because it is necessarily more authoritative but because such sources indicate what is perceived to be the continuing public interest in the matter, 40 or 50 years after the event. And this perceived interest is justified if only because, at the end of the line, the tourist waits, only too ready to travel to see such objects, often of intrinsic interest but now additionally interesting precisely because they are imbued with mystery and the subject of media coverage. And such coverage, among other things, has the effect of heightening interest simply because of implications that 'great treasures', part of the 'common cultural heritage', have been 'lost' and might not be seen again. There is too a slight 'miracle effect' when such objects, perhaps tantalizingly glimpsed in old photographs published in the press dur-ing the course of the 'quest', are eventually 'found' and repositioned in the public gaze in all their physical authenticity. Think, for example, of the scale of public demand to see the well-illustrated 'Amber Room', 'the priceless decorative chamber stripped [in 1941] from a palace [Catherine the Great's palace at Tsarskoe Selo] in St Petersburg [formerly Leningrad]',[3] should disputed reports of its rediscovery prove true. The 'moving object'? – '12 [six according to *The Sunday Times*] *tons* of intricately carved amber tiles' presented by Friedrich Wilhelm of Prussia in 1717 to Peter the Great of Russia are alleged to have been 'looted by the Nazis during World War II [and] buried on a Red army base in Thuringia, formerly in East Germany' (now of course in Germany).[4]

Everything seems to be moving around in that instance, cognitively as well as physically. Though objects move, however, and their contexts, environments, meanings and political significances change, some facets of their acquired iconography remain for a long time. A new, but essentially similar, story relates to the former contents of the Bremen Kunsthalle.[5] 'Soviet opinion remains deeply divided' on the question of repatriating cultural and art objects moved from Germany. This was the case despite the Soviet–German treaty of November 1990, in which the signatories agreed 'that art treasures that disappeared or were unlawfully appropriated, which are now in their territory, will be returned'. Why such hostility to the return of cultural and art treasures from the West? – because 'the Germans themselves conducted a similarly ruthless campaign of pillage and destruction . . . after Hitler's May 1941 invasion, and . . . the emotional scars . . . are fresh in the memory of millions of Russian and Ukrainian families'.

The 'Treasure of Priam' is only one other element in the Nazi-loot story but it stands out as having all the ingredients of a thumping good yarn. It also raises nice questions at a more philosophical level of who owns which bits of what past and, more pragmatically, who has the right now to show what to the public where? A further twist to the ambiguities is given by the fact that 'Troy', in the sense of the Homeric city of King Priam, as identified by the excavator as the second settlement of seven stratified in a tell (see p. 73) at Hissarlik in north-west Anatolia, has proved to be of the third millennium BC, long before the time Homer was writing about; so the 'Treasure of Priam', a powerfully evocative name, is nothing whatsoever to do with Priam. Present concern is, therefore, about a wrongly named hoard from a wrongly identified context, possibly on a site which is the wrong one anyway, for it is not certain that the literary Troy was at Hissarlik at all.

Despite wrong ascriptions, however, the 'Treasure' was undoubtedly found, though arguably it should not subsequently have been in Berlin to be lost. The Hissarlik tell was in part of the Ottoman Empire at the time of the discovery on the day before the end of the season's work in 1873, a part which became Turkish under the Treaty of Versailles of 1919. It is further arguable as to whose heritage the hoard really belonged to at any time from the second millennium BC up to the later-nineteenth century AD. The 'Treasure' came to be an ornament of Nazi

Germany simply because its excavator was Heinrich Schliemann, a retired German businessman with more money and antiquarian obsessiveness than scholarly disinterest or archaeological know-how. He smuggled the material from his Trojan diggings out of the country and it came to the Berlin Museum where it was viewable by visitors until 1939. From there it 'disappeared' in 1945, together with a great deal of other material, some, it was feared, destroyed in military action, some, it was suspected, moved and concealed. It has been estimated that some $10 billion worth of art treasures disappeared from Germany in the last stages of and immediately after the Second World War. Much hinges, so it now appears, on the alleged flight of a military plane from Berlin to Moscow in July 1945.

On 24 March 1991, the British Sunday newspaper, the *Observer*, anticipated the publication of an article in the April number of an American magazine *Artnews*. On its front page, it led with a summary of 'how the artworks were seized and taken to secret stores in Moscow, Leningrad, Kiev and Zagorsk'. These already much loved objects included, so it was claimed, works by Velázquez, El Greco, Goya, Cézanne, Monet, Degas and Renoir as well as 'Three crates of special archaeological treasures [which] came from the Berlin Museum'. These last 'are said to have included the Trojan gold excavated by Heinrich Schliemann, the sixth-century BC Eberswalde treasure, the fifth-century Kottbus treasure and the eleventh-century Holm treasure'. A hitherto unknown 1945 memoir of an American army officer 'gives some idea of the scale of the Soviet war trophy: "7,000 Greek vases, 1,800 statues, 9,000 antique gems, 6,500 terracottas and thousands of lesser objects were removed from the Department of Greek Antiquities alone" '. The *Observer* article concluded with the observation that 'What is new is the acknowledgement that many of [the objects] are under [Soviet] government control, a revelation which is bound to increase pressure by German museums for the return of *their* treasures'. The italics of '*their*' are the authors', for that one word begs many of the questions implicit in this whole field of the 'moving object'; particularly now that no sooner had this paragraph been keyed than 'Soviet government control' itself dissolved.

The temptation cannot be resisted to remark that, in line with our theme, if there was one particular moment symbolizing that dissolution then surely it was, to the watching world television audience, when a permanently fixed cultural object, rather like a Virgin Mary in a miracle, unbelievably moved. Who will ever forget that image of the huge statue of Felix Dzerzhinsky (see also Chapter 1), lurching stiffly and cumbrously from its plinth to swing so incongruously and terminally in mid-air?

That events in what is now the former USSR have changed the political situation there fairly fundamentally merely serves, for our purposes, to illustrate the general point that whatever the rights and wrongs of an object's location and ownership at any one point in time, its very being, its use and its availability are always subject to political circumstances. Reflecting the political change in the USSR, icons of the formerly great and good were taken to lie 'in disgrace in a "monster corner", apart from the other exhibits in a sculpture park'.[6] But so seriously regarded were the issues raised by the future of the visible and symbolic remains of Communist ideology that, in the midst of all the politicking, 'Moscow has set up a Commission on Cultural Heritage to deal with the statues. . . . Few [of the 123 Lenins] will be kept; most will go to the Museum of Totalitarian Art'. In similar vein, but an extreme example, an exhibition early in 1991 in Warsaw, Poland, consisted of 'Everyday articles from 45 years of Communism . . . satirically displayed as objets d'art'.

A further facet of the 'Nazi-loot' story exemplifies the complexities when one does get down to such particulars. Some other objects which 'disappeared' from Germany were the 'treasures' of Quedlinburg church, subsequently located in East Germany. They included the ninth-century Samuhel Gospel, 'one of the most precious of Germany's lost medieval works of art'.[7] The objects had last been seen in 1945 during the American occupation of the area when they had been hidden for safety in an abandoned mine guarded by a succession of American soldiers. 'When the army pulled out, handing the town over to Soviet forces, about half of the treasures went missing'. Necessarily telescoping a long and tortuous story here, the reappearance of the Gospel in 1988 on the international art market led to the discovery of a cache of 'almost all the missing Quedlinburg treasures' in a bank safe in Whitewright, a 'sleepy Texas town' north of Dallas. The items included 'a reliquary box . . . estimated to be worth $50 million, and six reliquaries made of rock crystal. Most came from 6th-century Egypt, were reworked in Germany. . . . Items not from Quedlinburg included Roman coins . . . and manuscripts'. The happy part of the ending is that locals and tourists can now see the Gospel and other manuscripts at the Bayerischer Staatsbibliothek, Ludwigstrasse, Munich. The unhappy part lies in the paradox that the investigator of this trail across three continents and several cultures can apparently only recoup his considerable personal expense in bringing back into the public arena these much travelled objects by suing the church at Quedlinburg – which could only afford to pay him by selling the treasures.

The movement of cultural objects as a result of military conflict is, then, by no means uncommon. This is illustrated by 1991 alone, a year in which our subject has been affected by military action in Iran, Iraq, Kuwait, Russia and Yugoslavia. These instances follow other 'movements' occasioned by like circumstances in recent years in, for example, Cyprus, Romania, Sri Lanka, Afghanistan, China, Cambodia and Lebanon.

It might well be asked 'So what?' But in fact the issues here really do seem to bite deep; they actually matter, being taken seriously by many individuals and institutions, not least governments. Take the Gulf War for example. 'Now the Gulf war is hopefully over', wrote Wolfgang Georg Fischer, 'it's time to count the cultural cost'.[8] He continued, making our point here:

> War destroys not just human lives, homes and countryside but also religious and cultural monuments like churches, mosques, open-air sculpture, museums and works of art of all kinds. A passionate art lover could argue, with cynical frankness, that human life and even the countryside can be regenerated or reproduced, while the great cultural monuments of human history are irreplaceable if destroyed. There is only one St Peter's, one Acropolis, one Mona Lisa.

Eschewing the temptation to discuss at some length the general implications of that paragraph, let us just keep to the Gulf War and its consequences in terms of moving objects. For one thing, Iraq complained to the United Nations that 'large sections of the Iraq Museum in Baghdad were destroyed in the first five days' of the War, a claim unsubstantiated at the time. Devastation of sites, and the movement of objects by various means and for various reasons, there certainly were. A result was Fischer's suggestion, articulating the deep concern felt throughout many sensitive parts of the cultural 'global village': 'the international forum of art historians, archaeologists and art-lovers will have to try to find a formula by which art protection in times of conflict can be adapted to the demands of highly mechanised war and sophisticated weapons technology'. Technically, his vision has substance, but whether it will be supported by the will is another matter. And in any case, it does not cover threat and disturbance occasioned by an old-fashioned low-tech, 'dirty' conflict, such as that filling the second half of the same year and on into 1992 in Yugoslavia (see Chapter 6). Nor does it provide for the continuous, but far less dramatic, movement of objects in quite different military circumstances.

Another example will have to illustrate that general point. While cultural objects of all sorts can be affected by military conflict, the conflict itself produces artefacts and many of these become highly desirable to collectors. These can range from the army units actually involved in the conflict who want institutional mementoes (above p. 104) through individual soldiers taking their private souvenirs, to the armies of museums and private collectors who all want a slice of the artefactual action. Militaria, therefore, have an immediate as well as a long-term collectability, an enhanced value through a range of significances over and above the practical reasons for their manufacture. The fields of the Battle of Waterloo were scoured within days of the event and were the subject of tourist visits later in 1815. Now the search for military-heritage objects is worldwide to meet a worldwide demand.

The year 1991 saw one aspect of it make world news, with Britain claiming centre stage as 'the main market for stolen relics'.[9] In this case they came from the graves of some 600 British soldiers killed on 22 January 1879 during the Battle of Isandhlwana, some 130 km north-east of Pietermaritzburg, South Africa. While the dead Zulus were dragged away, the British were left for over a month and their remains were only then buried in shallow graves covered by whitewashed stones. The hundred or so cairns are scattered over an area of more than 90 acres. 'Many of the burial sites belong to the 24th Regiment, later the South Wales Borderers and now the Royal Regiment of Wales', according to the curator of the regimental museum. No anonymous graves of prehistory, these, but of known context in a world saga which is still being played out as South Africa draws back from apartheid. Nevertheless, 'People have been taking away great sackfuls of stuff . . . to feed a growing black-market trade in Zulu war memorabilia', added *The Sunday Times* four months later when it extended the report of the desecration (though without stating evidence) from Isandhlwana to 'famous battle sites'.[10] 'The officials believe there is an organised ring offering large incentives to Zulus to collect the insignia. . . . "They move fast, at night . . . and bones are left scattered around. . . . Prices are high. You are talking about hundreds of dollars for metal remains from a Martini Henry rifle" ' – presumably when the relics become available in Britain 'where dealers and Zulu war enthusiasts pay handsomely for them'.

In that South African instance, the attraction was the objects buried with the dead; in other cases, it is the dead themselves which attract and become the focus of highly charged debate. In one sense, corpses are not of course objects; but once they are artificially preserved and used for iconographic purposes they become to all intents and purposes, and certainly from a tourist point of view, like a 'heritage object'. This becomes apparent especially when questions are being asked at one level about corporeal symbolism and simultaneously at another level about tourist potential. The embalmed corpse of Lenin is a classic contemporary example: should it be moved from the mausoleum in Red Square (a World Heritage Site incidentally)? What does the corpse now 'mean'? How will the collapse of Communism, or the removal of the corpse, affect tourism to one of the outstanding heritage centres in the world? To whom indeed does 'he' now belong?

Similar issues can arise at the other end of the global scale. In the village of Kampehl in eastern Germany, population 150, 'the corpse of a knight who died 300 years ago' is 'the community's only tourist attraction'. Indeed, the corpse, having failed to decompose, is 'a *lucrative* [our italics] tourist attraction, drawing thousands of visitors every year'.[11] The philosophical issue of proprietary claim was here a practical one: the vicar said the corpse belonged to the church, the mayor said it was council property. Here, however, there is no question of the corpse's moving; it is its significance which has moved. And the change has come about, not through any great academic insight into its history or some revelation from medical science about its preservation, but from the familiar pair of political and financial considerations. The corpse was formerly managed by the East German state, making a modest income and paying rent to the church. Now, in post-Communist times, free enterprise in true capitalist style has raised the entrance fee to the crypt containing the knight from 7p to £1. With more tourists arriving, the corpse has suddenly become relatively big business, with a rumoured 'take' of some £50,000 a year. It therefore matters a very great deal, at least locally, who owns him and hence the urgency and import of the dispute. It is also, behind the clash of politics and deutschmarks ostensibly over ownership, a dispute about a clash of global cultures. Meanwhile, the corpse remains unmoved.

Another corpse which *was* moved became much more famous in 1991. This was a corpse some 5,000 years old. As an addition to European heritage, it proved extremely controversial, not least because its tourist potential was a consideration from early in its international reincarnation. Attracting extensive media coverage (which we use eclectically in this discussion), it raised a number of issues: authenticity, conservation and access, fairly predictably, but also legal ownership and, therefore, which country was going to be able to show it to the public, gaining cash and kudos. 'The ice warrior . . . is a potential blockbuster on the intellectual tourist trail', presciently observed one writer at an early stage of the drama.[12] The hiker who found the corpse made a legal claim to 50 per cent of all profits arising from the body because he 'had realised early on that what we have here is a potential tourist goldmine'.[13]

Corpses have an intrinsic if morbid fascination: who is it? What sex is it? How old was he or she? How did he or she die? This corpse was discovered on 19 September 1991, some 3,280 m high in the Alps, frozen stiff. The Italian police showed little interest when it was reported to them because, not surprisingly as it turned out, there was no correlation with their list of 'missing persons'. Four months afterwards, a Swiss woman claimed she had recognized the corpse of her father, lost on the same glacier in the 1970s.[14] Very moving. Had there been a police report later, it would have run along these lines: 'A dark-skinned male person of unknown identity and no known address, in his late 20s, 1.57 m high, with a beard, hair 9 cm long, clipped finger nails and tatoos on the knee, ankle and back; wearing a grass cape and patched leather coat and shoes insulated with straw and grass, and jewellery made of stone beads on leather thongs; carrying a hazel rucksack, rope and two mushrooms, and equipped with a yew bow and arrows and a copper axe bound by leather thongs to a yew handle, a flint knife and a quiver of twelve unfinished arrows. May have been physically handicapped by former fractures to the knee and a pelvic growth; some internal cranial damage. Circumstances of death uncertain but, while neither assault nor ritual exposure can be ruled out, likely to have been accidental, perhaps involving a fall or avalanche resulting in injury followed by hypothermia. Likely time of death: about 3,300 BC'.[15] Further investigation was likely to be very expensive, it might have added, so, in fairness to the Austrian taxpayer, Japanese sponsorship was being sought.

All quite interesting, no doubt, and clearly of archaeological importance; but why all the fuss? Again, the answer lies in ownership. The find-spot was so remote that it was not at all clear whether the corpse had been found in Italy or Austria, and indeed both countries became involved in meticulous survey to try to establish exactly where on the ground their hitherto undisputed frontier lay, for the corpse was found very close to the line and could have been on either side of it. The find-spot proved to be 92.6 m inside Italy. Meanwhile, the corpse had been moved to Innsbruck, Austria, and a long process of detailed examination began; his associated artefacts were moved to Mainz, Germany, for conservation. Back on the icy spot on the mountain, barbed wire kept out the inevitable looters and, as a result of the survey, Austria agreed to return the corpse to Italy. There was another proprietorial complication. Since the corpse was in Italy, it was also in the Tyrol, a part of Italy which wants to be independent; so a strongly worded suggestion was made locally that the 5,000-year-old young man should be called 'Homo Tyroliensis'.

Bits of him meanwhile went off to Oxford for radio-carbon dating: that should have settled it, as it did for the Turin shroud and many a fake 'antique' moving around on the market; for the biggest question of all about the Man of Houslabjoch was: Is he a hoax? A lot was already at stake on that score by the time that laboratories at Oxford and Zurich came up with the double-checked answer. Far from being a fake, the corpse was even older, at around 3,300 BC, than he should have been on the basis of his associated artefacts (c. 2,000 BC). This has left something of an academic archaeological issue to be resolved but that can be left to the scholars; sufficient for the viewing public that the 'Iceman' is definitely prehistoric, his corporeal survival a miracle whether it has been for 4,000 or 5,000 years. The interplay of cultures here clashing in different ways – for example, scientific v public interest, international counter-claims, tourist and status potential – accord well with our theme, especially as the issues arose only when a very static object was moved. From among several historical and/or contemporary perspectives are culled different purposes, rendering this intensely complicated and unfinished story of far more than mere human interest and intrinsic fascination.

Another reason for objects to travel is to show them off not so much for their own sake, or to enhance their owner's status, as for fund-raising on behalf of their proprietorial institution. A classic example also illustrated some of the problems that can be encountered. It concerned what was thought to be a world-class original, the copy of Magna Carta belonging to Lincoln Cathedral, England. Like many of its kind, Lincoln Cathedral is chronically short of revenue, needing a considerable income not only to maintain the fabric of its structures but also large lump sums to carry out much needed, long-term repairs. At the moment, its magnificent west front is clad in scaffolding for work which will take many years to complete. Consequently, visitors to Lincoln, as to many other great religious buildings, are confronted by an obscured façade – and a request for a 'voluntary' entry charge. Entrepreneurial activities also encourage them to spend money, side by side with appeals to their charity.

It was to support the long-running need for cash that the Lincoln Magna Carta had several times been moved abroad: to America, for example, as part of the 1976 celebrations of independence when over $1m was raised (in part through the efforts of a young man called John Major). In 1988, the year of the World Expo in Brisbane, a sub-dean took the same copy of the Magna Carta, 'off to his homeland, Australia, on a six-month fund raising trip. He also took his wife . . . his . . . daughter . . . her friend . . . and his colleague . . . the managing director of the cathedral shops.'[16] Further, 'In Australia, he appointed a cousin to co-ordinate PR and another relative to organise volunteer help. Unfortunately, [they] failed to raise many Australian dollars for Lincoln's needy coffers. In fact, their fund raising sojourn [which netted £938 according to the *Weekend Guardian* report] set the cathedral back £56,075' (£80,775 according to a later account,[17] but other figures have been bandied about and the exact amount is immaterial to our use of the case here).

In this particular example, issues of the 'moving object', which were perhaps never paramount in the affair, became clouded by clashes concerning personalities, finance, the governance of a great cathedral and matters of religious observance in the Church of England. But Magna Carta itself, as an object rather than as a primary documentary source of fundamental significance to English history and rather more perhaps, was at the centre, giving rise to powerful emotions and dramatic events (and certainly appalling publicity about those who would be our leaders in rectitude). Focused on the claustrophobia of Lincoln's close, the affair nevertheless stretched across three continents and into very different cultures. As Jocelyn Targett observed, while 'Lincoln' meant a lot in the USA ('it's the capital of Nebraska, a president, and a long shiny limousine'), it neither brought any associations to Australia nor set up resonances there.[18] Whether the actual object has suffered from these peregrinations is a moot point; it can hardly have benefited from them, and one might well question the cultural stewardship of any organization which encourages such frequent and long-distance movements primarily for its own financial purposes.

On the other hand, of course, is the argument that the moving Magna Carta has enabled many hundreds of thousands, if not millions, of people to look at a prime piece of history which they would not have travelled to Lincoln to see. Two questions arise: can an object like the Magna Carta be properly appreciated not just out of context away from Lincoln Cathedral library but exposed in a created and alien environment as at Brisbane, where Lincoln's 'dressy pavilion' vied with the Vatican exhibition next door? And, on the conservation issue, is it valid to think of instances like this – wear and tear on an object through travel to take it to the public – as the mirror-image of the on-site situation where too much public visiting harms the physical remains, and probably environment, of a heritage structure? In the latter situation, it is the travelling tourist who threatens the desired but static object; in the former, it is the object which can suffer deterioration by becoming the tourist.

While we may doubt whether the consideration of such philosophical and pragmatic issues led to the decision, the saga of the Lincoln Magna Carta at least produced one happy landing. Incredibly, it was suggested that the great charter should make a further tour, this time to New Zealand. The Dean decided that 'Magna Carta's jetset, peripatetic lifestyle was over. From now on it was grounded'. So if you have not seized the opportunity to look on Lincoln's Magna Carta in the USA or Australia you will now have to be a tourist to Lincoln to see it (for a voluntary entry fee of course).

Most cathedrals have at least one main tourist attraction. At Hereford Cathedral, England, it was, and will fortunately continue to be, its map of the world. The *Mappa mundi* is of thirteenth-century date, one of the oldest maps in the world, as well as of the world; but of course its interest, not least in this book, lies as much in its depiction of a concept, a world-view 700 years ago, as in its cartography or early date as such. It ought to be perceived as a world-class heritage item; it certainly is a major item in the British heritage, and although tourists do not flock to Hereford in the same way as to Canterbury or York, many of those who do visit probably go as much to see this map as anything else. This access was recently threatened for, pleading as usual a pressing need for cash to maintain and repair a particularly friable complex of historic buildings and contents, including the medieval chained library in particular, the Dean and Chapter announced that the map would have to be sold. Though similar in some respects to the Lincoln case in proposing to exploit a heritage item to meet institutional financial needs, Hereford's intent apparently was to send its treasure off permanently it knew not where as distinct from sending it temporarily on tour to a predetermined destination.

Apart from fears about possible consequences to the object itself, the proposal raised questions about the right of a single institution to sell off for its own ends, however worthy, part of the British national heritage; and about the shame of such a nationally important object going abroad and even into private ownership where perhaps it would not be available to the public. It is in many respects a familiar scenario. Anyway, from the tourist point of view, why should a person wanting to see it have to travel to, say, Osaka, and what vibes would he or she receive from it in such a place, when all the historic and cultural associations of this particular object are, and always have been, with a place called Hereford, a name with its own and very pertinent resonances?

Again, the tale took some time and complexity to unfold but the eventual upshot was that the *Mappa* stayed in Hereford, the need to sell it having been largely obviated by donations of £1 million from the J. P. Getty fund and £2 million from the National Heritage Memorial Fund in Britain towards a new building to house both it and the library. The question of whether, *in extremis*, the Cathedral authorities would actually have sold the map remains unanswered, but the threat of doing so 'worked'. The Cathedral solved its immediate problem (providing for its medieval library) and simultaneously helped trigger changes in the provision of state aid for historic buildings. The case highlighted, once again, the power of a single object to move people, institutions, even government; in this case without itself moving, though important to our argument is that it might and could have done so. Tourists can, as it happens, continue to go to Hereford Cathedral to see the Hereford *Mappa mundi* as part of *their* heritage.

Nevertheless it is worth recalling, within our theme of the 'moving object', another incident in the immediate background to this development. The object did not in fact move, but that it *could* have done so is the interesting point in what turned out to be a deadly heritage game of institutional bluff and double bluff. The interests of heritage, global and national never mind local, were sidelined in the po-faced public stance of the needy proprietor, while the poor tourist, actual or potential, could only watch events as influentially as on a television screen.

Just as the ownership, location and movement of many objects are affected by war, so then can they also be affected by religious contexts. Lincoln and Hereford illustrate the case of world-class secular objects enmeshed in religious imbroglios, at one and the same time both powerfully local in their dynamic and yet driven by, and raising, matters external and general. Yet cash, not context, seems to be the common factor there. That is not, however, always the whole motivation. Few subjects, for example, raise tempers quite so fast as classical Greek antiquities, especially when regarded as 'art' in the modern world; and many of the pieces were after all originally religious in inspiration and function even if they now have to fight their way in very secular situations. Of course they are bought and sold, but they can also involve patriotism and repatriation. The Elgin marbles clearly loom here; though it is really the phenomenon of 'Elginism' which concerns us.

We understand this to mean the tensions inherent in a situation where one group, often a nation state, demands repatriation of part of what it sees as its heritage from another party, often another country, to which the objects in question have been moved, at some time in the past. Thus the Greek government's prolonged pursuit of those parts of the marble sculptured frieze formerly around the Parthenon on the Acropolis, Athens, which are currently in the British Museum, London, has led to this new word, 'Elginism'. It denies the right of the British Museum to 'own' the pieces even though Lord Elgin, technically the owner in that he had paid for them, legally sold the marbles to the Museum in 1816 for £35,000. On the one hand, Greece sees such works of art from its premier monument, a temple, as peculiarly its heritage, with the rider that this glory that was classical Greece should be on show in its homeland to the greater glory of present-day and tourist-attractive Greece. On the other, the British Museum is not allowed under its statute to dispose of parts of its collection and in any case, so it argues, it is a world museum which happens to be in Britain, not the British *sensu* 'National British' museum, holding material from the world for the world at a convenient place on the global tourist routes.

Furthermore, at the time of Lord Elgin's purchase of the pieces, the Acropolis was of course in the hands of the Turks, who were actually the legitimate rulers by conquest of that part of the Ottoman Empire to which the 30-year-old Elgin was in fact the British ambassador. Part of his motivation, estimated to have cost him some £4 million in today's terms, was to save the pieces from the rude soldiery, then using the temple as an ammunition store; and from the indigenes, then rendering large chunks of it into building mortar.[19] That he was successful in this, and indeed in accidentally thereby 'saving' the objects from the effects of modern pollution which has wreaked such havoc in twentieth-century Athens, is seen as beside the main Greek point.[20] This quite simply is that, matter not the detail, the marbles are theirs by a sort of natural (or should it be 'cultural'?) 'right of heritage'.

This is the inspiration for the building beside the Athenian Acropolis of a brand-new museum specifically to house the marbles: 'It will be the most beautiful museum in the world. When it is built the British will have no excuse not to give us the Elgin marbles back'.[21] Cultural interchange continues as the Greek government, after an international competition, awarded the contract for the £50 million museum to two Italian architects, the largest contract involving foreigners in modern Greek history. In the ensuing row, disparaging remarks have of course been made about both the design – 'Disneyland' – and Italians. They 'see the Acropolis as tourists', a Greek architect was reported as opining, a most interesting remark in our context; we take it to have meant that Italians do not empathize with Greek heritage, rather than being merely a rude remark about tourists (on which the Greek economy is fairly dependent). The further observation that the new museum 'will be so large that the world's most important sculptures will be lost in it' struck a particularly plangent note since most of them are not there nor, *pace* Mme Mercouri, are they likely to be in the near future; though an exhibition or temporary loan might be possible. Meanwhile, the new museum is planned with two empty rooms awaiting the marbles' return or arrival, depending on your point of view. The 'moving object' may be a commonplace but the power of objects once moved is, in the later twentieth century, becoming a major global issue.

Whatever the particulars, the case of the Elgin marbles, and hence 'Elginism', raise the general issue of whether, and if so, all or just some, cultural objects should remain in their indigenous context, their place of origin. To accept the argument that they should is to deny any concept of 'world heritage' or the practicalities of conservation and display for a mass public. To act on it would lead to as great a reverse movement of material as there has been centrifugally since Renaissance times. Most of the world's great museums would become the equivalent of parish chests and, conversely the world would see an enormous proliferation of thousands and thousands of site and local museums (and, though they have their own significant functions, international collecting and interchange is not, by and large, one of them: see Chapter 8). The effect of Elginism implemented would be to spread the tourist load globally, arguably desirable, but to deny the great majority of tourists the opportunity of seeing even a small proportion of the world's significant artefacts.

Perhaps most serious of all, to all but the best-funded scholars it would deny the study of culture through its artefacts on a world, intercontinental and even continental, scale because nowhere would one person, tourist or scholar, be able to see and study great collections and make comparisons and syntheses. Too much time and money would simply be taken up travelling, even in the age of 'the global village', for the effective creation of informed views, whether their purpose be personal edification or international scholarship. And undoubtedly the former would suffer if the latter were inhibited.

Nor would there be international exhibitions if the logic of Elginism were carried to its full conclusion. And all this assumes, of course, that 'Elginism' is practicable: it is not, in the sense that, to put it mildly, it is by no means clear who owns what in heritage terms even if the premise of repatriation is admitted. To sort out questions of appropriate ownership would require superb records of context and 'object history', considerable scholarship and the judgement of Solomon even when the 'facts' had been established. To move the objects back, not so much to a place as to an owner, in such a major act of global self-denial would take decades, enormous negotiating skill and a great deal of goodwill. The last would in practice be virtually impossible to engender in a field so emotively bound up with status, pride and image, never mind the monetary value of the object itself and its potential as a revenue-earner in touristic terms. Yet some things are on the move as a result of the Elgin bandwagon. The repatriation of heritage objects, including human bones, to the indigenous Americans from the 'white man's museums' is perhaps the outstanding example so far, though that has been triggered by other considerations too.

'Elginism' or no, another major factor has to be considered: the international market for antiquities. Despite the respectability assumed by its leading lights, the role of too many auction houses and dealers has too often been shown to be open to question, for example with regard to context, for the trade to have unquestioned credibility in matters of ethics and propriety. Money-making accompanied by an economy with the truth sometimes seems to be a hallmark of a mechanism which does, nevertheless, indeed make, if not the world go round, then heritage objects move around the world.

From numerous examples which have been reported in the news-papers (and many more, with more and perhaps greater authenticity, have appeared in professional journals), we choose just a few illus-trations of objects being moved, minimally across national frontiers. The rape of Irish heritage, for example, was a sad but well-known phenomenon of the 1980s. It was fired by the discovery of the Derryflan treasure, an eighth-century silver chalice and other liturgical objects, by a father and son using a metal detector. At the time the law was unclear as to ownership – though clearly the treasure was part of Ireland's early Christian heritage – and a seven-year court battle to determine the question only served to encourage others into the field. Cultural objects have subsequently been moved out of Ireland in great quantity, turning up, if at all, mainly in the USA and Britain but also in Germany and Australia. The private and institutional market reach-able through dealers was being serviced. A Bronze Age gold torque, for example, worth millions of pounds on the market, was retrieved from Christie's, the London auctioneers, by the personal intervention of the Irish Prime Minister. He simply said that it was stolen property and threatened a law suit; it is now in the National Museum, Dublin. Ownership? – what ownership? Context? – what context?

That is merely one item from 'countless treasures of Viking silver,

Celtic stonework, Bronze age gold, and Armada and Tudor weaponry and coins' which have disappeared from Ireland in just a few years. As a result, changes in the law and realistic fines (£50,000 for unauthorized digging on a historic site) have been imposed, while the personal interest of the Taoiseach and co-operation between the Gardai and the FBI have combined to tackle the problem both at source and at the point of distribution.[22]

Not perhaps the headline to engender national pride wherever it applies, 'World's leading city for looted antiquities' happens to refer to London.[23] Any passing tourist has but to stroll round St James's in London to sample the cultural richness of the world and realize the substance in the headline's claim; but of course it is some auction rooms rather than antiquities shops that normally catch the headlines. The case of the Keros sculptures was an example; it was widely reported in the weeks leading up to, and especially around, 9 July 1990. In Greece, as now in Ireland and many other countries, heritage objects found in the soil of that country belong to the state. How Sotheby's therefore came to be auctioning 4,500-year-old sculptures from the Greek island of Keros is an interesting question, answered by the fact, sufficient from the auctioneer's point of view, that the objects had already moved into a private collection. However, the Greek government argued that they had arrived there as a result of looting in the late 1950s or 1960s and should be returned to their rightful owners; an argument that was lost in the High Court in Britain before the sale, but which led to a compromise whereby three objects (out of 180) were withdrawn from the auction and sold privately to the Greek government on condition that it withdrew its action to stop the sale altogether. The proceeds of the sale were themselves destined for an animal welfare foundation in Switzerland.

There can be no doubt that the trade in antiquities fuels the looting of sites, or that the network and attitudes of some dealers provide the mechanism whereby objects make the early moves in their post-discovery history. It seems little answer to say that the trade merely supplies demand; nor does it seem a major philosophical contribution to the debate for the owner of a New York gallery, Ariadne, to charge archaeologists with a lack of realism 'for not accepting the existence of a booming market'.[24] Academic value of most cultural objects apart, how could anyone, archaeologist or not, approve of a field of activity in which receiving important and intrinsically valuable cultural objects, known to have been looted from an archaeological site on private land against the wishes of the landowner, is justified with the euphemism that the objects have been acquired legally from a reputable source?

If reported correctly, however, then Ariadne's owner should indeed be listened to when 'he forecast that the market [for antiquities] in Europe would be uncontrollable after 1992'. That prediction contains much to cause trepidation among both heritage and tourist interests, for ultimately neither may be served, as far as antiquities are concerned, by the private collector and his infrastructure.

These matters are of great concern to the cultural professionals responsible for acting in the public interest – the curators of public museums and of sites out in the field in particular. As but one example of such professional concern, a European conference of such people discussed the issues at Canterbury, Kent, in September 1991, under the auspices of the Museum Documentation Association. One aspect of such official control as there is involves legal provision, variously covering work on sites and the movement of cultural property thereafter, but of course also trying to embrace 'old' material long removed from its depositional context. Many countries have such provision to a lesser or greater extent and it is variously effective. Canada can serve as example.

The Canadian Cultural Property Export and Import Act 1974–5–6 (like all official documents in Canada, in French and English) is about 'respecting the export from Canada of cultural property and the import into Canada of cultural property illegally exported from foreign states'. For practical purposes this is supported by 'Regulations respecting the Export from Canada of Cultural Property' and a 'Cultural Property Export Guide', the latter being 'A guide to procedures to be followed by persons exporting cultural property under the Cultural Property Export and Import Act and in accordance with the Cultural Property Export Regulations'. There is also a 'Canadian Cultural Property Export Control List', unlike the two documents just listed, actually dated (March 1988), and a helpful volume of 'Guidelines and Information' for 'Applications for Certification of Cultural Property for Income Tax Purposes' (July 1991). This paper edifice is administered by the Canadian Cultural Property Export Review Board, reporting annually to the Minister of Communications (whose department produced the middle three publications listed above, the first being an Act of Parliament, the last friendly advice to its constituency from the Board itself). Within the department is a Heritage Policy Branch, part of which is the Movable Cultural Property Program whose 'major activities' are also picked out in the Board's Annual Report.

The detail of such bureaucracy seldom makes gripping reading but that briefest of outlines of provision in one country, typical in some respects, idiosyncratic in others, serves to emphasize that there now is over many parts of the world an official stake in the control of the 'moving object'. Basically, countries do not want their movable heritage to cross their frontiers; equally, the good ones are not prepared to play host to others' moving objects, either in transit or in providing a domicile. In principle, gone are the days of the big battalions being able to acquire without let or hindrance whatever they wanted from wherever they chose provided they could pay for it; and in addition to statute, the museum profession itself internationally and in many countries, and many individual museums in their stated collecting policies, have bound themselves by codes of conduct, for example, on the necessity to establish cultural context as well as legal ownership before acquisition.

A UNESCO Convention on the Means of Prohibiting and Preventing the Illicit Import, Export and Transfer of Ownership of Cultural Property (1970) also claims the high ground of principle, in this case for the behaviour of its signatories as members of the international community, but not all members of the United Nations have yet signed it, for example the UK. The Convention puts the responsibility on each signatory to make its own provision to protect and preserve its own cultural heritage and to act appropriately in the matter of others' heritage property. The Canadian Act therefore 'includes procedures for the recovery and return of foreign cultural property which has been illegally exported from its own country'. The crucial word here is, of course, 'illegally', for what is illegal in one country with respect to exports may be legal, or at least not illegal, in another.

Obviously, there are, and always will be, difficulties in administering whatever provision is made in this field, though that should not discourage the attempt, as Britain has done with the UNESCO Convention on the grounds that it is unworkable. The statutory provision, or its regulations, may themselves be defective: in the UK, for example, the authorities do not prevent the great bulk of archaeological material destined for abroad from leaving the country. Any provision is also up against determined opposition, devious, playing for high monetary stakes and supplying the wherewithal to meet the basic human attributes of greed, obsessivensss and self-glory. It may seem a slight bastion of decency that in the Canadian example, as elsewhere, the Act seeks not only to regulate the import and export of cultural property but also 'provides special tax incentives to encourage Canadians to donate or sell important objects to public institutions in Canada'. Maybe that provision is itself misconceived: it is, after all, based on the same principle of personal monetary advantage as the very evil it is designed to counter. Nevertheless, the control envisaged extends to an ambitious range of material, itself in effect defining what Canada sees as its portable heritage.

'Objects recovered from the soil or waters of Canada' embrace arte-facts ('any object made or worked by man, associated with historic or prehistoric cultures'), fossils of several types, 'described mineral speci-mens' ('a mineral specimen for which scientific data, illustrations or descriptions appear in a professional publication') and minerals in the sense of 'any element or chemical compound that occurs naturally in soil or water'. The range expands to include 'Objects of Ethnographic Art or Ethnography', themselves defined, *inter alia*, as including ones with

(c). . . a fair market value in Canada of more than five thousand dollars and . . . made, reworked or adapted for use by a person who is an aboriginal person of the territory that is now
(i) Africa south of the Sahara
(ii) Australasia
(iii) Melanesia
(iv) Polynesia
(v) South and Central America, or
(vi) Micronesia, and
(d) has a fair market value in Canada of more than fifteen thousand dollars and . . . made . . . [etc., as above] by . . . an aboriginal person of a territory other than a territory listed in paragraphs (a), (b) or (c).

Bear in mind that the definition covers objects which are *not* to be exported from Canada without licence on the ground that such are Canadian cultural property. The list of controlled categories of cul-tural property continues at some length – military objects, objects of decorative art, of fine art, scientific or technological objects, books, records, documents, photographic positives and negatives and sound recordings – each and every sub-group being related to a specified 'fair market value in Canada' as a measure of definition.

The whole is a magnificent attempt at the impossible, not just to define cultural property in one country but to define it for administrative purposes by price. What about inflation? What about fluctuations in the market? What about changing perceptions of heritage itself, changes which can occur as much outside as inside a particular country? Such changes, the product of cultural evolution, fashion, taste, trends demographic and economic – basically matters outside government control – themselves affect the market: a cultural Catch 22; and all this to stop the object moving. Why? Because it is now generally accepted throughout much of the world that indigenous and 'historic' (not quite the same thing: the Elgin marbles are now 'historically' British) cultural property is best conserved and displayed in the country of origin or 'historic possession'. And why is that seen to be important, even by government? Basically because culture is seen as integral to identity, especially of statehood at official level, and because of its economic significance in terms of tourism around 'the global village'. To put it crudely, if you have not got heritage, can you exist in any meaningful, particularly political, sense? And if you have not kept your 'cultural loot', how can you capture a segment of international cultural tourism?

The 'moving object' indeed represents a problem, a cultural phenomenon pursued as always by the mass of tourists. Perhaps the tourists who actually have seen what they wanted to see where they expected to see it, and found that it 'meant' what they wanted, should count themselves lucky; for, in the clash of public and private interests, of money and culture, of ownership and location, physical and interpretive mobility in cultural property is actually quite as much the norm as stasis.

Global products 10

The idea of developing a product that is all things to all men is naturally an attractive one to anyone with even a modicum of aspiration to be a business-person. We report in Chapter 1 the comment of the head of a conglomerate on the necessity to think globally in producing a new product if only because of contemporary costs associated with such a launch.

In tourism terms, presenting a single product to a global audience is a seriously 'hot potato'. The travel industry appears to be well aware that, so often, niche-marketing is an unavoidable requirement. It appears that heritage-presenters are often less enlightened. Frequently their approach seems to be, in either ignorance or ill-founded optimism, to plonk down a heritage statement and wait for the visitors to turn up. As is apparent from studying closely the marketing of supposedly global products, the reality is that, in many instances, a product is carefully tailored into 'sub-products' honed by the cultural predilections of the miasma of sub-audiences. As an authority on the subject, Kenichi Ohmae, has said, 'in most cases creating a global product means building the capability to understand and respond to customer needs and business system requirements in each critical market'.[1]

Of course, no heritage-presenter can know with certainty who is going to visit his 'product'. In theory, the whole world could beat a path to his door; though in practice, as we shall discuss more fully in Chapter 11, generally, visitors are drawn principally from among the rich industrialized nations of the West and East, though these countries demonstrate a considerable, indeed sometimes surprising, variety of attitudes towards international travel.

Even an airport can be portrayed as a global product, representing a melding-into-one attempt in tourist and heritage terms. Marketed as

'Airtropolis – global hub that's a destination in itself', is the 'international airport with eight different cuisines' in the small country of Singapore, 'a tropical island with four different cultures'. Here we see shown the airport as a commodity to serve the world. Similar in concept is the description by its chief executive of that element within American Express which handles travel as 'a global boutique'.[2]

The 1991 World Arts Summit, meanwhile, has 'questioned the existence of such a thing as "world culture" '. By some, 'Coca-Cola culture was thought to be nearer the mark'; wheareas 'another participant . . . described McDonalds as a handy "means of cultural interaction" '.[3]

The two giants of cola are among those products perceived as global. Of interest to us is their association with heritage and tourism. Recent instances that have attracted attention are connected with the hostilities in the Gulf and the 1996 Olympics. The one having 'secured a bridgehead in Saudi Arabia in 1955', the other bragging of its 'long history of association with the US military', both rivals distributed their respective cans to US troops. The final victor appeared to have been Coca-Cola which managed to get its drink on the tables of a post-War 'heroes' lunch[4] attended, to massed media attention, by the Prince and Princess of Wales.

A backlash came later when Athens was publicly miffed at the choice of Atlanta, headquarters town of Coca-Cola, as the venue for the 100th anniversary Olympics. Feelings ran high: Coca-Cola and Pepsi-Cola slugged it out in advertisements in the Greek press, Coca-Cola's denying any influence upon the decision, and Pepsi-Cola's crowing: 'Now you know Pepsi is the right choice'[5]; actress Melina Mercouri, bidding to become mayor of Athens, reportedly called the decision 'the victory of Coca-Cola over the Parthenon'.[6]

Before the decision had been made the Black mayor of Atlanta, Andrew Young, an ex-US ambassador, went to Africa to canvass support for his city's candidature as host to the Olympics. He drew attention to the fact of Coca-Cola's headquarters' being in Atlanta, commenting aferwards: 'Coke is sold all over the world. Everybody knew the name immediately.'[7] Once back in Atlanta, he invited members of the Olympic committee there, saying: 'Half our people are of African descent. So when African delegates came and walked down our street, they saw people who looked like those back home.' All in all, the activity was a clever use of heritage presentation to attract visitors to Atlanta.

Benetton is a company which has chosen to present a universal face often using heritage imagery, though, interestingly, occasionally causing culture-clash upset in particular countries with its global advertisements. Third-world items in a shopping catalogue *mean* something on their home ground. Images from the Eskimo culture, colonized by the United Colours of Benetton for its replica ethnic clothing in turn to be worn by citizens of the world, have a cultural significance to Eskimos. They are, in a sense, cultural cuckoos in the market-place of the world, separated from context and their heritage story. Many culturally derived products have been separated from their heritage in this way and become world commodities, global brands; an example is Levis. Sometimes the cultural resonance has been accentuated as a marketing tool; in the instance of Levis, the purchaser is encouraged to believe that he is buying an American West open-roadist attitude, all swagger and individualism. A happy by-product, for the American tourist industry, is a perpetuation of the idea that the American West is a desirable place to be.

By means of food items, all the countries of the world can be presented on our table at one time and, in theory, by implication, so can their associated heritages: for example, taramasalata, Camembert, pizza, pitta, pasta, waffles, English [American] muffins, curry, chow-mein, cous-cous, tortillas, kiwi-fruit, pineapple, mango, coffee, tea, wines and whisky. What an exhibition of many cultures, or is it that they are all neutralized by being divorced from their contexts? And perhaps we enlightened peoples would not care to be told the true story behind the production of these items for our delectation; some of it might be unappetizing. The tales of ancient peasant cultures presented in advertisements are altogether more romantic and suited to our predilections. An exotic crisp from Medomsley Road, Consett, a former steel-manufacturing town in the UK, is in much the same way a sanitized simulacrum of a heritage product as a theme-park heritage presentation.

Is there, then, a heritage product suited to anyone from anywhere?

World Heritage Sites (see also Chapter 7) might be expected to be, *par excellence*, global-heritage products. In practice, in some instances, 'packaging' of World Heritage Sites to cater to a world market appears to be subservient to the needs and criteria of the individual nations in which the Sites are to be found. It is people from these nations, after all, who, almost certainly, will have proposed the sites as worthy of designation as World Heritage Sites in the first place. In many cases, such sites are places of significance to a particular group, for example religious sites or sites of relevance to a political faction. It is therefore not difficult to see what considerations, other than that of not giving offence to audiences of many kinds, will occupy first place in determining the presentational strategy for World Heritage Sites.

The Getty Museum (to which we have referred in several chapters) in California is an American oil-man's memorial. It is located, literally and metaphorically, in an elevated position. Because of the sheer financial might that it can bring to its collecting across the world, the Getty Museum has effectively taken on a role as global keeper of global-heritage artefacts. As is known, and with considerable effect, it can afford to build a collection of the best in the world. The Getty Museum can afford to be *the* superior world museum, a global-product museum. However, it is scarcely a feature of the mass-tourism itinerary, as is, for example, the Louvre Museum (see Chapter 8) in Paris.

If such a thing as a global-heritage product for tourists exists, it is that formed by Disney. In the words of a current Disney slogan, we are invited to 'Discover the World According to Disney'. In the presentation of heritage to the world, few would deny that the most 'high-profile' endeavour is Disney's. Essentially, the famous Disney 'Imagineering' approach, using such means as a 'show project producer' and 'theatre professionals', has given rise to the phenomenon of the 'heritage industry' which emerged into prominence in the 1980s. Perhaps the best-known heritage attraction to which this in the circumstances novel approach was first applied academically is Jorvik Viking Centre in the city of York, England. The Jorvik Viking Centre, which sought overtly to make heritage entertaining and thus, by association, a tourist attraction, spawned a host of imitations, not all of which have given the same close attention to basing their presentations on the best-available historical information.

To go back to the start: predictably, it all began in California where in 1955 the first big Disney theme park, Disneyland, was established. A precursor, in the specific instance of mingling on a grand scale historical re-creation and public recreation, was the colonial city of Williamsburg, which 'opened its doors' in 1934, the project made possible by Rockefeller funding. That, by 1971, Disney had realized the potential of its product for world penetration is perhaps suggested by the ambitious naming of the next Disney theme park to open, in Florida, as Walt Disney World.

Looking, in hindsight, at the features of Disneyland, Thomas Hine, in his book *Populuxe*,[8] said of 'The exotic Adventureland [which] sums up Africa, South America and South East Asia as places of lush plants, large verandas, fierce animals and headhunters . . . [that] unfortunately, it probably is an accurate reflection of the nation's view of what was to become known as the Third World'. He continued with a searing follow-up: 'During the 1960s and 1970s, the US fought a war in Adventureland.' It is also Hine's opinion that Disneyland influenced 'developments like Boston's Faneuil Hall and Baltimore's Harborplace', both major heritage tourist attractions.

Consideration of an American (commercial) view of heritages, such as that of Disney, is very instructive, both because of the proliferation of 'Americanization' across the world, and because the Disney theme parks, two in America, one in Japan and one, so far, in Europe, attract so many visitors to look at their presentations. For example, Walt Disney World may be visited by as many as 150,000 people a day;[9] in its first year of operation 11 million visitors were expected at the EuroDisney Resort outside Paris.[10]

The potential of Disney for influencing/indoctrinating is further indicated by Monica Charlot when she opines of the EuroDisney Resort, 'It is a fair bet that no child in Europe will grow up during the next century without having visited the site or dreamed of going there'.[11]

The Epcot Centre, in Disney World opened in 1982. The presentation of nations called the World Showcase is predictably engaging to people who are looking at heritage. Many visitors to the World Showcase from the countries presented must look forward to relaxing in 'familiar' surroundings, to seeing their 'home territory' – albeit in the unlikely situation of the Florida swamps.

The opportunity on offer is more than that of looking, as it were, at a geography book. Visitors are invited to travel the globe. The Disney experience is to 'sail through *El Rio Del Tiempo* in Mexico. Discover the mysteries of the East in China. Stroll through a Japanese garden. Sail in a *Maelstrom* in Norway'. Sightseers, in other words, are invited, as Disney sees it, to be there.

It is interesting to speculate on the criteria for selecting the countries displayed in the World Showcase. Are the chosen countries selected because they represent the main visitor catchment areas for this particular Disney attraction or for their qualities of picturesqueness? The countries include Canada, the UK, Norway, Italy, Japan, China, Mexico, France, Morocco (this last, almost as if to underline a perception of the separateness between the French and 'fuzzy-wuzzies' of a former French colony; a distinction that has considerably less clarity in reality, as indicated by civil unrest in 1991 in outer areas of the French capital).

In France itself, the threat of acculturation by Disney is taken seriously. Some of the Paris intelligentsia are reported to have gone so far as to describe the new EuroDisney as 'a "cultural Chernobyl" '.[12] A representative of Disney had admitted that 'Disney has its heritage in the US and *much of the theme park will be seen as through the eyes of an American* [our italics], but there will be touches of a more European element to the park'.[13] American theme imagery is used at the EuroDisney Resort for the six hotels and the 'pretending with the help of a cow-town that you are on the prairies'[14] campground. Significantly, perhaps, the section at EuroDisney about the future has been named Discoveryland rather than Futureland 'because researchers found Europeans to have an ambivalent attitude about change'.[15]

Reading between the lines of the voluminous press comment about EuroDisney, one can maybe see a glimmer of an indication that the commonplace penetration of the world with an Americanized, supposedly global, product, may have reached, has perhaps even gone beyond, its limit; and that a re-trenchment may even have begun. In the context of heritage and tourism, the increase in enthusiasm for so-called eco-tourism could perhaps be indicating something not dissimilar. A straw in the wind too may be the situation which has occurred in relation to the projected theme park, Millenium [sic].[16] Reporting in an article with the delightful title 'Mouse traps laid for Mickey's parks',[17] Ruth Sullivan described the pre-natal aggravations of Millenium, destined to be built in the Po valley in Italy. The theme park has had to be relocated, Sullivan said, 'after the environmental watchdog Europa Nostra complained to a court that the original site threatened the Po Delta Park and a Benedictine monastery'.[18]

On their home ground, at least, the Americans seem undaunted. They are even on to the next stage. In the Californian desert, the site of the 'Egyptian' City of the Pharaoh film set of Cecil B. De Mille's 1923 epic *The Ten Commandments* is being excavated.[19] The Santa Barbara Trust for Historical Preservation's executive director, Jarell Jackman, reportedly said of the dig: ' "This is utterly unique and it gives you a sense of time having passed – that movies are now part of history. . . . Don't they know that in 500 years some archaeologist may be uncovering Disneyland?" '[20]

Just imagine what approaches in heritage presentation might be adopted, and by whom, to present that old product of America, which in time attained global penetration, to the world of AD 2491.

Heritage, tourism and 'the village' 11

In preceding chapters we have tried to indicate, with many examples, some types of difficulty to which presentations of heritage to a global audience are prone. Essentially, what we are highlighting is culture clash.

By communications' becoming fast, 'the global village' came into being. By the global village's coming into existence, global glasnöst has been produced. Of glasnöst, and its fellow term perestroika, Keith Waterhouse opined in 1991,[1] 'there can hardly be a person on this planet outside the Brazilian rain forests or the snowy wastes of Greenland who has not heard the words and does not understand their meaning'.

In effect, we now live in a 'new world'. An important function in this different global environment is that of the media, as Alvin Toffler has so convincingly explained.[2] As he says, 'the new global media system has, in fact, become the prime tool of revolution in today's fast changing world'.

As more and more people travel, to more and more places, as more and more of these persons are conditioned to expect instantaneous transmission and easy assimilability of information, so ever more ripe may the circumstances for a mass of different understandings become. A one-world view might be an ideal, but, as we have tried to show, in reality it is not – yet, anyway – on the agenda. Our descriptions in Chapter 5 of our individual reactions to the same experience demonstrate that not even so few as two people will necessarily see the same thing the same way.

It is generally accepted that in the conduct of their business global travellers need to be aware that the same thing can mean different things to different peoples. It is much less clear whether those in the tourist industry who cater through heritage interpretation to the inter-cultural variety of the world's travellers have recognized that prin-ciple. The difficulties associated with making statements acceptable to a wide span of world society apply just as much to their endeavours, and probably more so in such a highly sensitive area as is heritage interpretation. Our many examples attempt to show not so much the range of sensitivities themselves as the range of situations and circum-stances in which sensitivities can be, and are, aroused. By and large, our impression is that this whole dimension is simply ignored by the commercial tourist industry, not so much with intent to offend as out of a lack of understanding. Offence may, nevertheless, be caused; and, even more importantly, opportunities are missed every day in every bus and at every site and museum to increase the world's understand-ing of itself by relating across cultures through cultural-heritage interpretation.

The difference between the old and the new touristic situation, apart from the sheer numbers of travellers, is that it is now the fashion to formulate a heritage message, perforce of selected information, for their entertainment and, perhaps also, education. In this circumstance, the utmost sophistication on the part of presenters and their, probably mixed, audience is necessary if mis-information, and possibly offence, is not to be given. In the good old days, a historic site was a preserved old monument; and a museum was a collection, a selected collection of course, but nonetheless one which allowed individual interpretation of it. In both instances, the visitor was usually aided by the provision of a certain basic number of 'facts'. It can, of course, be argued that in no media of communication, not even the old-style ones, such as books or newspapers, can information be objective; it could be said that there has *always* been a process of selection. One reason for writing this book, however, is that we believe the new circumstance of *a* heritage presentation to a world audience comprised of peoples not just from many countries but also of many different cultural com-ponents, is an intrinsically perilous situation. We hope that we have provided some indication of why those who embark upon the presen-tation of heritage to the global traveller should regard themselves as addressing an extremely difficult and hazardous task.

Of the variety and complexity of humans, Herbert Muschamp wrote: 'The fact is that we *are* echoes of earlier voices – walking data bases of aphorisms, snapshots, songs, and recipes, composites not only of voices heard in childhood but also of the reverberations of ideas through cultural history.'[3] Heritage has been described by Dr Germaine Greer as 'the cultural expression of what makes us what we are, our spiritual DNA'.[4]

The 'presentation', for example, of a Third-World-scape to an audience through a Hilton or tour-bus window can be of a community scene that is picturesque and engagingly and reassuringly simple and naive. However, tourist 'engagement' on the streets of New York, a mass of interlaced cultural zones, can be a somewhat different, more complicated and more confrontational experience. In that Babylonian metropolis, heritage 'presentations' overlie one another and intertwine. Behind the Chinatown for the tourists is Chinatown for the Chinese immigrant residents. Entering Hispanic and Negro territory, to visit the literate presentation at the Museum of the American Indian is almost to find a White refuge rather than seek objective information about North America's first citizens. In New York, gung-ho *Bonfire of the Vanities* style is out of style for those wise to the tales from the streets. That city perhaps has more heritage stories than any other place on earth; and a lot of them conflict.

Two new US heritage presentations, both concerning recent ex-Presidents, have interested us particularly. The one, 'already . . . a top tourist attraction',[5] is the Sixth Floor Museum in Dallas, apparently a tourist-led provision, whose subject is the assassination – ' "the shot that was heard round the world" . . . [is the] notice above the main exhibit' – of President John Kennedy. This Museum, with its 'window . . . symbolically half-open' is clearly no white-wash job. In the words of the *Weekend Guardian*, 'The Museum acts as grief therapy for America'. The other, high in the California hills, is the Reagan Library. Outside the Library is a dramatic spectacle: a huge monolithic portion of the Berlin Wall commanding the view which extends over wave upon wave of hills to far horizons. The whole is symbolism on a monumental scale. What is interesting to us about these sights, and the reason for their inclusion here, is their relevance, we believe, for the world in general. After all, it has been said that the US sees itself as caretaker of the world. Kennedy and Reagan *are* part of the world-heritage pantheon.

One of these presentations serves to remind us that any heritage anywhere in the world, not least that of heroes, will continually be reassessed; and that in the *modern* world a person will likely have a global as well as local/national heritage. He or she will be a world citizen – Kennedy in Berlin in 1963, 'All free men, wherever they may live, are citizens of Berlin. . . . Ich bin ein Berliner'. The other, aside from demonstrating humankind's general yearning to leave lasting footprints upon the world, shows that someone wants this man to be seen as an exalted being with far-reaching vision going beyond temporal boundaries, a Master of the Universe.

Catering to mass audiences naturally means that a heritage presentation must be comprehensible to a wide diversity of people. This can lead, of itself, even without the conditioning occasioned by the form of the medium of transmission, to a tendency towards simplification of information and therefore the loss of the subtlety of nuance. Emphasis upon the visual in contrast to written words will be a likely characteristic. Richard Hoggart, British doyen of commentators upon the place and relevance of literacy in human conditions, and former United Nations official, wrote recently, 'The literacy given to most people is insufficient for the needs of increasingly complex societies and, more important, inadequate in ways essential to democracy. Most leave school critically, culturally and imaginatively sub-literate.'[6] The past has tended in the past to élitism; now it tends to be populist. This should be good; but it may be a different past as a result and regarding heritage presentations the heritage tourist should be alert to the misleadingly simplistic masquerading as informed simplicity.

Divisions and differences between groups, whatever the reason for their coming into being, are liable to lead to difficulty. As the author of *Wanting Everything* (1991), Dorothy Rowe, said, 'Whenever we organise a system for living which cuts us off from contact with a wide range of people . . . we do damage to ourselves, because when we lose touch with the complexity of human life, we are less and less able to construct meanings which closely approximate reality'.[7] In other words, in our context: the rudiment to most successful heritage interpretation does not lie only in historicity; it lies as much in sensitivity to the present.

Yet despite warnings such as these, often we want to be exclusive. Often it suits us to see places stereotypically and culturally clichéd. Many outsiders want to see America as the Land of the Levi and Australia as the country of Fosters and 'Four X'. Writing in 1983, advertising expert David Ogilvy provided in his book *Ogilvy on Advertising* an example of foreign visitors wanting to see what they want to see: 'Research told me that what American tourists wanted to see in Britain was history and tradition. . . . So that is what I featured in the advertisements, only to be slaughtered in the British press for projecting an image of a country living in its past.'[8] Now, it appears, there are new 'storylines' in the making. It is reported that, 'The traditional Beefeater and thatched cottage image of Britain is to be elbowed aside under a £6 million British Tourist Authority campaign which will cater for the whims of different nationalities'. Among the projected initiatives described are: 'In literature aimed at German tourists . . . pubs become inns, while for the Japanese, who the authority discovered were admirers of Beatrix Potter, the Lake District becomes Peter Rabbit's Country.'[9] We would but remark that if you regard acculturated differences as mere 'whims' then of course you will come up with such triteness. While they indicate a superficial cognizance of the attitudes of outsiders, these examples actually represent the antithesis of our argument, for they demonstrate a deep lack of understanding of what heritage and tourism should, and could, be about.

The presentation of England's next-door country, Scotland, has been subject to outside influence. The major exhibition in Glasgow during its designation as European City of Culture was called 'Scotland Creates: 500 Years of Art and Design'. A culturally collaborative venture put together by relevant organizations in rival cities Edinburgh and Glasgow, it sought to reintroduce home-nation views. In the book of the same name[10] accompanying the exhibition, Tom Normand opined, 'the popularly projected images of Scottish "customs", such as the paraphernalia of tartanry, are a cruel parody of actual Scottish life. In consequence an authentic expression has been absent from the cultural life of the nation.' He commented ruefully, 'In the absence of a clearly defined national identity . . . artists and intellectuals have generally accepted, at second hand, the insights of more confident national cultures'.

Fear of cultural ravishment by invading tourists was reported in 1983. Ogilvy told of 'a prayer . . . read from the pulpit of every church in Greece, asking the Almighty to spare the Greeks from the "scourge" of foreign tourism'.[11] It is a resilient community that can withstand the effects of strong invasion from outside. Authors of *The Good Tourist*, Wood and House, say unequivocally, 'Inevitably, constant contact with alien customs and cultures results in a weakening of native traditions and values'.[12] And that the Third World is particularly susceptible to becoming victim to tourism is readily apparent. Wood and House enquire uncompromisingly in their Preface, 'How much cultural (and, indeed, physical) prostitution can these societies be expected to take before seeing the tourist industry as a latter day colonial power, over which they have no control and which adversely affects their lives in far-reaching ways?'

The visitors from outside are easy candidates for blame. But it can be conceived that a proportion of tourists at least have the capacity to make individual assessments of sites, to see through and beyond false, simplistic, incomplete or unbalanced images. As Donald Horne said optimistically in his book *The Great Museum*, 'it is intellectually possible to train ourselves to swim against the tide. To be able to contemplate a monument not just according to the present stereotype, but to give it one's own meanings – and to know something about the other meanings it has had – is one of the ways of sharpening intellectual acuteness.'[13] Yes, but how many agencies providing for tourism, whether it be physically or interpretively, allow for that, never mind encourage it?

It would perhaps be unfair to expect the tourist industry as such to provide for 'sharpening intellectual acuteness'. Horne nevertheless raises a profound issue, one even more relevant in a world which has moved further into post-modernist mode and even bulkier tourism since he wrote. One of the many paradoxes of a world with an embryonic 'global culture' is that while communications have improved, enabling even more people to talk to and visit one another as global villagers, so their appetites and perceptions have fragmented. On the one hand, many starve while others pick their convenient way across global platters; on the other, the concept of 'world heritage' is promoted by UNESCO while everywhere locals, often for the first time, look to their own particular patrimony, not least in economic hope.[14]

Such fragmentation, whether cultural or political, may well be one of the worldwide characteristics of the post-modernist state, but even more typical seems to be the re-assembly, on a platter, in a new building, and especially in tourism, of new, eclectic packages made up of previously unassociated components. Clearly such a process is at work in the marketing of heritage tourism: 'theming' at one place is an example; specially contrived trails and tours making links where none existed before, be they personal or conglomerate, 'historical' or 'literary', is another. In trying to relate heritage and tourism within the concept of a 'global village', we are clearly surveying a highly complex scene, involved essentially both with variables and with different levels of activity and perception. Activities, for example, range from the ultimate passivity of armchair video to the hopefully controlled hardship of small-group, post-colonial adventure backpacking on the roofs of the world; perceptions range from the deeply personal about the local to attempted objectivity about the global.

Like 'the global village', of course such a 'global culture' does not exist in the sense of being confined to one area or one group of people with a particular historical or ethnic background; indeed among its characteristics might well be an absence of some conventional criteria of culture. Nevertheless, as with an archaeologically defined culture, e.g. the 'Beaker culture' which gave rise to the idea of a 'Beaker folk', 'global culture' may well be related to characteristic artefacts (see

Chapter 10) in which future archaeologists might come to recognize 'global folk'; but its hallmarks are rather denationalized life styles reflecting an attitude of mind and access to fast communications. Rapid movement of messages, images and bodies is part of it, and maybe mass tourism itself is a facet of the phenomenon. Whether so or not, the thought follows that perhaps we have yet another anthropologically definable cultural manifestation on our hands, not so much tourism itself as 'tourist culture'.

Tourism after all has its own idiosyncratic way of behaving, and it produces characteristic results. People also tend to behave in a touristic sort of way, differently from their domestic lives; as tourists, they inhabit and use characteristic artefacts. We ourselves when at home can spot a tourist a mile off; and then become one the next day as we zoom off not just to a different geography and a new daily life deriving from the *locale* but to a different patterning of our own behaviour which, *as that of a tourist*, is pretty much the same wherever we alight. Present here therefore are the elements of a definable culture, unfixed in place or race or history but very definitely of the later twentieth century. Perhaps here lies a clue to an understanding of this global phenomenon of our time, not as the tourist industry but as the 'tourism culture'. And it might be helpful to recall that in normal scientific parlance, an 'industry' is but a sub-set of a 'culture'.

Each of our three main components – heritage, tourism and 'the global village' – comprises a whole range of sub-sets and each is itself a variable. Variation is expressed not just physically but perceptually too; so immediately, even if each component were 'fixed' geographically, bilateral relationships between any two of them will be dynamic because each one is changing through time and in how it is perceived. Make the relationship between all *three* components, and obviously complexity becomes greater. In crude terms, even if one or all of the components stood still for a moment, their relationships would still be dynamic because perceptions of the static scene would be different, and shifting, at that moment. But of course each of the three is actually jumping up and down, changing shape and character, and being mobile in 'meaning', merely with the passage of time, never mind simultaneously changing in the perceptions of increasing millions of ever more poly-ethnic, multi-cultural people. Add the dimension of movement in space – tourists by definition travel, objects, even monuments, move, and movement itself engenders differences in status and perception – and all the ingredients are there for a powerful phenomenon. It is one difficult to pin down for dissection and therefore, as our humanistic, non-analytical discussion implicitly illustrates, to comprehend.

One of the most significant variables is not actually any of the three main components of our inter-relational triangle, but perceptions of them. These perceptions vary: they have done in the past and they continue to do so. One man's under-capitalized, run-down country estate is another's heritage time-capsule; a politician's post-industrial dereliction is the conservationist's wonderful industrial heritage. Such perceptions change from person to person and, for each individual, through his or her life. Hence, for example, the theoretical base for the marketing ploy of 'repeat visits': visit the Pyramids this year, and they'll look different next. Still the same heritage, note, but you will have changed and/or the circumstances of your return will be different. Perceptions also change depending on whether the visitor is alone, in a small group, or with a large party; whether he or she is visiting privately or in some official guise. What we say and do, what we think we think, is conditioned by our immediate social context: the self-effacing person can become aggressive in the security of a group, a committee can take the most remarkable decisons that not one of its members would agree to alone. An analogous process occurs in heritage tourism.

We (the authors) do not like visiting sites together. What we 'see' and take away is very much dependent on that condition of by-one-self-ness. Others need company; the past, after all, *is* a foreign country[15] and tourists to it may need comfort and help. Some cannot apparently move without a guide to tell them what to 'see' and what it 'means', and their impressions, the 'messages' they take away, are likewise conditioned. As we have noted, some tourism marketing is predicated not just on group travel but on social tourism with others of like sort. Other tours are marketed around the idea of the academic expert, he (and there seem few she's of this ilk) who 'knows' all about it and will tell you authoritatively what it all 'means'. Meanwhile, the heritage visited, so differently perceived, stays exactly the same. Or does it?

The globe, *sensu* the earth as a planet, physically exists (for the purposes of the present argument at any rate); 'the global village' has an existence as a high-tech communications network, a motivating force, and a 'dream'. 'Tourism' exists too: its hardware, its hyperbole, and the personal experiences of many of us bear that out; yet even the abstract noun itself has many different connotations – 'good', 'bad' and 'ambivalent'. 'Heritage' also exists: we visit it, we read about and teleview it, we react to it as interesting or boring, we are even probably proud of 'our' bits of it at personal, local, national and possibly global levels. But we have to ask not so much 'What is its meaning?' as 'Can it have a meaning?' At one level, clearly the answer is 'Yes': 'that building marks the site where my religion was founded' or 'that hill saw the decisive battle in which my country repulsed the invaders'. A building, however, is but an assemblage of materials, a hill but a hill. Any 'meaning' beyond that is acculturated, that is it is conceptualized by the human mind, applied to the object, and passed on to other humans. The hill does not see itself as a battlefield; nor is it perceived as one by the sheep grazing on it.

Indeed, nor would the hill be perceived as the site of a battlefield, and therefore as having a cultural value as well as a meaning, by anyone who had not learnt to perceive it in those terms. An Easter Islander arriving at Bosworth Field would see but typical English Midland countryside without the presentational hardware of information boards and fluttering flags, just as the significance of the Easter Island statues has been so signally difficult for the Western mind to grasp. Indeed, pursuing the line of different *levels* of perception, even English visitors to Bosworth need the interpretation to convert perception of those ordinary-looking fields into significant, value-laden 'heritage fields'. Here, this is not just because their knowledge of the English Wars of the Roses may be hazy but also because they are of a country long unfamiliar with the very idea of civil war, let alone one fought over regal succession. Yet the 'meaning' conveyed in the site interpretation is entirely in English, and militaristic and tactical: not unreasonable, one might think, of an English battlefield interpretation, but what about the non-English reader and those who want to know about the farming of those fields at the time?

This variability of perception lies behind one of the practical problems faced by archaeologists arriving on a farm to tell the landowner that he is ploughing over a prehistoric settlement or arguing in committee that a particular development is ill-advised because it will destroy a well-known Roman site. 'Well-known' to whom? – the archaeologist 'knows' the site is there and has given it a 'meaning' by judging it to be 'significant' in cultural terms; but neither the farmer nor the developer 'know' anything of the sort. Both know their land well and are therefore disinclined to believe this new information, partly because of the financial implications but basically because it requires a different mind-set to assimilate. Each is therefore in no position to perceive a physical reality which has actually been present for 2,000 years, let alone give any 'meaning' to this extra item on their land in terms of its 'worth'. The sites have existed in one sense for a long time yet in other senses they now come to be both perceived and not perceived, 'existing' for archaeologists but not the landowners. In one of those senses, the Pyramids, visited by millions of tourists every year and a very real conservation problem for the Egyptian authorities, do not exist for someone who has not heard of them. Communicating with great difficulty with an old Navajo lady, we could not explain where we came from because not only had she not heard of London but she was unfamiliar with the concept of 'sea'. For her, one of the world's great cities and much of its surface did not 'exist'.

Similarly, because it has no intrinsic 'meaning', heritage has no existence either. Of course it is there as bits of stone and mud, metal and wood; but it only becomes 'heritage' when we, and we alone, give it a value-laden significance in anthropogenic terms. In other words, tourists go to see, not just artefacts, but psychological artefacts, their meanings created, differentially and a million and more times over, in the minds of each and every one of us. One of the problems for us all as individuals is that, along the tourism trail, many of the popular 'pyscho-facts' have already accreted layers and facets of meaning before we arrive. 'Meanings' come with the artefact, through signage, guide and leaflet, maybe even background reading beforehand; they may indeed be part of the attraction which has brought us there in the first place. Whether the prepared messages come as supposedly neutral 'information' or well-meaning but inevitably biased 'interpretation', they pre-condition and condition our responses; and yet, at even the most visited of sites and museums, one cardinal factor is that for each of us, there is a first time, a personal journey of discovery and exploration. And by that we mean intellectually as well as emotionally and physically. We have not been to the Pyramids yet. Despite our pre-perceptions, our clutter of already acquired 'meanings', we believe that there must be an idiosyncratic 'meaning' there for us and therefore that to visit the Pyramids would be worthwhile.

Tourism is a mechanism posited on this phenomenon of the human condition. It exploits the creative urge to give meaning, it demands meaning as its lubricant, it invents meaning by default and sometimes in cynicism. Yet tourism is also the medium enabling global villagers to visit their patch at the other ends of the earth, not just to go to see but to give the buildings and the hills a significance, as many 'meanings' as the villagers needs. Tourism is the mechanism; but interpretation is the means, for everything has to be sifted through our minds. Professional interpreters have a key role, not just on individual sites but in presenting a region or a culture; but essentially each tourist, if he or she has a gram of cerebration for every kilogram of flesh, not only takes away a personal interpretation but also contributes to the 'meaning' of the heritage perceived.

As tourism develops further, we can but hope that it will come to recognize its proper place as gentle giant, and accept the responsibilities of its role in a highly complex and very sensitive process of human interaction in a matrix of psychology, ecology, culture and time. This is an enormous intellectual and ethical challenge to an industry preoccupied with logistics, marketing and profit-margins. Maybe it will not be able to cope, but if it would *try*. . . . With the world its oyster, the tourism industry has enormous power to affect circumstances within our global village, and that industry is, after all, comprised of villagers too. They have to live in the village, locally with their heritage as well as globally with nowhere else to go.

So, in which direction is heritage tourism now travelling? Many regard new departures in green, or eco-, tourism as positive developments towards a less disruptive future. In Chapter 2 we refer to the 'alternative' package tours, which we think, simply because they are still packages, in basic concept differ not so very much from old-style tours; though this does not mean that they do not, at the very least try to, avoid cultural damage to the visited environment and to limit the environmental demands made by their presence. But little that we have seen or read persuades us that the thinking behind such 'good' practice is other than intellectually 'soft' for it rarely extends much into the cultural province of the mind. Eco-tourism on the ground is much to be welcomed, but that is only half the journey. The rest of the tour, much the more difficult, is an intellectual matter, involving issues of ethics and aesthetics, understanding and interpretation, way beyond the thinking in most of mass tourism. If a slogan is needed, try: 'Be friendly to Nature, *and* be kind to the mind'.

The managing of heritage tourism to green ends can mean that it is by its nature exclusive of the mass of people. The six-village Laona Project in Cyprus is a case in point. Described as 'a research hatchery',[16] the attempt is, with financial support from such organizations as Friends of the Earth and the European Community, to regenerate the area by various means which include accommodating holidaymakers during their stay, in restored buildings, within the traditional life ways of the village communities.

The escalation of types of development already tried is another way forward. The creation of an image as a cultural resort has been seen by many cities as a way to a secure future. Notable among them are those, such as Glasgow, seeking a post-industrial role. Now, Venice is trying to become 'the international cultural supermarket of the world'.[17] Already, as reporter Martin Kettle said, 'all Venice trades on its reinterpretation of history'; but the effort is now that much more deliberate, with the presentation there of such events as the ambitious

Celtic Europe exhibition, 'I Celti' (see also Chapter 8). Kettle commented of the exhibition, 'It is ironic that the descendants of the Romans . . . should be so enthusiastic about the cultures which their distant ancestors destroyed. But this is typical of the post-modernist mood in Italy, in which world culture has become an ever expanding pick-and-mix buffet to which all are welcome.'

Meanwhile, Paris, which has a reputation of pre-eminent cultural sophistication ready established, is providing an innovative lead in its high-tech museological and educational activity allied with socio-economic engineering of a particularly sensitive and responsible type. In a run-down working district, provision has been made of a new ultra-modern-style cultural park, the parc de la Villette. It houses the Cité des Sciences et de l'Industrie, highlights of which are the unique Géode, a cinema in a sphere, and a multi-media library available to all visitors. Its centre-piece is the permanent exhibition 'Explora'. Of fundamental interest in the search for suitable models for the successful transmission of information to a general audience is that the Cités slogan is 'le plaisir de comprendre'. It is clear that, through the media and content of its presentations, not least their sheer verve and style, the Cité amply fulfills the expectation the slogan engenders. Private sponsorship features at la Villette. As a source of optimism, indeed excitement, in relation to the matters with which this book is concerned, the Cité is a prototype probably, we believe, without equal. In essence, it is a high-tech, high-style, highly-approachable, highly informative, highly entertaining, presentation.

It is perhaps not a coincidence that a number of the latest and most innovative museological projects have been located as 'off-shore experiences'. Could it be that they are unconsciously perceived as being less subject to cultural influences, for, in a sense, such presentations are off cultural limits? In the waters of Ustica, an island close to Sicily, for example, an archaeological park has been established by 'the Antiquities Department, the Palermo tourist board, and *Archeologia Viva*, a journal which promotes tours and courses in underwater archaeology'.[18] Locals are pleased to have the new attraction; 'The risk of theft is therefore reduced by the vigilance of hoteliers, shop-owners, and all those who have an interest in protecting their cultural heritage'. Elsewhere in the Mediterranean, off Monaco, replica reefs, real amphorae and a bogus 'Roman Merchant galley' have been scattered about, ready for inspection by visitors travelling by underwater bus. Along the coast near Marseilles is a genuine, and major, heritage find in the water. This is the cave with its not-in-the-water prehistoric wallpaintings (see Chapter 7). It was reported that 'bars have been placed at the underwater entrance to the "museum" . . . to keep out amateur divers'.[19] The cave has been designated a historic monument by Jack Lang, the dynamic Minister of Culture in France, so it will be particularly interesting to see how, if at all, this important discovery is handled in touristic terms.

Perhaps the most innovative water-based experience will be the Groninger Museum, currently being constructed in a canal in Holland. The Museum is a combined Dutch, Italian, American (Frank Stella) and French (Philippe Starck) creation in the form of a ship. The Museum, scheduled to open in October 1992, will break new museo-logical ground. Its lead architect, Alessandro Mendini, has said: 'A museum should be an invention, an ideal place abounding in surprises, not a necrophiliac depository of cultural power.'[20] Artist Frank Stella has said: 'the building works in a parallel way with my wavy, *Moby Dick* series. You move through this New Wave Museum as though making a voyage.'[21] And Philippe Starck has said: 'This museum is like a ghost train – at every stage you find a surprise. Intuition prepares you for enlightenment, not audio-visual lectures. There's less to read, more to feel.'[22]

Technological innovation and attitudinal change are likely to be key-stones of advances in heritage presentations. In both these categories, the Japanese seem well equipped to lead. Of particular interest to this book's theme is that Japan is a literate nation. An important character-istic of Japan, aside from its facility with technology, is 'the way it finds, in a way we [the British] do not, the confidence to absorb cultural revolutions. ... Nothing in Japan stands still for a moment.'[23]

We have discussed the existing propensity towards the hyper-real experience. Technology is now poised to allow us a replicated experi-ence so almost real as to be dubbed Virtual Reality (VR). The potential of this type of simulation for the presention of heritage is obvious. In his book on the subject of VR,[24] Howard Rheingold drew attention to related matters. He says: 'Given the rate of development of VR technologies, we don't have much time to tackle questions of morality, privacy, *personal identity and the prospect of fundamental change in human nature*' (our italics). The relationship to the matters we address in these pages of the consequences to which Rheingold alludes are clear to see. Meanwhile CD-I, Compact Disc Interactive, a system whereby the experience of interactivity, with an amalgam of sound and video text, graphics and animation, may take place with TV screens, has already been launched. In a newspaper report, it was described how 'consumers can interact with television to tour museums'.[25]

Such departures seem worlds apart from the other new, gentle, approaches to the touristic heritage experience as exemplified by the best endeavours at eco-tourism. That in our global village heritage tourism is both so prevalent and in so dynamic a situation must surely make it worthy of continuing consideration. It is therefore reassuring to find that in Britain among the GCSE subjects available to students is 'Travel and Tourism', and the more so to know that among the study options is 'culture and tourism'. All the commodification and packaging has the capacity to encourage laziness, to blunt an impulse to enquire, on an individual or mass basis. If, in line with one of our motivations in attempting this discussion, 'culture and tourism' as a global phenomenon with implications for us all comes not merely to be taught but to be considered within an intellectual, academic framework, then so much the better. Tourism is so much more than being looked after in body; it is also about the mind and spirit.

Already, in 1975, Turner and Ash were stating: 'Tourism is the industrialisation of a delusory mythology and the effects of this on tourist generating centres and host countries alike are equally ambivalent.'[26] Of course, we now know that to be true, only more so because some of the 1970s' 'ambivalences' have proved disastrous; but we also now know how to mitigate some of those bad 'effects', and how to generate some 'good' aspects of tourism.

It is the premise of this book that the development of a heritage presentation which will offend no tourist, anywhere, is an impossibility. In their book *Megatrends 2000*, John Naisbitt and Patricia Aburdene have predicted that, 'In the face of growing homogenization, we shall all seek to preserve our national identities, be they religious, cultural, national, linguistic, or racial'.[27] They take up the theme later, saying:

> The more humanity sees itself as inhabiting a single planet, the greater the need for each culture on that globe to own a unique heritage. It is desirable to taste each other's cuisine, fun to dress in blue denim, to enjoy some of the same entertainment. But if that outer process begins to erode the sphere of deeper cultural values, people will return to stressing their differences, and suffer a sort of cultural backlash.[28]

We agree with the principle of that prognostication, though we suspect – and events recently provide pointers to the trend – that the 'heritage units' in which people will be seeking their 'identities' will be either smaller, or larger, than 'national'.[29]

The warning has been sounded by Naisbitt and Aburdene. But their projection is a particular projection to a particular point in future time. Perhaps the underlying theme, running through much of the comment and many of the examples that we quote, is that of the extreme variability and changeability of the external circumstances in the world, and of the complexity of our responses, as individuals and as members of cultural groups, to the situations across the globe that we encounter.

In the Prologue to his book Donald Horne described the dilemma that is being addressed, and related it to the interaction between the tourist and heritage. He said this: 'Since "reality" does not exist in itself, we create it – with the result that each society and each age has different versions of what "reality" might be. This makes the tourist experience a voyage through many different "dreamlands" '.[30] Turner and Ash described the problems thus: 'If the suppression of the present life of a country, in favour of its monuments reduces the reality of the past, then equally the suppression of the past reduces the reality of the present'.[31]

Essentially, the requirement of the tourist industry in the heritage business is that it should play a game, in which it shows courteous appreciation of frontiers, and due recognition of their multiplicity and diversity, across a terrain ostensibly without boundaries. That it will not be an easy tight-rope act is indicated in this book. Our concern is that those concerned should be aware of the need for the act.

For the presenter of heritage to tourists across the world, the task is to tell it like it is, and was, for everybody. For all the world's a heritage stage; and everyone's a player.

Notes

1 Introduction: Setting the global scene

1 Mumford, L., *The City in History*, Harmondsworth, Penguin, 1961, Harmondsworth, Pelican, 1984 ed., p. 653.
2 *W* magazine, 14–21 May 1990, p. 23.
3 *Observer*, 4 August 1991, p. 26.
4 Wood, K. and House, S., *The Good Tourist*, London, Mandarin, 1991, Preface.
5 Turner, L. and Ash, J., *The Golden Hordes: International Tourism and the Pleasure Periphery*, London, Constable, 1975, p. 197.
6 ibid., p. 204
7 Hall, E. T., *The Hidden Dimension*, Doubleday 1966, New York, Anchor, 1990 (1982 ed.), p. 129.
8 ibid., p. 181.
9 ibid., p. 189.
10 Morris, D., *The Pocket Guide to Manwatching*, London, Triad Grafton, 1982 ed., p. 193.
11 ibid.
12 Thompson, J. B., *Ideology and Modern Culture*, Cambridge and Oxford, Policy Press in association with Basil Blackwell, 1990, pp. 16–17.
13 Hudson, K. and Nicholls, A., *The Cambridge Guide to the Museums of Europe*, Cambridge, Cambridge University Press, 1991.
14 Alex Hamilton reviewing the book *Thomas Cook: 150 Years of Popular Tourism* by P. Brendon, 1991, in *Weekend Guardian*, 2–3 March 1991.
15 Thompson, op. cit., p. 277.
16 Hall, S., in *Redemption Song*, BBC2, 11 August 1991.
17 Pearce, D., *Tourist Development*, Harlow, Longman, 2nd ed., 1989, p. 53.
18 ibid., p. 217, from Smith, V. (ed.), *Hosts and Guests: the Anthropology of Tourism*, Philadelphia, Pennsylvania Press, 1977.
19 Chesshyre, R., 'Caught in the sun trap', *Telegraph Magazine*, 13 April 1991, p. 40.
20 Turner and Ash, op. cit., p. 208.
21 Frater, A., 'Rebel yell for the Olde Civil War', *Observer*, 21 April 1991, p. 63.
22 Greenberg, K. E., 'Pilgrims resist progress', *The European*, 11–13 January 1991, p. 12.
23 Advertisement in *The Mail on Sunday*, 14 April 1991, p. 55.
24 O'Neill, S., 'Shoot to thrill', *Weekend Guardian*, 15–16 December 1990, p. 24.
25 Ashdown, P., 'Europe: the only thing we have to fear is fear itself', *Daily Mail*, 19 June 1991, p. 6.
26 Advertisement in *Weekend Guardian*, 16–17 March 1991, p. 13.
27 Advertisement in *The Mail on Sunday*, 7 April 1991, p. 41.
28 Paris, J., 'Grim summer faces Greek tourism', *The European*, 24–6 May 1991, p. 22.
29 *The European*, 5–7 April 1991, p. 2.
30 Mayle, P., *A Year in Provence*, London, Hamish Hamilton, 1989, and *Toujours Provence*, London, Hamish Hamilton, 1991.
31 *The European*, 19–21 April 1991, p. 14.

32 Report in Helgadottir, B., 'Vikings take on Columbus', *The European*, 19–21 April 1991, p. 4.

33 Report by Vora, K., 'Slow boat to America!', *The European*, 24–6 May 1991, p. 3.

34 Advertisement in *The Mail on Sunday*, 3 March 1991, p. 48.

35 Gordon, G., 'Any colour so long as it's black' *Daily Mail*, 14 June 1991, p. 6.

36 *The Journal* (Newcastle upon Tyne), 4 October 1990, p. 9.

37 Burchill, J., 'Crusading for culture in the Club Ed playpen', *The Mail on Sunday*, 19 August 1990, p. 17.

2 Home thoughts

1 Johnston, B., 'Chianti turns sour for British expats', *The Sunday Times*, 23 September 1990, p.25.

2 Severignini, B., author of *Inglesi* (Rizzoli, 1990), interviewed by S. Kelly in the *élan* section of *The European*, 23–5 August, 1991.

3 *The Journal* (Newcastle upon Tyne), 14 February 1991, p. 3.

4 Montgomery-Massingberd, H., 'Old times of the New World', *Weekend Telegraph*, 31 August 1991, p. xiii.

3 Indigenous and colonial

1 Blake, M., *Dances with Wolves*, New York, Ballantine Books, 1988; UK ed., Harmondsworth, Penguin, 1991. 'Repatriation' as a statutory requirement is reviewed in the light of experience at the Smithsonian by Baugh, T. G. et al., 'Native communities and repatriation; the Smithsonian Institution perspective', *Federal Archaeology Report*, 5, 1, Washington D.C., National Park Service, March 1992, pp. 23–4.

2 For Britain, see Fowler, P. J., *The Past in Contemporary Society: Then, Now*, London, Routledge, 1992, p. 161.

3 This and the other quotations, facts and figures in this passage are taken from *National Parks*, vol. 65, May–June 1991, a Special Issue to commemorate the 75th Anniversary of the National Park Service, Washington D.C., National Parks and Conservation Association.

4 *Australian National Parks*, Canberra, Australian National Parks & Wildlife Service, 1990.

5 *Time* magazine, Special Issue, 'California, the endangered dream', 18 November 1991. The 'flickering dream' burst into flames in the Los Angeles riots of 29–30 April/1 May 1992.

6 Walker, M., 'How the West was won, or was it?' *The Guardian*, 13 June 1991, p. 23. Among the mass of relevant literature, particularly helpful in its point of view, is a 1991 Special Edition of *Historama*, no. 21: *Les Indiens d'Amérique, Le Massacre des Peaux-Rouges*, Paris, Loft International. Bailey, E., 'Sitting Bull's lost army', *Telegraph Magazine*, 24 November 1991, gives another useful contemporary, journalistic assessment. See also Lopez, B., 'This land is our land', *Weekend Guardian*, 4–5 January, 1992, pp. 4–7.

7 *National Historic Park, Skagway, Alaska*, Washington D.C., National Park Service, 1990.

8 ibid., p. 14.

9 Faldbakken, K., 'Hello Bristol, and Goodbye Columbus', *The Guardian*, 10 May 1991. The authoritative study is Fernández-Armesto, F., *Before Columbus: Exploration and Colonisation from the Mediterranean to the Atlantic, 1229–1492*, London, Macmillan Education, 1987.

10 These quotations, and other material here, are taken from an article by Clerici, N. and Faldini, L., 'To celebrate Columbus . . .', *European Review of Native American Studies*, 4, 2, Wien, Austria. C. F. Feest, 1990, pp. 37–9, a journal which, like *Historama*, edited above in note 6, provides a perspective interestingly different from a more familiar Anglo-American one. See also Plenel, E., 'Voyage avec Colomb', *Le Monde*, Paris, *numero spécial*, Septembre 1991.

Notes

11 *The European, Weekend*, 29–31 March 1991, p. 9.

12 Not least because it reviews many recent additions to a range of books about Columbus, the Special 500th Anniversary Issue of *History Today*, 42, May 1992, is particularly useful: 'New Worlds for Old. Columbus and his consequences, 1492–1992'. It is thoroughly recommended, especially for putting the 'Indian question' in a long global and cultural context.

13 Wood, J., 'Farewell! a long farewell, to all my greatness!' *The Guardian*, 13 December 1990, p. 23.

14 Grier, P., 'Still searching for the Fertile Verges', *The Guardian, New Worlds* supplement, 13 December 1991, p. 21.

15 As identified in Fowler, op. cit., p. 58.

16 Morris, B., 'Wild West pins its hopes on Europe's tourist gold', *The Independent on Sunday*, 26 May 1991, p. 8.

17 *International Herald Tribune*, 29 October 1990, p. 3.

18 See Bailey, op. cit.; and Perry G., 'The first face of America', *The Sunday Times Magazine*, 3 February 1991, pp. 19–24.

19 Horwell, V., 'Truckin' down to Taos', *Weekend Guardian*, 16–17 March 1991, p. 31.

20 Southworth, J., 'Stone Age wife', *Daily Mail*, 2 February 1991, p. 13.

21 Phillips, C., *The European Tribe*, London, Faber, 1987, p. 121.

22 Turner, L. and Ash, J., *The Golden Hordes: International Tourism and the Pleasure Periphery*, London, Constable, 1975, p. 204.

23 ibid., p. 246.

24 Norman, P., in an article 'God save our Island of Fantasy', *Daily Mail*, 3 March 1990, pp. 15–16, adapted from his book *The Age of Parody*, London, Hamish Hamilton, 1990.

25 Wright, P., *On Living in an Old Country: The National Past in Contemporary Britain*, London, Verso, 1985, p. 81.

26 Theroux, P., 'Walkabout', *Observer Magazine*, 30 December 1990, p. 11.

27 Chatwin, B., *The Songlines*, 1987, London, Pan, 1988, p. 16.

28 Hilton, T., 'Sacred and commercial', *The Guardian*, 28 August 1991, p. 27.

29 Chiastacz, M., 'Station at the end of the line' (for *Libération*), *The Guardian*, 28 June, 1991, p. 26.

30 Lowry, S., 'The British tribes of France', *Weekend Telegraph*, 17 August 1991, p. i.

31 Advertisements under the heading 'Overseas travel' in *The Daily Telegraph*'s *Weekend Telegraph*, 19 October 1991, p. xiv.

32 Among books related to the topics under discussion are: Maybury-Lewis, D., *Millennium: Tribal Wisdom and the Modern Age*, New York, Viking, 1992; and Pieterse, J. N., *White on Black: Images of Africa and Blacks in Western Popular Culture*, London, Yale, 1992.

4   East and West

1 Kipling, R., 'The Ballad of East and West', 1889.

2 See Bishop, P., *The Myth of Shangri-La; Tibet, Travel Writing and the Western Creation of Sacred Landscape*, London, Athlone, 1989.

3 Kipling, R., 'The Man Who Was', 1890.

4 Ignatieff, M., 'A voice that cries in the wilderness', *Observer*, 9 September 1990, p. 11.

5 Widdicombe, R., '$100m. Forbidden City Chinese park planned in Barcelona', *The European*, 15–17 March 1991, p. 19.

6 Willis, R., 'Bath time in Budapest', British *Vogue*, April 1991, p. 111.

5   The *aloha* experience: Hawaii

1 Kirch, P. V., *Feathered Gods and Fishhooks: an Introduction to Hawaiian Archaeology and Prehistory*, Honolulu, University of Hawaii Press, 1985, p. 22; and the source of much of the pre-visit background here.

2 ibid., p. 308.

3 Pukui, M. K., Egbert, S. H. and

Mookini, E. T., *The Pocket Hawaiian Dictionary*, Honolulu, The University of Hawaii Press, 1975, p. 11.

4 Lodge, D., *Paradise News*, London, Secker & Warburg, 1991.

5 The *Official Program* of the Third Global Congress of Heritage Interpretation International, 1991, p. 4.

6 Turner, L. and Ash, J., *The Golden Hordes: International Tourism and the Pleasure Periphery*, London, Constable, 1975.

7 ibid., p. 162.

8 ibid., p. 162.

9 Blake, D., 'Losing the unequal battle', *The European*, 13–15 December 1991, p. 10.

10 Honolulu, Waikiki records, WC-307.

11 This and other facts here are from a leaflet, *Facts and Figures 1991 Edition*, Honolulu, Department of Business, Economic Development and Tourism, State of Hawaii, 1991.

12 A particularly helpful article is Zinsser, W., 'At Pearl Harbor there are new ways to remember', *Smithsonian*, 22, 9, December 1991, pp. 73–83.

13 *The Gabby Pahinui Hawaiian Band*, volume 1, produced by Panini Records, 1975 ED CD 241, was manufactured in England for Edsel Records, a division of Demon Records Ltd, Brentford, Middlesex, 1987.

14 *The 1989 Hawai'i Declaration of the Hawai'i Ecumenical Coalition on Tourism Conference [on] 'Tourism in Hawaii': Its Impact on Native Hawaiians and Its Challenge to the Churches.*

15 Kirch, op. cit., ch. 9.

16 Prepared by Community Resources, Inc., Honolulu, for the Tourism Branch of the Department of Business and Economic Development, State of Hawaii, August 1989.

6 Urbane and streetwise

1 *Guía Turistica de Mérida*, Mérida, Impresora Artística SRL, 1990. Spelling follows the original.

2 *Provence*, Harrow, Michelin Tyre plc, 1989, p. 44.

3 *The Borough of Castle Morpeth* (England Mini Guide), London, English Tourist Board, 1988.

4 Montpellier in *Gorges du Tarn: Cévennes, Bas Languedoc*, Paris, Pneu Michelin, pp. 111–19.

5 Montpellier Herault Synergie, 75, September 1991, p. 3.

6 All the quotations in this and the next paragraphs are from information leaflets, tourist brochures, etc., available in 1991, except for the Indian quotations which are from Keys, D., 'Ancient treasures', *High Life*, London, British Airways, March 1992, p. 65.

7 Cunningham, V., 'Creativity with the purse strings' (an article in review of the book *The Need to Give* by A. Sinclair), *Observer*, 23 September 1990, p. 39.

8 Rocca, T., 'Bardot whips up debate on world's oldest horse race', in the *élan* section of *The European*, 9–11 August 1991, p. 7.

9 *The Guardian*, 5 July 1991.

10 *The European*, 28–30 June 1991, p. 4.

11 Rocca, op. cit.

12 *Take Time Off in Swiss Cities 1991/2*, London, Time Off Ltd, 1991.

13 Payne, D., 'See all the sights and feel the terror', *The European*, 27 February 1992.

14 *Federal Archaeology Report*, Washington D.C., National Park Service, 4, 3, September 1991, pp. 10–13.

15 *The European*, 11–13 October, 1991, p. 6. For a total contrast, compare a recently discovered 'negroes' burial ground' now in downtown New York but, when closed in 1790, 'on the most desolate edge of town'. Described as 'one of the oldest remnants of a black community', and as 'a major find', attempts to commemorate it in some appropriate way naturally clash with the redevelopment proposals which led to its discovery. '[n]ot only could African-Americans not hope to govern New York City, they could not hope to be buried within its boundaries', Mayor David Dinkins was reported as saying, *The Guardian*, 11 October 1991.

Notes

7 The rural scene

1 Speaight, G. (ed.), *The New Shell Guide to Britain*, London, Ebury Press, 1985 (rev. ed.), p. 271.
2 Rogers, P., 'Introduction' to *A Tour Through the Whole Island of Great Britain 1724–6*, Harmondsworth, Penguin, 1971, p. 29.
3 A considerable library exists about Hadrian's Wall as a Roman frontier: best for academic entry points are Breeze, D. J. and Dobson, B., *Hadrian's Wall*, Harmondsworth, Penguin, 3rd ed., 1987 (reprint 1991), and Johnson, S., *English Heritage Book of Hadrian's Wall*, London, Batsford/English Heritage, 1989, both with good bibliographies.
4 Hegewisch, H., 'Shakespeare inspires Utopia on Rhodes', *The European*, 18–20 October 1991, p. 13.
5 *Le Causse Méjean. Elévage Tourisme* (1972), Meyrueis, 'Le Méjean' Association Caussenarde, 3rd ed., 1982. All facts and figures here are from it unless otherwise stated.
6 *Le Méjean. Villages d'hier et d'aujourd'hui*, place of publication and publisher not identified but printed at Le Parc National de Cevennes (Florac), 1986, p. 16.
7 Crewe, Q., 'Pens are deadlier than swords', in the *élan* section of *The European*, 13–15 December 1991.
8 Advertisement in *The Sunday Times*, 4 June 1989, p. B13.
9 *Annual Report 1989–90*, Fayetteville, Arkansas Archaeological Survey, October 1990, p. 129.
10 *The Independent*, 24 October 1991.
11 Montgomery-Massingberd, H., 'An inspiration for all souls', *Weekend Telegraph*, 26 October 1991, p. xiii.
12 *The Journal* (Newcastle upon Tyne), 28 March 1991, p. 3.
13 Widely published in Spring 1991; here quoted from *Observer Magazine*, 10 February 1991, inside back cover.
14 Clough, J., 'A need for heroes', *Weekend Telegraph*, 8 December 1990, p. x.
15 *Daily Mail*, 23 April 1991.
16 *The European*, 18–20 October 1991, p. 3.
17 *The European*, 1–3 November 1991.
18 *The European*, 22–4 March 1991, p. 3.
19 *The European*, 20–3 August 1992, p. 1.

8 In the museum direction

1 Quotes from *Concise Oxford Dictionary*, 7th ed., Oxford, Oxford University Press, 1982 (reprinted 1985).
2 McGurk, T., 'Rumours rule amid debris of Afghan war', *The Independent*, 24 September 1991, p. 10.
3 Ward, D., 'Thousands flock to captivating war museum', *The Guardian*, 27 May 1991, p. 6.
4 Watts, J., 'The nuns of Dachau', *Observer Magazine*, 9 December 1990, pp. 30–4.
5 Neatly described in Rellstab, U., 'East End on the mend', *The Guardian*, 11 January 1991, p. 27.
6 Markov, V. et al., *Russian Holograms Treasure Trapped in Light*, York, Cultural Resource Management Ltd for York Archaeological Trust, 1989.
7 Willett, F., 'Museums; two case studies of reaction to colonialism', in Gathercole, P. and Lowenthal, D., eds, *The Politics of the Past*, London, Unwin Hyman, 1990, pp. 172–83.
8 Keys, D., 'Celtic art gets a European platform', *The Independent*, 26 March 1991, p. 5.
9 ibid. For the full academic treatment, see Kruta, V. et al., *The Celts*, London, Thames & Hudson, 1991.
10 Hughes, C., 'Gone are the days of "do not touch" ', *The Independent*, 24 October 1991, p. 15.
11 Corbishley, M., ed., *Archaeology in the National Curriculum*, London, English Heritage/Council for British Archaeology, 1992. See also Halkon, P. et al., eds, *The Archaeology Resource Book 1992*, London, English Heritage/Council for British Archaeology, 1992.
12 See discussion about Japan in Buck, L. and Dodd, P., *Relative Values*, London, BBC Books, 1991, pp. 88–100.
13 Malraux, A., *Museum Without Walls* (1949) quoted in Bayley, S., *Commerce*

and Culture: From Pre-Industrial Art to Post-Industrial Value, Tunbridge Wells, Penshurst Press Ltd, 1989, p. 15.
14 McGill, P., 'Japan's colossus of history calls out to the capital that lost its memory', Observer, 23 February 1992, p. 18.
15 ibid.
16 Telegraph Magazine, 24 August 1991, p. 38.
17 Alberta Past, Edmonton, April 1990.

9   The 'moving object'

1 See, generally, Chamberlin, R., Loot! The Heritage of Plunder, London, Thames & Hudson, 1983; and Meyer, K. E., The Plundered Past, London, Hamish Hamilton, 1973.
2 Wickman, R., 'Spain braced to repel armada of gold-hunters', The European, 22–4 November 1991, p. 3.
3 The Sunday Times, 24 November 1991.
4 Daily Mail, 23 November 1991, p. 10.
5 Marks, L. and Bailey, M., 'Red Army Spoils', Observer Magazine, 15 December 1991, pp. 14–22.
6 The Guardian, 11 October 1991. Six months later, also moving was the replica of a statue of Kaiser Wilhelm I to a site overlooking the Rhine at Düsseldorf in the new, united Germany. The original was destroyed by the USA in 1945; the move was criticized as glorifying the imperial past: what are tourists to make of this?
7 The European, 15–17 February 1991.
8 The Guardian, 1 March 1991.
9 The Guardian, 25 March 1991.
10 The Sunday Times, 2 June 1991, p. 13.
11 Lees, G., 'Knight's relics caught in German tug of war', The Sunday Times, 4 August 1991.
12 Daley, J., 'Giving the bodies to voyeurism', The Times, 1 October 1991, p. 14.
13 Pile, S., 'Messenger from the past', Telegraph Magazine, 19 October 1991, pp. 32–8.
14 Daily Mail, 10 January 1992, p. 13.
15 Details here and elsewhere are updated from The European, 5 March 1992, and

a BBC television 'Horizon' programme, 'Iceman', broadcast on 27 April 1992. 'Horizon' showed the original 'excavation' to have been an absolute shambles, and four months later a German TV team was suggesting the whole assemblage to be 'an elaborate hoax' using an Egyptian mummy. The Sunday Times, 14 August 1992, p. 14.
16 Targett, J., 'The Lincoln handicap', Weekend Guardian, 23–4 March 1991, pp. 4–7.
17 The Guardian, 20 April 1991.
18 Targett, op. cit., p. 5.
19 Letter from Adam Bruce, Daily Telegraph, 7 July 1990. See McNeal, R. A., 'Archaeology and the destruction of the later Athenian acropolis', Antiquity, 65, 1991, pp. 49–63.
20 cf. 'We are in some ways fortunate that so much was preserved overseas', a remark by the Assistant Director of the Auckland Institute, New Zealand, about Maori canoe carvings. Well-carved canoes ceased to be a prestige symbol in 1860 and some carvings survived by being sold to European collectors. Quoted in Chamberlin, op. cit., p. 235.
21 Melina Mercouri, former Minister of Culture, quoted in The Guardian, 22 April 1991, p. 6.
22 Sharrock, D., 'US court case highlights plunder of Ireland's cultural treasures', The Guardian, 26 August 1991, p. 8.
23 The Guardian, 7 July 1990.
24 ibid.

10   Global products

1 Ohmae, K., The Borderless World: Power and Strategy in the Interlinked Economy, Collins, 1990; London, Fontana, 1992, p. 38.
2 Marti, S., reprint of Le Monde article 'Amex joins the club', The Guardian, 29 March 1991, p. 26.
3 The Guardian, 6 September 1991.
4 Levy, G., 'Operation Coke', Daily Mail, 12 June, 1991, p. 6.
5 Daily Mail, 27 September 1990, p. 15.
6 ibid.

Notes

7. *Daily Mail*, 20 September 1990, p. 10.
8 Hine, T., *Populuxe*, 1986; London, Bloomsbury, 1990, p. 152.
9 *Steve Birnbaum's Guide to Walt Disney World 1991*, Avon Books & Hearst Professional Magazines, Inc., 1990, p. 5.
10 Charlot, M., 'La grande illusion', *The Guardian*, 3 May 1991, p. 27.
11 ibid.
12 Crabbe, M., 'Disney magic under fire', *The European*, 3–5 May 1991, p. 19.
13 Wise, D., 'The fun starts here', *The Guardian*, 1 March 1991, p. 26.
14 British *Metropolitan Home*, October 1990, p. 71.
15 ibid.
16 Sullivan, R., 'Mouse traps laid for Mickey's parks', *The European*, 15–17 February 1991, p. 22.
17 ibid.
18 ibid.
19 The subject of Thompson, D., 'Thou shalt dig up graven images', *The Mail on Sunday, You Magazine*, 26 May 1991, pp. 26–8.
20 ibid. p. 28.

11   Heritage, tourism and 'the village'

1 Waterhouse, K., 'Just two big words', *Daily Mail*, 22 August 1991, p. 8.
2 Toffler, A., *Powershift*, New York, Bantam, 1990; paperback ed., 1991, p. 338.
3 Muschamp, H., 'now & then', American *Vogue*, January 1991, p. 219.
4 Greer, G., 'Turn for the worse is just not cricket', *The Mail on Sunday*, 21 August 1988, p. 18.
5 Phillips, P., 'In the last steps of JFK', *Weekend Guardian*, 7–8 December 1991, p. 27.
6 Hoggart, R., 'The pursuit of quality', *The Bookseller*, 14 June 1991, p. 1700.
7 Rowe, D., 'Power is the right to define reality', *The Guardian*, 23 August 1991, p. 24.
8 Ogilvy, D., *Ogilvy on Advertising*, London, Pan 1983, p. 127.
9 *The Guardian*, 13 September 1991, p. 3.
10 Normand, T., 'Scottish modernism and Scottish identity', in Kaplan, W., ed., *Scotland Creates: 500 Years of Art and Design*, London, George Weidenfeld & Nicolson Ltd (in association with Glasgow Museums & Art Galleries), p. 162.
11 Ogilvy, op. cit., p. 133.
12 Wood, K. and House, S., *The Good Tourist*, London, Mandarin, 1991, p. 28.
13 Horne, D., *The Great Museum: The Representation of History*, London, Pluto, 1984, p. 251.
14 Featherstone, M., ed., *Global Culture, Nationalism, Globalization and Modernity*, London, Sage Publications, 1990. A good example of a 'local heritage' being redefined and made more accessible through international co-operation specifically to create a global attraction is the 'Mundo Maya' project, aiming 'to spread the tourists, and their dollars, more evenly across the five participating nations' of Central America supported by about $1 million from the European Community': Hammond. N., 'Nations unite to put Mayan past on world tourist map', *The Times*, 27 June 1991.
15 See the book by Lowenthal, D., *The Past is a Foreign Country*, Cambridge, Cambridge University Press, 1985.
16 Nettell, S., 'Giving the green light to tourism', *Weekend Guardian*, 3–4 August 1991, p. 26.
17 Kettle, M., 'The Venetian version', *The Guardian*, 18 October 1991, p. 25.
18 Trove, T., 'A magical museum of the deep', *The European*, 5–7 July 1991, p. 27.
19 *Daily Mail*, 19 October 1991, p. 10.
20 Niesewand, N., 'Voyage of Discovery', British *Vogue*, April 1991, p. 209.
21 ibid., p. 211.
22 ibid., pp. 210 and 211.
23 Spencer, P., 'I see our future – and it's Japan', *The Mail on Sunday*, 26 May 1991, p. 17.
24 Rheingold, H., *Virtual Reality*, London, Secker & Warburg, 1991.
25 *The European*, 18–20 October 1991, p. 17.
26 Turner, L. and Ash, J., *The Golden Hordes: International Tourism and the*

Pleasure Periphery, London, Constable, 1975, pp. 150–1.

27 Naisbitt, J. and Aburdene, P., *Megatrends 2000*, 1988; London, Sidgwick & Jackson, 1990, p. 126.

28 ibid., p. 133.

29 Fowler, P. J., 'A sense of belonging', *The Times Higher Education Supplement*, 19 July 1991.

30 Horne, op. cit., Prologue, p. 1.

31 Turner and Ash, op. cit., p. 278.

Further reading

Adorno, T. W., *The Culture Industry. Selected Essays on Mass Culture*, London, Routledge, 1991.

Boyne, R. and Rattansi, A., eds, *Postmodernism and Society*, London, Macmillan, London, 1990.

Furnham, A. and Bochner, S., *Culture Shock: Psychological Reactions to Unfamiliar Environments*, London, Routledge, 1989.

Lunn, J. et al., eds, *Proceedings of the First World Congress on Heritage Presentation and Interpretation*, Alberta, Heritage Interpretation International and Alberta Culture and Multiculturalism, 1988.

MacCannell, D., *The Tourist: A New Theory of the Leisure Class*, New York, Schocken, 1976.

Mitchell, R., 'Tourism Management', *British Book News*, July 1989, pp. 468–73 (a 'book survey' with professionally prepared bibliography).

Ryan, C., *Recreational Tourism: A Social Science Perspective*, London, Routledge, 1991.

Tabata, R. and Cherem, G., eds, *Proceedings of the Third Global Congress of Heritage Interpretation International*, Chicago and Hawaii, University of Chicago Press and The University of Hawaii Press, 1992.

Urry, J., *The Tourist Gaze, Leisure and Travel in Contemporary Societies*, London, Sage, 1990.

Uzzell, D., ed., *Heritage Interpretation. Volume One: The Nature & Built Environment. Volume Two: The Visitor Experience*, London, Belhaven, 1989.

We also recommend relevant titles in the *One World Archaeology* series, originally published by Unwin Hyman, London, and now taken over by Routledge; and the publications, including a bulletin *Environmental Interpretation*, of the Centre for Environmental Interpretation (CEI), Manchester Polytechnic, United Kingdom.

Index to places

(by continent/region-country, then specifics)

Index to places

Index to subjects